Fruits of the Harvest

Also by Eric V. Copage

Fruits of the Harvest

RECIPES TO CELEBRATE KWANZAA AND OTHER HOLIDAYS

Eric V. Copage

Illustrations by
Cheryl Carrington

Amistad
An *Imprint of* HarperCollins*Publishers*

HarperCollins books may be purchased for educational, business, or sales promotional use. For information, please write: Special Markets Department, HarperCollins Publishers, 10 East 53rd Street, New York, NY 10022.

An extension of this copyright page appears on pages 341-42.

Originally published in 1991 as *Kwanzaa: An African-American Celebration of Culture and Cooking* by William Morrow and Company, Inc.

FIRST AMISTAD EDITION PUBLISHED IN 2005.

Designed by Cheryl Carrington

Printed on acid-free paper

Library of Congress Cataloging-in-Publication Data
Copage, Eric V.
  [Kwanzaa]
  Fruits of the harvest : recipes to celebrate Kwanzaa and other holidays / Eric V. Copage.
      p. cm.
  Originally published under title: Kwanzaa. Morrow, 1991.
  Includes index.
  ISBN-10: 0-06-083324-6
  ISBN-13: 978-0-06-083324-4
  1. African American cookery. 2. Holiday cookery—United States. 3. Kwanzaa. I. Title.

  TX715.C7865 2005
  641.5'68'08996073—dc22   2005048188

---

05 06 07 08 09 QUE 10 9 8 7 6 5 4 3 2 1

To my father, John E. Copage,
who encouraged me to dream.
To my children, Evan and Siobhán,
for their prosperous future.
And to those of African descent
around the world and throughout history.

ACKNOWLEDGMENTS

It's usually said that too many cooks spoil the broth. But in the case of this book, there wouldn't be any broth (not to mention much meat, fish, or drink) if it weren't for the score or so of caterers, cooks, and food lovers, and of course Kwanzaa celebrants, who so generously gave their time and not only shared their recipes but sometimes allowed us to adapt them for consistency. I am especially grateful to my featured contributors: **Hiram Bonner,** who attended the Cordon Bleu and the French Culinary Institute and is weekend chef for David Dinkins, Mayor of New York City, as well as supervisor for the executive dining room of the *New York Times.* Hiram took time out from his own project, preparing a culinary curriculum for public school children, to ask his family to give up treasured recipes and indulge me as I queried him about his family's culinary history. **Audie Odum-Stallato,** a cooking instructor who has worked as an assistant chef in various New Jersey restaurants. (She lives in my hometown, Montclair, New Jersey.) She is the owner of "Catering by Audie." And **Mavis Young** and her sister **Cynthia Lewis,** owners of Mavis' and Cyn's Restaurant and Catering in La Mesa, California. When Mavis first described some of the dishes they were going to contribute, my stomach growled, *"Want some! Want some!"*

Great thanks to **Empress Akweke,** owner of EGUSI, Royal African and International Caterers, a Brooklyn-based catering company specializing in food of the African diaspora, who immediately saw the

culinary and cultural value of this book. And to **Saalik Cuevas,** a fellow Kwanzaa celebrant, for his insights into being a Puerto Rican proud of the African part of his heritage and for his vision of Kwanzaa. And I'd like to thank the other contributors, **Catherine Bailey, Steven Barboza, Karen Grigsby Bates, Roscoe Betsill, Isabella Bravim, Dee Dee Dailey, Georgia Dunn, Gwen Foster, Paula Yaa Johnson, Frieda Jones, Maggie Marenga, John Moore, Diana N'Diaye, Lincoln Pattaway, Rita Springer, Enoch Thompson,** and **Gwendolyn Tonge,** for their recipes and passion.

At William Morrow and Company, I'd like to thank my editor, **Maria Guarnaschelli,** and director of special projects **Will Schwalbe.** Their confidence in me and their enthusiasm made the book possible. Specifically, I appreciate Maria's insightful comments about the manuscript and Will's patience in coaxing this book out of me. And three cheers for **Rick Rodgers,** cook and food tester extraordinaire, for his many hours of polishing family recipes to a cookbook shine—adapting them and translating them into cookbook language so that we all might share. I'll never be able to thank him enough.

Thanks to **Penelope Green,** for assigning me to write the *New York Times* magazine food article on Kwanzaa that helped ignite interest in the creation of this book, and for prying the lid off my writing in her editing of that initial piece. And thanks to **Warren Hoge,** editor of the *New York Times* magazine, for his indulgence and belief that I could juggle writing a book and my duties as an editor at the magazine.

And, of course, my profound thanks to **Maulana Karenga,** who gave an invaluable gift to the community with his creation of Kwanzaa.

Last, I'd like to thank my wife, **Kathleen,** for a priceless ten years of patience, support, and love.

CONTENTS

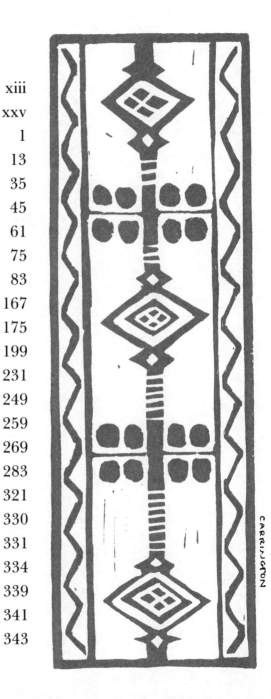

CARRINGTON

INTRODUCTION

Before eating, open your mouth.

Proverb, Mauritania

I was never a holiday kind of guy. Perhaps it was because we observed few holiday rituals of any kind. Although we put up a Christmas tree every year, there was no ceremony to it—no drinking of eggnog or listening to carols while hanging ornaments. To me the tree seemed more or less like another piece of furniture. Over the past few years, however, the holiday season has taken on a new meaning for me as my family sits at the dinner table the week following Christmas to celebrate Kwanzaa.

This cultural observance for black Americans and others of African descent was created in 1966 by Maulana (Ron) Karenga, who is currently chairman of black studies at California State University in Long Beach. *Kwanzaa* means "first fruits of the harvest" in Swahili, but there is no festival of that name in any African society. Karenga chose Swahili, the lingua franca of much of East Africa, to emphasize that black Americans come from many parts of Africa. Karenga synthesized elements from many African harvest festivals to create a unique celebration that is now observed in some way by more than 5 million Americans.

When I first told my wife I was thinking about observing Kwanzaa, she barred the way to our attic and said she'd never chuck our Christmas tree lights and antique ornaments. I told her that wouldn't be necessary. Kwanzaa, which runs from December 26 to New Year's

Day, does not replace Christmas and is not a religious holiday. (We now celebrate both.) It is a time to focus on Africa and African-inspired culture and to reinforce a value system that goes back for generations.

Like many people, I was introduced to Kwanzaa by chance, in late December a few years back. I was visiting the American Museum of Natural History when I heard the sibilant sound of African rattles. It was coming from a dance performance, part of the Kwanzaa celebration that has been held annually at the museum since 1978. The holiday didn't make much of an impression on me then, but I returned to it after the birth of my son, Evan, in 1987.

I wanted Evan to have a three-dimensional sense of his African heritage. I wanted him to experience the pride of learning about the sublime Russian poet Aleksander Pushkin, the extraordinary American composer Duke Ellington, and Alexandre Dumas, author of *The Three Musketeers*. I wanted Evan to learn about the West African medieval empires—Songhai, Mali, and Ghana—and about the African explorers such as Esteban, who traveled throughout what is now Arizona and New Mexico in the sixteenth century, and about inventors like the mechanical engineer Elijah McCoy (who was the original "real McCoy"). I wanted him to understand that through tenacity, hard work, and purposefulness—all of which are grounded in the African and African-American ethos—blacks have flourished as well as survived. I wanted to train Evan to look for opportunity, and to prepare for it. And I wanted to have a forum for showing him examples of past successes, and for showing him that those people inevitably gave back to the black community in particular and to the general community in which they lived.

But how to do this? I could have made up some ritual. But then we'd miss the communal aspect, the idea that in households similar to ours people were involved in similar activities. We'd miss one of the major reasons for celebrating a cultural holiday, the hoped-for metaphysical bonding with other African-Americans.

There is Black History Month, of course, which I've always enjoyed. I look forward to being enveloped for four weeks in the membrane of black accomplishment as it comes to me from special radio and television programs and is represented in the special displays in bookstores. But this Gatling gun approach to black culture, laudable as it is, seems to lack focus. And unlike other long observances—Lent, for instance, or Ramadan—Black History Month has no agreed-upon ritual, structure, or climax.

I thought about my goals for Evan and decided that Kwanzaa was the best lens through which to view the landscape of the African diaspora and the lessons it has to teach. Because it is only one week long, and because of the ceremony, and because it climaxes with a glorious feast, Kwanzaa has an intensity and focus that provides the perfect atmosphere for my son to experience the joys of being black.

Kwanzaa also has the celebratory aspect that will provide memories for Evan and now my daughter, Siobhán, to savor as adults and to pass on to their children.

If you want to adhere strictly to the Kwanzaa program as Karenga conceived it, here is what you need to have and what they mean:

1. **Mazao:** fruits and vegetables, which stand for the product of unified effort.
2. **Mkeka:** a straw place mat, which represents the reverence for tradition.
3. **Vibunzi:** an ear of corn for each child in the family.
4. **Zawadi:** simple gifts, preferably related to education or to things African or African-influenced.
5. **Kikombe cha umoja:** a communal cup for the libation (I like to look at this as a kind of homage to past, present, and future black Americans).
6. **Kinara:** a seven-branched candleholder, which symbolizes the continent and peoples of Africa.

7. **Mishumaa saba:** the seven candles, each one symbolizing one of the Nguzo Saba, or seven principles, that black Americans should live by on a daily basis and which are reinforced during Kwanzaa.

On each day of Kwanzaa, a family member lights a candle, then discusses one of those seven principles. The principles, along with Karenga's elucidation of them in 1965, are:

1. **Umoja (Unity):** To strive for and maintain unity in the family, community, nation, and race.
2. **Kujichagulia (Self-determination):** To define ourselves, name ourselves, create for ourselves, and speak for ourselves instead of being defined, named, created for, and spoken for by others.
3. **Ujima (Collective Work and Responsibility):** To build and maintain our community together, and to make our sisters' and brothers' problems our problems and to solve them together.
4. **Ujamaa (Cooperative Economics):** To build and maintain our own stores, shops, and other businesses and to profit from them together.
5. **Nia (Purpose):** To make our collective vocation the building and developing of our community in order to restore our people to their traditional greatness.
6. **Kuumba (Creativity):** To do always as much as we can, in whatever way we can, in order to leave our community more beautiful and beneficial than we inherited it.
7. **Imani (Faith):** To believe with all our heart in our people, our parents, our teachers, our leaders, and in the righteousness and victory of our struggle.

The next-to-last day of the holiday, December 31, is marked by a lavish feast, the *Kwanzaa Karamu*, which, in keeping with the theme of black unity, may draw on the cuisines of the Caribbean, Africa, South America . . . wherever Africans were taken. In addition to food, the Karamu is an opportunity for a confetti storm of cultural expression: dance and music, readings, remembrances. Here is Karenga's suggested way of conducting a Karamu as enlarged upon by Cedric McClester:

1. **Kukaribisha (Welcoming)**
   Introductory remarks and recognition of distinguished guests and elders.
   Cultural expression through songs, music, dance, unity circles, etc.

2. **Kukumbuka (Remembering)**
   Reflections of a man, a woman, and a child.
   Cultural expression

3. **Kuchunguza tena na kutoa ahadi tena (Reassessment and Recommitment)**
   Introduction of distinguished guest lecturer, and short talk.

4. **Kushangilia (Rejoicing)**
   Tamshi la tambiko (libation statement)
   Kikombe cha umoja (unity cup)
   Kutoa majina (calling names of family ancestors and black heroes)
   Ngoma (drums)
   Karamu (feast)
   Cultural expression

5. **Tamshi la tutaonana** (Farewell Statement)

When my family lights the black, red, and green Kwanzaa candles the last week of December, we do so with millions other black Americans around the nation. Major community celebrations are held in just about every city that has any kind of black population: Atlanta, Chicago, Philadelphia, Milwaukee, Dayton, Durham, and Charleston, to name just a few. The people who celebrate Kwanzaa comprise a cross-section of black America. They include Catherine Bailey of Boston, a teacher who has been celebrating since 1969; Saalik Cuevas, a

Puerto Rican–American computer programmer who is as proud of his African heritage as he is of his Spanish and Indian backgrounds; and Diana N'Diaye, a folklorist at the Smithsonian Institution. Audie Odum-Stallato, a cooking instructor and caterer, has invited non–African-Americans to Kwanzaa as her way of sharing African culture. There are others for whom the idea of sharing Kwanzaa with anyone other than a fellow African-American would be anathema.

Some people, such as New York City caterers Carol and Norma Jean Darden, "Kwanzafy" their Christmas by using African-inspired Yuletide decorations and ornaments on their Christmas tree. Gwen Foster, an Oakland, California, social worker, also uses African-inspired Christmas decorations—including a straw wreath wrapped with red, black, and green ribbon that she hangs on her front door—in addition to holding a small Kwanzaa ceremony with her family on each of the seven days. Lincoln Pattaway and his family celebrate Kwanzaa in lieu of Christmas. Like Foster, the Pattaways, who live in Houston, also have an intimate family celebration—but on only one night of Kwanzaa. The other nights they do the town:

> We meet in different areas: in schools, community centers. One of the reasons we move around is because the city is so vast and you want to make it available to everyone. The historical society I belong to sponsors one night. The other nights are sponsored by other groups. During our last celebration, there were about two hundred people. It was standing-room-only.
>
> There are big banners and beautiful signs. There is also a table set the same way we would set it at home, with the candles, mat, fruit, and vegetables. Most people are dressed in African garb. We're seated in front of the stage. Whoever is conducting the program for that night comes out to introduce themselves and the group. We are given a brief explanation of Kwanzaa. We light one of the candles and somebody speaks about that night's principle. This year we sponsored self-determination (*Kujicha-*

gulia) and our speaker, a local product, was an Egyptologist. After he spoke about Egypt, we had the libation. Then we asked the audience to make a circle. We drank from the unity cup and talked about commitment for the following year.

Because it's a large group and so many people want to participate, we start at 7:00 P.M., and with the entertainment and activities, sometimes we're still there at midnight.

Saalik Cuevas takes a much more intimate approach. Over the past twelve years that Saalik, his wife, Isha, and their two sons, Sha'ir and Na'im, have celebrated Kwanzaa, they have usually kept their observance to a family affair.

We had gotten to a point that we started getting more in touch with our African selves. A good friend invited us to a Kwanzaa celebration. We didn't know anything about it, but were immediately struck by the spirituality of the affair. We made up our minds then and there to incorporate Kwanzaa into our lives. We started reading up on it. That first year everything was homemade. For the kinara, for instance, I used a piece of wood and seven apple juice caps covered with aluminum foil. The unity cup was a gourd we had bought. And that fall we bought what is called Indian corn, to represent our first son.

Our first Kwanzaa consisted of my wife, myself, and our eldest child. The second year we invited a few other family members. By then we had bought a kinara. It's made of wood and lacquered red. It's about 2 feet across and nearly 3 feet high. I got long tapered red, black, and green candles for it. We bought another straw mat that just about covers our whole table. Our unity cup is a white porcelain chalice.

Our Kwanzaa table now takes up the whole server in our dining room. We add to it year after year. We have African sculptures on the table, a basket of fruit, a separate basket with vegetables. The boys came up with the idea of having little baskets

of rice and beans and corn. After the seven days of Kwanzaa, we use that rice, beans, and corn to make the first meal of the year.

We spend the whole day after Christmas setting up the Kwanzaa table and decorating the house. By sunset we are dressed in African clothes and ready to light the candle for Umoja. We pour a drop or two of water right on the rug for the ancestors. Then we pass around the cup. Traditionally I start it off since I am the eldest male in the household. We discuss the principle. For instance, I said last year that not only African-Americans need unity, but the entire human race needs unity, so that there won't be war, poverty, and hunger. After that I'll say a short prayer. It could be the Lord's Prayer or an African prayer. Then we snuff out the candles, and that signifies the end of the ceremony for that day. The ceremony lasts about twenty minutes. Then we eat.

Instead of a slew of gifts at the end of Kwanzaa, we give the children a few gifts each day. The first day will be something simple like fruit, books, a dashiki. We want them to get into the feel of this African holiday. The third or fourth day we might give them a cartoon book about the pyramids or Sun Man [a black hero-figure toy like the "He Man" toy] or something like that. On the last day, since this is America and we know that when they go back to school they are going to be asked what they got, we give the more commercial Nintendo, Ninja turtle video, train set—type presents. My wife and I feel that if we try to force Kwanzaa on our two sons, they might push it away. But if we try to incorporate it into our lives, it might take better.

We like to celebrate the last day of Kwanzaa. We might have forty-five people over to our house, close friends and family. What we do is supply basic foods for a mega Kwanzaa buffet and ask other people to bring salads. We go over all the Kwanzaa principles in detail, not just that day's principle. For instance, last year we talked about Mandela as an example of Umoja because with him, it was the first time in a long time that black people had a common focus. This ceremony can last almost an hour.

After the ceremony, we ask people who are creative to do something. My mother-in-law, for instance, is a good speaker, and as an elder she will read from Kahlil Gibran about children. We might have someone who is a good singer lead us in an old spiritual.

As for the recorded music, we always play Sweet Honey in the Rock, who sing a song about the Nguzo Saba. And then we might play Olatunji, Marvin Gaye, the Supremes, or KRS-One. A woman once came up to me and asked me to give her a list of Kwanzaa songs. I gave her a copy of *Billboard* magazine, turned to the R and B charts, and said, "Here, choose any of these." Any of those musics are part of the black experience, as are reggae, traditional African music, Afro-Cuban jazz. . . .

One year we were lucky enough to have someone who was into the traditional African belief system, that of the Yoruba people in particular, and he did a blessing for us. And once we had someone who told traditional stories. Between the playing of music, dancing, and eating, the party can last all night.

The other days of Kwanzaa we snuff out the candles. But on Imani we let the candles burn down. It signifies the end of the holiday.

Catherine Bailey describes her personalized celebration:

My family and I celebrated our first Kwanzaa around 1969, with only the family as guests. But by 1972 we had a network of about fifty friends who were interested in sharing the festival with us. We had lots of teenagers and children along with more senior guests. My eldest son was not particularly interested in either Kwanzaa or Christmas, but my second son, especially after his return from Vietnam in 1972, participated actively in all of the aspects of Kwanzaa. We were especially blessed that my father

CARRINGTON

CARRINGTON

lived to see a semblance of "Ethiopia stretching forth her hand." My greatest regret was that our mother had passed away in the early 1940s. She would have loved Kwanzaa.

One of the most innovative features of Kwanzaa is the Zawadi tray filled with gifts for guests to take home. None of these gifts, with the exception of books, should be bought, according to Karenga. All of them should be homemade. For that purpose I have knitted, crocheted, sewn, baked, and wrapped my gifts, all tied with the red, black, and green liberation colors. Guests make their own selection from the tray.

I have worked out a well-organized procedure that over the years has resulted in fun-filled and very satisfying anticipatory pleasure for me and my guests. To all offers of "What would you like me to bring?" my answer is always "Bring yourself and, if you like, a friend." I make sure I have the kind of music for listening and dancing that appeals to young and old. Letta M'Bulu, Olatunji, Nina Simone, and Hugh Masekela are perennial favorites. I am addicted to do-it-yourself projects, so I design the menus, always typed, with a map of the Motherland.

As you can see, there is a wide spectrum of ways to observe Kwanzaa. My family, like many others, takes an à la carte approach. We decided we'd have one Kwanzaa meal in the middle of the weeklong holiday.

Our first meal consisted of dishes that brought forth sweet memories of my childhood. I remembered helping my grandmother make collard greens, especially the arduous task of washing dirt from the leaves (and getting bawled out if someone got a gritty mouthful during dinner), and I remembered sorting and discarding the bad black-eyed peas for the Hoppin' John she cooked. I remembered visiting West Africa when I was eighteen and tasting the spicy tingle of peanut soup for the first time. And of course there was a lifetime of cornbread.

Like our Christmas, our Kwanzaa tends to be a small celebration comprised of our nuclear family of four, although we do go to the daytime Kwanzaa cultural exhibits—dance performances and the like—held at the American Museum of Natural History or the Studio Museum of Harlem. After our Kwanzaa meal I relate the biography of a black man or woman or tell a black folktale, myth, or historical event. Every night during Kwanzaa, I talk about the principles as a bedtime story. Along with many other African-Americans, I interpret the Nguzo Saba in a broader way than Karenga did. For instance, I have defined Kuumba (Creativity) not only as leaving our community a "more beautiful place than we inherited it" but also as finding solutions to seemingly unsolvable problems. In other words, the house paintings of the Ndebele people of South Africa exhibit Kuumba, as do the bluesy strains of the late Charles Mingus. But so did director/producer Robert Townsend when he took cash advances on all his credit cards (using his wit to come up with an unorthodox financial source) and used them to finance his first film, *Hollywood Shuffle*. I also define Nia (Purpose) not just as restoring "our people to their traditional greatness," but also as focusing on a task and not getting distracted. Thus Townsend also showed Nia, or purpose, by using the money only for his film. And Frederick Douglass showed creativity and purpose in overcoming the institution of slavery that forbade him from learning how to read.

During my family's Kwanzaa we don't drink from the unity cup, but rather pour a small libation into it and leave it in the center of the table; and we prefer to use freestanding candles instead of putting them in a kinara. That may change, however, with this coming Kwanzaa or the Kwanzaa after that. It took several years for me to feel comfortable saying "Happy Kwanzaa." But I think that is only natural. Any holiday, and the rituals that go with it, derives its symbolic and social power from its cultural context. It takes time for a cultural context to crystallize. It's easy for someone to devise a holiday from on high, but it takes time for the buzz to develop, for people to find out if their neighbors are celebrating the holiday, and if so, how.

Since the celebration of Kwanzaa is only a quarter of a century

old this year, it is still very dynamic. There are even those agitating to have it moved to February (Black History Month), May (Malcolm X's birthday), or almost any time but that crazy month of December. I don't think the people who want to move the holiday will prevail. But I know Kwanzaa is destined to transform further, as African-Americans calibrate their observances to what they are comfortable with and to the needs of their individual families.

To be sure, celebrating Kwanzaa is not an end in itself. Neither is having an Africa medallion swinging from your neck, wearing a kente cloth hat, or giving your children African names. Medallions, clothes, and newly created rites should remind us of our collective strength, and of the fact that this strength is manifest only through individual effort. What we are doing with Kwanzaa and "Afrocentricity" in general is using our culture as an ideal that each of us tries to live up to. The seven principles, or Nguzo Saba, are practical tools, guides for helping us live these ideals throughout the year. That, for me, is the ultimate benefit of Kwanzaa. As Saalik Cuevas says, "You take those principles and use them all year, and by the end of the year you will be a changed person."

HOW TO USE THIS BOOK

There is a jazzy quality to everything black people do, a spirit of improvisation and self-creation. It is part of the African aesthetic. And it is very much a part of Kwanzaa.

This book is designed to provide all the components for your Kwanzaa celebration: stories to illustrate the principles of Kwanzaa and recipes for the special meals. It is to be used as a resource, a garden from which you can pick and choose the elements you want for your own Kwanzaa celebration.

Food is a big part of the holiday, and here you will find more than 125 treasured recipes, passed on through families but changed by each generation and each cook. There are no set menus or combinations that you have to follow, no rigid schedule of when to serve which food. Putting together your own Kwanzaa feasts is part of the joy of the holiday.

You can celebrate a different country of the African diaspora each day by cooking only foods of that country. On the first night you might serve Jamaican dishes, on the second food from the American South, on the third African, and so on . . . ending with a glorious all-out multinational banquet on the last night.

Or you can put together a menu for each night with no two recipes coming from the same land.

You can do a potluck supper and have everyone contribute a course that comes from the place where they were born, or the country their ancestors came from, or a place they have visited. This is a great way to start people talking about their particular families and history.

All-vegetarian dishes can be served, or you can create meals for special dietary requirements. You can even take one type of food, such as rice, and cook all the different recipes that use that food for one meal.

The possibilities are as wide as your imagination.

And you don't have to save these recipes for Kwanzaa—you can cook from them year-round. But I like to save certain favorite recipes just for Kwanzaa.

In all the excitement of the food preparation, with all the delicious smells coming from the kitchen, and in the bustle of everyone pitching in, it is easy to delay planning the ceremony to the last minute. But planning the ceremony should be the very first thing you do.

Long after the foods are consumed, and the dishes stacked and put away, it is the stories and ceremony that everyone will remember. Kwanzaa is first and foremost a celebration of heritage and culture.

There are seven chapters of text in this book, just as there are seven principles celebrated in Kwanzaa. Each chapter starts with a list of all the principles, because each chapter contains stories that touch on all of them. There are few pieces of history, stories, or folktales that only have one moral, one point to make, one principle to illustrate. Most represent many principles—or all of them.

You can choose a principle to talk about—maybe one a night, in the order that Karenga established, as described in the Introduction—and then read a particular story or series of stories and talk about how that one principle applies to everything just heard.

Or you can read a story, or a few stories, and then have a spontaneous discussion about the principle or principles that the listeners think they represent.

If you have a small child, you may want to read only the folktales and the proverbs. And then you can tie them into simple lessons—how these principles relate to the child's daily life.

Older children may want to hunt through the book themselves, choosing a story to read to you.

I have suggested some of the principles that I think are illustrated in each story. There is no one right answer, but rather as many right answers as there are people present.

One way to use the book is to read a few of the stories from each chapter in order, chapter by chapter, on each successive night. You can then talk about the principles in order, one by one, and see how that night's principle is reflected in that group of readings.

Another way is to turn over each night's readings to a different member of the family and have them search through the book for the stories they want to read to illustrate a particular principle.

The joy, the togetherness, the affirmation, come not only from a well-planned Kwanzaa but from the preparation process itself.

Nguzo Saba

Umoja (Unity)
Kujichagulia (Self-determination)
Ujima (Collective Work and Responsibility)
Ujamaa (Cooperative Economics)
Nia (Purpose)
Kuumba (Creativity)
Imani (Faith)

CARRINGTON

A single bracelet does not jingle.

Proverb, Congo

The principle of Unity (Umoja), sounded in this proverb, came to life during the Montgomery bus boycott. The boycott was successful, not because one person boycotted the bus lines, not because twenty did, but because the entire black population of Montgomery did. The black citizens also showed Creativity (Kuumba) in the various plans they concocted to sustain the boycott under intense pressure to end it.

In the 1950s the African-American community in Montgomery, Alabama, paid the same bus fare as the city's white citizens, yet they were forced to sit in the back of the bus or to stand if a white person boarded when all the seats were filled. This ended in 1956 after the yearlong Montgomery bus boycott, arguably the most significant boycott of the Civil Rights era.

Many people think civil rights boycotts originated in Montgomery, but it was an ongoing tactic in an ongoing battle. The most recent actions against segregation of public transportation had taken place in Baton Rouge just three years earlier. One was a daylong boycott protesting the segregation of city buses, which ended unsuccessfully. A weeklong boycott three months later ended with a compromise.

The Montgomery boycott was not a spontaneous response in support of Rosa Parks's refusal to give up her seat to a white man. It was a deliberate act and part of a historical continuum. It was yet another example of the resolve, discipline, and dignity of the African-Americans.

In this excerpt from the book *Eyes on the Prize* by Juan Williams, we pick up after the success of the one-day boycott that had been called by leaders of the African-American community in Montgomery, and after the vote by the people of that community to extend the boycott.

On Thursday, December 8, 1955, only four days into the boycott, the Montgomery Improvement Association (MIA), which included Dr. Martin Luther King, Jr., met with the city commissioners and representatives of the bus company to present their demands, which included seating on a first-come, first-served basis and the hiring of black drivers on black routes. The commissioners rejected the demands and hinted that the city's 210 black cab drivers, who had been charging black riders the 10¢ bus fare, would be heavily fined if they didn't charge every passenger the minimum 45¢ cab fare.

The boycott leaders now had to face the possibility that the taxicabs—their main source of alternative transportation—would no longer be available at low fares. King call Baton Rouge, Louisiana, to speak with those who had successfully staged a bus boycott months before. Rev. T. J. Jemison there had worked out a detailed strategy for transporting boycotters, a complex system of carpooling with drop-off and pick-up points and a communications network to connect those needing rides with those offering them. Jemison suggested that the MIA form a private taxi system. This could be done only if blacks in Montgomery could be convinced to use their cars to ferry maids and laborers to work. It was feared that this would be a tough sell. To many blacks, car ownership was a status symbol that distinguished them from the less privileged. But at a mass meeting of boycotters, more than 150 people volunteered their cars.

The MIA appointed a Transportation Committee to work with some black postal workers who knew the layout of the streets. They

CARRINGTON

developed an efficient plan for transporting the boycotters. Within one week of the meeting at which people volunteered their cars, the MIA had organized forty-eight dispatch and forty-two pick-up stations.

The boycott had withstood its first assault. But setting up this elaborate system required funding. Mass meetings were held twice a week to keep the boycotters informed, to keep spirits high, and to collect contributions.

"This movement was made up of just ordinary black people, some of whom made as little as five dollars a week, but would give one dollar of that to help support the boycott," a local reporter recalled.

In time the MIA bought several station wagons to use as taxis. The churches put their names on the side of many of the cars, which became known as "rolling churches."

Days turned into weeks, and the boycott continued unabated. Yet the Montgomery city fathers and the police were undaunted. When their first attempt at breaking the boycott by pressuring cab drivers failed, they turned to other means. They would try to divide the leadership, set well-to-do blacks against poor blacks, and support segregationist organizations like the Ku Klux Klan, which would strike violently at the boycotters.

The City Commission met with three black ministers, none of whom represented the MIA. The commission's hope was that the MIA did not truly reflect the will of the blacks in Montgomery. If more "reasonable" ministers were to agree to a compromise—the first ten seats in the bus for whites, the last ten seats for blacks, the middle section first-come first-served—perhaps the boycotters would stop their protest. The three ministers accepted the proposal, and the commission then leaked news of the agreement to a local newspaper, which ran bold headlines on the Sunday paper's front page falsely announcing the end of the boycott.

But the leaders of the protesters heard about the hoax and went barhopping on Saturday night, passing the word that the story to appear in the morning paper was a lie—the boycott was still on. On

Monday the bus manager announced tightly that there was "no no-
ticeable increase on the Negro routes."

Although the bus company was feeling the economic costs of the
boycott and downtown businesses were also suffering, letters sup-
porting the mayor's "no talk" and "get tough" policy poured into City
Hall. Many of the most prominent city fathers publicly and pointedly
joined segregationist organizations. King's house was bombed; his wife
fled to a back room with their seven-week-old baby to escape injury.
Two days later the house of another boycott leader was bombed. By
the time the boycott was three months old, the white Citizens Council
membership had doubled to twelve thousand. During that same time,
a group of prominent white lawyers in Montgomery suggested that
the city enforce an old and seldom-used law prohibiting boycotts.
Eighty-nine blacks—including King and twenty-four other
ministers—were indicted for conspiring to boycott.

Meanwhile, the boycott's leaders were pursuing their own court
case, filed on behalf of five women who were challenging the constitu-
tionality of bus segregation. The boycott leaders now considered
whether they might call an end to the strike. The best chance of victory
lay with the courts, not in negotiations with city officials or the bus
company. But King and others insisted on continuing the boycott. If
the court did not rule in their favor, the boycott would still offer some
chance of success. The boycotters stayed off the buses. They carpooled
and walked through winter, spring, and on into the summer of 1956.

In June the five women won their suit, but the city commissioners
appealed the decision to the Supreme Court. The buses remained
segregated, and blacks did not ride them. Meanwhile, whites tried
another way to choke off the boycott: preventing the "rolling churches"
from getting insurance. Without insurance, these church-owned cars
could not operate legally.

The liability insurance was canceled four times in as many months,
and insurance agents throughout the South were pressured by the city
commissioners, the white Citizens Council, and their supporters to

refuse the boycotters coverage. But King arranged for insurance through a black agent in Atlanta, who found a British underwriter who agreed to sell the boycotters a policy. Blacks stayed off the buses through that autumn.

But the segregationists did not quit. In October the mayor sought a restraining order to prevent blacks from gathering on street corners while waiting for the "rolling churches." The mayor claimed that the blacks were singing loudly and bothering residents, thus constituting a public nuisance.

He won a small victory on November 13, when a court granted the order. But on that same day the boycotters won a far greater triumph. The United States Supreme Court affirmed the lower court's decision outlawing segregation on buses. The segregationists challenged the ruling, arguing that it violated states' rights. The Supreme Court, however, refused to reconsider the case.

The written mandate from the Supreme Court did not arrive in Montgomery until December 20. The next day, nearly thirteen months after the boycott began, blacks boarded Montgomery City Lines buses. Nearly a year after Rosa Parks had defied James Blake's order to move to the back of the bus—after months of walking, carpooling, litigation, and intimidation—the boycotters had won.

Years later, Jo Ann Robinson, who had helped initiate the boycott, said, "We felt that we were somebody."

But long before the Montgomery boycott, there had been black resistance to segregated travel. Toward the end of the nineteenth century, blacks had boycotted streetcar lines in more than twenty-seven cities. Montgomery itself had witnessed a two-year-long boycott of segregated car lines in 1900. In the end the local transportation companies acceded to the boycotters' demands, but segregated seating was soon reinstated through city ordinances. So this story may not yet be over.

The trickster character is a familiar one in folklore around the world. This character—among the most popular animals are coyotes, rabbits, and monkeys—uses his wits to escape the clutches of stronger or more numerous foes. In black folktales one of the most famous tricksters is Anansi the spider (Brer Rabbit is a close second), who comes from the folklore of the Ashanti people of southern Ghana, Togo, and Ivory Coast. Anansi stories spread in great profusion to the West Indies, where he is known by many names, among them Nancy, Aunt Nancy, and Sis' Nancy.

I chose this adapted folktale because for me it embraces the principles of Unity (Umoja), Collective Work and Responsibility (Ujima), Purpose (Nia), and Faith (Imani). While each of the sons has an individual talent, it is by being united and working collectively and singlemindedly (with purpose) that they succeed in helping their father. On a more symbolic and metaphysical level, Anansi's misfortunes represent for me the buffeting of the spirit that we as African-descended people have suffered. But through the resourcefulness and united effort of millions of anonymous black men and women over hundreds of years, our spirit continues to shine.

Anansi and his wife, Aso, had six sons. To their parents' surprise, at birth each son announced his name. First there was See Trouble, then Road Builder, then River Drinker, then Game Skinner, then Stone Thrower, and finally Cushion.

They lived happily and uneventfully for many years. Then one afternoon, while returning home from town, Anansi spotted a bright, beautiful, glowing sphere. He tucked it under his arm and was continuing on his way home when he slipped and fell into a lake. A big fish who lived in the lake swam by and swallowed him up.

"Oh, how I would give this glowing ball of light to the person who can rescue me," Anansi thought, very much afraid.

Time passed. The sun fell behind the trees. It grew dark. But Anansi did not come home. Fearing for their father, the brothers asked See Trouble to close his eyes and find out what the matter was. He could hardly believe what he saw. "Our father is in the belly of a large fish," he cried out. Immediately Road Builder cut a path to the lake through the dense forest, and his brothers followed it into the dark, starry night. When they arrived at the lake, River Drinker took a deep breath and sucked up all the water in the lake. There in the mud at the bottom of the lake lay the big fish, pumping its gills frantically and flailing about. Now it was Game Skinner's turn. He jumped down into the mud and sliced open the fish. Anansi stepped out, the great ball of light nestled safely under his shirt.

Suddenly, an immense bird dove from a nearby tree and grabbed Anansi. It took him up into the sky. Stone Thrower grabbed a rock, threw it, and stunned the bird, who dropped Anansi. Down Anansi went. He sped down like a bead of rain. He thought surely this would be the end. But an instant before he hit the ground, Cushion placed himself at the precise spot were his father fell. Anansi was saved.

True to his promise, Anansi looked around, trying to decide which of his six sons should to get the bright, bright ball of light as a prize for having rescued him.

"If it weren't for you," he said to See Trouble, "nobody would have known where I was."

"But if it weren't for you," he said to Road Builder, "nobody would have been able to go through the dense forest to save me."

"And if it weren't for you," he said to River Drinker, "nobody would have been able to get to the bottom of the lake to fetch me."

"And if it weren't for you," he said to Game Skinner, "I would never have gotten out of the body of the fish."

"But if it weren't for you," he said to Stone Thrower, "all their work would have been lost, because that gigantic bird would have eaten me up."

"And if it weren't for you," he said to Cushion, "surely I would have died when the bird released me and I fell to earth. So whom should I give the prize to?"

The brothers and their father looked at each other, puzzled. They scratched their heads. Finally Anansi said, "Let the Great Spirit put the prize up in the sky for you all to share."

And it is still in the sky to this day. You can see it at night.

During the time of the Middle Ages in Europe, beacons of high culture issued from three great African empires: Ghana, Mali, and Songhai. This is the story of how the last of those kingdoms, Songhai, located in the northwestern region of Africa in what is now called Mali, rose to power under one of its greatest rulers. What impressed me about this story, which I got from a book called *Afro-Americans, Then and Now* by Jane Hurley and Doris McGee Haynes, was that Asikya surrounded himself with good counsel and helpers, which speaks not only to the principle of Collective Work and Responsibility (Ujima) but also to the principle of Faith (Imani) in the character of the people you choose as counsel.

There was a wise king named Askiya Muhammad, whose thirty-six-year reign began in 1493, the year after Columbus first arrived in the Americas. With the help of his friends and family, he restored the city of Timbuktu to its position as a world center of scholarship and trade and made the entire kingdom of Songhai great.

When Askiya became king, the country was in disarray. The roads were not safe for travelers because of robbers. People were afraid to come to Timbuktu.

Askiya attacked the problems of his country by first stopping the thieves. He built a powerful army to protect his people. It was said that Askiya's army was so vast and swift that when they rode across the desert they seemed to fly off "like a cloud of grasshoppers." Soon all of the robbers were subdued and the roads were again safe for travelers.

Merchants came to Timbuktu from many countries—by ship from Portugal and the Mediterranean countries, by camel from Cairo, Algiers, Morocco, and Baghdad. They traded their goods for gold, copper, wood, and hides. Students in Songhai were sent to Moslem universities, and the most brilliant of them were invited to stay at Timbuktu, where they were so well respected that they were given handsome endowments to continue their academic pursuits. Timbuktu became a rich and important city once more.

Askiya was also an excellent statesman and administrator. To help him rule more efficiently, he divided his kingdom and appointed directors, usually relatives or trusted friends.

As the ruler of the most powerful empire in the western Sudan, Askiya Muhammad considered it his sacred duty to spread Islam throughout the regions under his command. He saw himself as the "Renewer of the Faith." First he sought to renew and deepen his own faith by embarking on a *hajj*, or holy pilgrimage, to Mecca.

The Songhai emperor was accompanied by 500 horsemen and 1,000 foot soldiers on his journey. He also took 300,000 pieces of gold, one third of which was reserved for the distribution of alms (gifts to the poor) in the holy cities of Mecca and Medina and for the support of a shelter for Sudanese pilgrims in Mecca. From all accounts Askiya Muhammad's generosity on his pilgrimage came close to matching that of Mansa Musa, ruler of the West African kingdom of Mali, two and a half centuries earlier. After a two-year absence on his pilgrimage, Askiya returned to his kingdom and continued to make it a center of civilization.

Without debating the merits of America's western expansion in the nineteenth century, the fact is that African-Americans were there and participated in almost every way imaginable. We were cooks, cowboys, soldiers, settlers, and outlaws. We even had an Indian chief or two. We fought with Native Americans against American troops and with American troops against Native Americans. Tales of Nat Love, Bill Pickett, and Mary Fields should be as interwoven into the lore of the Old West as those tales of Pat Garrett, Buffalo Bill, Sitting Bull, and Chief Dan George.

Clara Brown exhibited the strength and tenacity that was typical of black pioneers. She demonstrated the principles of Purpose (Nia) in her determination to find her daughter, Creativity (Kuumba) and Purpose (Nia) in accumulating money to finance her search, Faith (Imani) in her belief that she would eventually find her daughter and other relatives, and Collective Work and Responsibility (Ujima) in sponsoring her relatives and other blacks to take advantage of the opportunities of the West. The following excerpt was adapted from William Loren Katz's book, *The Black West*.

Clara Brown, who saw her husband, two daughters, and son sold to different slaveowners, was destined to become a leading citizen of Central City, Colorado. She was born in Virginia in 1803 and three years later was sold with her mother to an owner who headed west. Several owners later, she was able to purchase her freedom. In 1859 she made her way to St. Louis, Missouri, where she persuaded a party of gold prospectors to hire her as a cook.

At the age of fifty-nine she found herself in the back seat of a covered wagon, one in a caravan of thirty wagons slowly making their

way across the plains to Denver. In June, after eight weeks of travel, the wagon train reached West Denver. There she helped two Methodist ministers found the Union Sunday School, and she then headed toward Central City, hoping to earn enough money to purchase her family from slavery.

In Central City Mrs. Brown opened a laundry (50¢ for a blue or red flannel shirt), served as a nurse, and organized the first Sunday school. By 1866, and despite the fact that she never refused to help anyone in need, she had earned $10,000, including investments in mining claims. After the Civil War she searched in vain for her family. She did locate thirty-four other relatives, whom she brought to Denver by steamboat and wagon. It was only the first of many black wagon trains she would sponsor. Shortly before her death, Clara Brown was reunited with her daughter.

Clara Brown's name is remembered with respect in Central City. The Colorado Pioneers Association buried her with honors; a bronze plaque in the St. James Methodist Church tells of how she provided her home for worship before the church was built; a chair at the Opera House is named in her memory. But undoubtedly she was remembered best in the hearts of those many she helped.

APPETIZERS

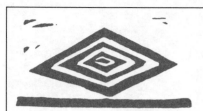

SPICED OKRA "SALSA"
(AFRICA)

Sheila Johnson got this recipe from *African Cooking*, one of the volumes in the Time-Life "Foods of the World" series. "What I try to do when I make my Kwanzaa menu," says Johnson, who works with the education and job information center of the New York City Public Library, "is to choose ingredients that have some African connection. There are certain foods that I make sure I use: sweet potato, greens, rice, and okra. I choose okra because I grew up with it, served steamed and stewed. It is also common to Africa and has spread throughout the world because we have spread throughout the world."

SPICED OKRA "SALSA"

Cook's Notes: We serve this spiced okra in a bowl to spoon onto crisp whole-wheat crackers as a kind of African salsa. Don't make this too far ahead or the okra will discolor.

Makes about 2 cups

3 cups water
1 small onion, finely chopped
2 garlic cloves, minced
1 teaspoon salt
½ teaspoon cayenne pepper
½ teaspoon freshly ground white pepper
1 pound fresh okra, stems and tips trimmed, cut crosswise into 3 pieces

1. In a medium saucepan, bring the water, onion, garlic, salt, cayenne, and white pepper to a boil over medium-high heat. Add the okra and boil, stirring occasionally, until the liquid has almost completely evaporated, about 15 minutes.
2. Drain the okra in a fine sieve, and rinse it under cold running water; drain well again. Transfer the okra to a bowl, cover, and refrigerate for at least 1 hour or up to 6 hours before serving.

FRIED OKRA

Cook's Notes: Even the most dedicated okra-hater will enjoy these crisp treats. While they always hit the spot at dinnertime, they also make a satisfying nibble to serve with cocktails.

Makes about 30

1 pound fresh okra, stems and tips trimmed
2 large eggs
1 cup all-purpose flour
⅔ cup water
½ teaspoon salt
¼ teaspoon cayenne pepper
Vegetable oil for frying

1. Wash the okra well, then pat completely dry with paper towels.
2. In a medium bowl, whisk the eggs well. Add the flour, water, salt, and cayenne, and whisk until smooth.
3. In a large skillet, heat enough oil to reach ½ inch up the sides until it is hot but not smoking (an electric skillet set at 375° works well). In batches, toss the okra in the batter to coat completely. Fry until golden brown on all sides, turning occasionally, about 4 minutes. Transfer the fried okra to drain briefly on paper towels, then serve hot.

FRIED OKRA
(WEST AFRICA)

"This is my favorite way to eat okra," says Audie Odum-Stallato, a New Jersey–based cook and caterer. "When okra is made like this and not sliced up, the vegetable's juices don't have a chance to get slippery. It's a perfect way to enjoy okra if you like its taste but not its texture."

According to Waverley Root, okra was introduced to the New World by African captives four hundred years ago. One vestige of this connection (and there are many) can be seen in Brazil, where a religious sect known as Candomblé uses okra as a main ingredient in one of its consecrated dishes. It is prepared by its priestesses, Root writes, for ritual observances and must be made according to a rigid formula. To prepare the dish in accordance with the sacred rules takes several hours and deviation from that formula would be sacrilege.

Luckily Audie's dish is faster, simpler and, if you fear the wrath of the gods, safer.

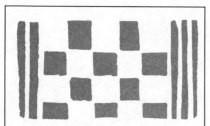

CURRIED LAMB SAMOOSAS WITH CHUTNEY DIP
(SOUTH AFRICA)

Samoosas, which originated in East India as "samosas," are meat- or vegetable-filled pastries. They are popular as snacks in much of eastern and southern Africa, where they are sold at street stands. "I make them bite-size so they can be served at parties as hors d'oeuvres," Audie Odum-Stallato explains. "I made them for Kwanzaa and they went like crazy!" Audie suggests that when you fill the wonton skins, make sure you squeeze out all the air. "If you don't, a bubble might form in the skin and burst open in the oven."

CURRIED LAMB SAMOOSAS WITH CHUTNEY DIP

Cook's Notes: These bite-size pastries bursting with a tasty lamb filling, and served with a chutney dip, would be a hit at any holiday celebration. You can make the filling up to a day ahead, and fill the samoosas up to 4 hours before deep-frying.

Makes about 40

1 tablespoon vegetable oil
1 small onion, minced
1 garlic clove, minced
1 pound ground lamb or ground beef round
1 teaspoon ground cinnamon
1 teaspoon salt
½ teaspoon ground cumin
¼ teaspoon curry powder
¼ teaspoon chili powder
¼ teaspoon freshly ground black pepper
⅛ teaspoon ground cloves
1 cup store-bought mango chutney
3 tablespoons orange juice
40 wonton skins, about 3½ inches square
Vegetable oil for deep-frying

1. In a medium skillet, heat the oil over medium heat. Add the onion and cook until softened, about 3 minutes. Add the garlic and stir 1 minute. Add the ground lamb and cook, stirring often, until the meat loses its pink color, about 5 minutes. Drain off any excess fat. Add

the cinnamon, salt, cumin, curry powder, chili powder, pepper, and cloves, and stir for 1 minute. Remove from the heat and let the lamb filling cool completely.

2. Meanwhile, in a blender or food processor, process the chutney and orange juice until smooth. Cover, and let stand at room temperature until ready to serve.

3. Place a wonton skin on a work surface. Place about 2 teaspoons of lamb filling in the center. Moisten the edges of the wonton with water, fold it over diagonally to form a triangle, and press the edges to seal. Repeat the procedure with the remaining skins and filling.

4. Preheat the oven to 200°.

5. In a large skillet, pour enough vegetable oil to reach ½ inch up the sides. Heat the oil over medium-high heat until it is hot but not smoking. (An electric skillet set at 350° works well.) In batches, fry the samoosas, turning once, until golden brown, about 4 minutes. Using a slotted spoon, transfer the fried samoosas to a paper towel–lined baking sheet, and keep them warm in the oven while frying the remaining samoosas.

6. Serve the samoosas warm, with the chutney dip on the side.

BACALAITOS FRITOS WITH CILANTRO DIP
Garlicky Salt Cod Fritters
(BARBADOS)

Like so many foods of the African diaspora, saltfish—codfish salted so as to preserve it without refrigeration—was devised to provide cheap and efficient nutrition for African captives. It is eaten today throughout the Caribbean.

   "This is one of the most popular finger foods in Puerto Rico," enthuses Saalik Cuevas, a computer programmer. "It's usually eaten as a side dish, or for lunch as an easily made meat substitute. When I visited my grandmother as a child, she would bring us a platter of bacalaitos in the mid-afternoon and they would tide us over until dinner."

BACALAITOS FRITOS WITH CILANTRO DIP
Garlicky Salt Cod Fritters

Cook's Notes: In Puerto Rico these would be enjoyed as a side dish, but their crispy richness led us to use them as an appetizer, dipped into a verdant green mayonnaise. When choosing salt cod, be sure to get the boneless, skinless variety. While it's more expensive, it is easier to work with. And pick out a nice thick piece with a snowy white coating. A yellowish tinge indicates age, and it will have a strong fishy taste.

Makes about 32

1 pound boneless, skinless salt cod
⅔ cup mayonnaise
¼ cup chopped fresh cilantro
3 garlic cloves, crushed through a garlic press
1 fresh hot chile pepper, such as jalapeño, seeded and minced
2 scallions, minced
1 tablespoon fresh lemon juice
2 cups all-purpose flour
2 cups water
¼ cup achiote oil (see page 178)
1 teaspoon salt
¼ teaspoon cayenne pepper
¼ teaspoon freshly ground black pepper
½ cup olive oil

1. Rinse the salt cod well under cold running water, then place it in a bowl and cover with cold water. Refrigerate for at least 24 hours, changing the water four or five times during that period.

2. Drain the cod, place it in a large skillet, and add enough cold water to barely cover. Bring it to a simmer over medium-high heat; then reduce the heat to low and simmer, uncovered, until the cod flakes easily with a fork, 30 to 40 minutes. Using a slotted spatula, transfer the salt cod to a bowl and allow it to cool completely. Flake the fish with a fork.

3. Meanwhile, in a medium bowl, stir together the mayonnaise, cilantro, one third of the garlic, the chile pepper, scallions, and lemon juice. Cover and refrigerate for at least 1 hour or up to overnight.

4. In a medium bowl, whisk the flour, water, achiote oil, remaining garlic, salt, cayenne, and black pepper to form a smooth batter. Stir in the flaked fish.

5. Preheat the oven to 200°.

6. In a large skillet, heat the oil over medium-high heat until it is hot but not smoking. In batches, drop tablespoons of the batter into the skillet to form small fritters. Cook, turning once, until golden brown, about 4 minutes. Using a slotted spatula transfer the fritters to a paper towel–lined baking sheet, and keep warm in the oven while preparing the remaining fritters.

7. Serve the fritters immediately, as a finger food, with the cilantro sauce served on the side for dipping.

OVEN-BARBECUED DRUMETTES WITH DEE DEE'S BBQ SAUCE
(UNITED STATES)

"Barbecue is something in the tradition from the southern side of my family," says Dee Dee Dailey, who also has relatives from the West Indies. Dailey owns the Brooklyn-based catering service, Dee Dee Dailey's Fine Catering. "My father's mother was from Virginia. My barbecue sauce is medium-hot, not scalding. If you want it hotter, you can add a dash of red pepper. You should use only apple cider vinegar— never distilled white vinegar, because it tastes acrid."

OVEN BARBECUED DRUMETTES WITH DEE DEE'S BBQ SAUCE

Cook's Notes: *Real* barbecue must be slow-cooked outdoors over smoldering hardwood coals. But this method produces tasty "indoor" BBQ, and everyone will love nibbling on these sauce-drenched mini-drumsticks (they're really cut-up chicken wings).

Makes about 3 cups sauce, about 30 drumettes

DEE DEE'S BBQ SAUCE:
¼ cup olive oil
1 large onion, finely chopped
5 garlic cloves, minced
2 cups tomato purée
½ cup cider vinegar
½ cup packed dark brown sugar
1 tablespoon Worcestershire sauce
2 teaspoons dry mustard
1 teaspoon dried oregano
½ teaspoon chili powder
½ teaspoon salt
¼ teaspoon freshly ground black pepper
1 bay leaf

DRUMETTES:
15 whole chicken wings (about 3¼ pounds), or 2¾ pounds precut
    chicken drumettes
2 quarts water
½ cup cider vinegar

1 medium onion, sliced
2 garlic cloves, crushed through a garlic press

1. Prepare the sauce: In a large saucepan, heat the oil over medium heat. Add the onion and cook, stirring often, until softened, about 3 minutes. Add the garlic and cook, stirring, 1 minute longer. Stir in all the remaining ingredients and bring to a simmer. Reduce the heat to low and simmer, uncovered, until slightly thickened, about 1 hour. The sauce can be used immediately, but it will improve in flavor if cooled to room temperature, covered, and refrigerated overnight. (The sauce can be made up to 1 week ahead; keep covered and refrigerated.)
2. Prepare the drumettes: Using a cleaver or a heavy knife, chop the whole chicken wings through the joints into three pieces. (Precut chicken drumettes need no chopping.) Discard the pointed wing tips (or reserve them for another use, such as chicken stock).
3. In a large saucepan, bring the water, vinegar, onion, and garlic to a boil over high heat. Add the drumettes, return to boil, and reduce the heat to low. Cook for 10 minutes. Drain the drumettes, discarding the cooking liquid.
4. Place Dee Dee's BBQ Sauce in a large bowl, add the drained drumettes, and toss to coat well with the sauce. Cover, and refrigerate for at least 1 hour or up to 4 hours.
5. Position a rack in the top third of the oven, and preheat to 375°.
6. Lift the coated drumettes out of the sauce, and arrange them on a large lightly greased baking sheet. Bake, basting occasionally with the remaining sauce, until the drumettes show no sign of pink at the bone when prodded with the tip of a small sharp knife, about 30 minutes. Serve hot, warm, or at room temperature.

CONCH EMPANADAS
(UNITED STATES)

Here Dee Dee Dailey takes the Mexican version of the turnover —similar to Samoosas (page 16) and Kingston Meat Patties (page 114)—and as a salute to the West Indian side of her family, fills it with conch, a mollusk found in the Caribbean and popular as a food there.

CONCH EMPANADAS

Cook's Notes: Conch (pronounced "conk") can be found in Italian neighborhood fish markets under the name *scungilli*. Tough as an old tire when raw, it must be pounded with a mallet, then long-simmered to reach tenderness, but luckily it is normally sold precooked. If conch is unavailable, substitute 1½ cups chopped cooked shrimp (about ¾ pound).

Makes about 30

CURRIED PASTRY:

2 cups all-purpose flour
1 teaspoon curry powder
½ teaspoon salt
12 tablespoons (1½ sticks) unsalted butter, cut into ¼-inch cubes
⅓ cup ice water

FILLING:

2 tablespoons olive oil
1 small onion, finely chopped
¼ cup finely chopped green bell pepper
2 garlic cloves, minced
¾ pound precooked conch (*scungilli*), finely chopped (a food
    processor works best)
2 tablespoons chopped fresh cilantro
2 tablespoons chopped fresh parsley
2 tablespoons bottled clam juice or water
2 teaspoons Old Bay Seasoning
1 teaspoon dried thyme
¼ teaspoon freshly ground black pepper

1 large egg, beaten

1. Make the pastry dough: In a medium bowl, stir together the flour, curry powder, and salt. Using a pastry blender or two knives, cut the butter into the flour until the mixture resembles coarse meal. Tossing the mixture with a fork, gradually sprinkle in the ice water, mixing just until the dough is moist enough to hold together when pinched between your thumb and forefinger. (You may need to add more water.) Form the dough into a thick flat disk, wrap it in waxed paper, and chill for at least 1 hour or overnight.
2. Make the filling: In a large skillet, heat the oil over medium heat. Add the onion and bell pepper and cook, stirring often, until softened, about 3 minutes. Add the garlic and stir for 1 minute. Stir in the conch, cilantro, parsley, clam juice or water, Old Bay Seasoning, thyme, and pepper. Cook, stirring often, until heated through, 1 to 2 minutes. (As conch has a distinctive "salt-of-the-sea" flavor, the filling probably will not need salt, but taste now to check for seasoning.) Remove from the heat and allow the filling to cool completely.
3. Preheat the oven to 400°.
4. On a lightly floured work surface, roll the dough out to form a 14-inch circle about ⅛ inch thick. Using a 3-inch round cookie cutter, cut out about twelve circles. Gather up and reserve the scraps.
5. Lightly brush the edges of the rounds with some of the beaten egg. Place about 2 teaspoons filling in the center of each round. Fold the rounds in half to enclose the filling, and press the edges with a fork to seal them. Transfer the empanadas to a lightly greased baking sheet. Repeat this procedure with the remaining dough and filling, combining the dough scraps and rolling them out last.
6. Lightly brush the tops of the empanadas with beaten egg. Bake until golden brown, 15 to 20 minutes. Serve hot, warm, or at room temperature.

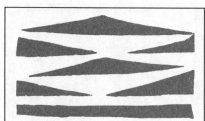

RED SNAPPER SALAD ON CUCUMBER SLICES
(UNITED STATES)

This delightful hors d'oeuvre is from Dee Dee Dailey's extensive repertoire.

RED SNAPPER SALAD ON CUCUMBER SLICES

Cook's Notes: A Caribbean-inspired hors d'oeuvre for your fanciest Kwanzaa celebration—poached red snapper fillet salad dressed with a lime-cilantro vinaigrette.

Makes about 30

COURT BOUILLON:

1 quart water

½ cup dry white wine

1 medium onion, thickly sliced

1 medium celery rib, thickly sliced

1 medium carrot, coarsely chopped

1 parsley sprig

½ teaspoon salt

¼ teaspoon dried thyme

¼ teaspoon peppercorns

1 bay leaf

RED SNAPPER SALAD:

2 red snapper fillets (about ½ pound each)

1 tablespoon fresh lime juice

1 garlic clove, crushed through a garlic press

½ teaspoon salt

¼ teaspoon chili powder

¼ teaspoon freshly ground black pepper

2 tablespoons olive oil

¼ cup chopped fresh cilantro

3 tablespoons minced red bell pepper

1 English (seedless) cucumber, cut into 30 ¼-inch-thick slices
Cilantro leaves, for garnish

1. Make the court bouillon: In a large saucepan, bring all the ingredients to a boil over high heat. Reduce the heat to low and simmer for 30 minutes. Drain the court bouillon through a sieve set over a large bowl, reserving the liquid and discarding the solids. (The court bouillon can be made up to 1 day ahead; allow it to cool, then cover and refrigerate.)

2. Make the salad: In a large skillet, bring the court bouillon to a simmer over medium-high heat. Add the snapper fillets, reduce the heat to low, and simmer until the fish is just opaque in the center when prodded with the tip of a sharp knife, about 5 minutes. Using a slotted spatula, transfer the cooked fillets to a bowl and cool completely. Using a fork, flake the fillets.

3. In a small bowl, whisk together the lime juice, garlic, salt, chili powder, and pepper. Whisk in the oil until combined. Then stir in the cilantro and bell pepper. Pour this dressing over the cooled fish and toss well to combine. Cover, and refrigerate for at least 1 hour or up to 8 hours.

4. To serve, place about 2 teaspoons of the salad in the center of each cucumber round, and top with a cilantro leaf.

KELEWELE
Spicy Fried Plantain
(CARIBBEAN)

Plantain in various guises is a popular snack throughout West Africa and the Caribbean. This variation was contributed by Dee Dee Dailey.

KELEWELE
Spicy Fried Plantain

Cook's Notes: Use yellow-ripe, not-too-firm plantains for these marvelously seasoned nibbles. They could easily become a favorite cocktail-time hors d'oeuvre, especially when served with a Caribbean rum drink like Mavis's Pineapple-Papaya Punch (page 267).

Makes about 60

4 large yellow-ripe plantains, peeled (see page 230)
2 tablespoons grated fresh ginger
1 tablespoon ground cloves
½ teaspoon cayenne pepper, or more to taste
¼ teaspoon grated nutmeg
¼ teaspoon ground cinnamon
½ teaspoon salt
2 tablespoons warm water
Vegetable oil for frying

1. Cut the plantains into diagonal slices about ½ inch thick. In a medium bowl, combine the ginger, cloves, cayenne, nutmeg, cinnamon, and salt. Stir in the water to form a paste. Add the plantain slices and toss to coat well. Let stand 30 minutes.
2. Preheat the oven to 200°.
3. Pour enough vegetable oil into a large skillet to reach ½ inch up the sides. Heat the oil over medium-high heat until hot but not smoking. (An electric skillet set at 350° works well.) In batches, fry the plantain slices, turning once, until golden brown, about 5 minutes. Using a slotted spoon, transfer the fried plantains to a paper towel–lined baking sheet, and keep warm in the oven while frying the remaining plantains. Serve warm.

SPINACH-LEEK DIP WITH CRUDITÉS

Cook's Notes: Many cooks have a version of this chunky dip, swirled with emerald-green spinach, and you can personalize this one with your choice of herbs. Try ¼ cup of chopped fresh dill, basil, or tarragon.

Makes about 2½ cups

1 (8-ounce) package cream cheese, at room temperature
½ cup mayonnaise
½ cup sour cream
1 (10-ounce) package frozen chopped spinach, defrosted and drained
2 scallions, chopped
½ package dried leek soup
1 (8-ounce) can water chestnuts, drained and chopped
¼ teaspoon hot pepper sauce
1 large acorn squash (about 1½ pounds)
Assorted fresh vegetables for dipping

1. In a medium bowl, cream the cream cheese, mayonnaise, and sour cream together with a wooden spoon until smooth.
2. In a sieve, press the defrosted spinach with your hands to remove as much moisture as possible. Add the spinach, scallions, dried leek soup, water chestnuts, and hot pepper sauce to the cream cheese mixture, and combine well. Cover, and refrigerate for at least 1 hour or up to 2 days.
3. Cut the acorn squash in half vertically. Using a large spoon, scoop out the seeds and enough flesh to create a large cavity in each half. Place the squash halves side by side in a large basket. Fill them with the dip, surround with fresh vegetables, and serve.

SPINACH-LEEK DIP WITH CRUDITÉS
(UNITED STATES)

Mavis Young, who co-owns a restaurant and catering company in La Mesa, California, gives this cooking hint: "We prepare this dip a day ahead of time and keep it in the refrigerator because that allows the seasonings to blend better."

SWEET POTATO FRIES WITH CURRIED MAYONNAISE DIP
(UNITED STATES)

Africa meets India in this dip, which marries the sweet potato —a food almost synonymous with the presence of black people —and curry.

SWEET POTATO FRIES WITH CURRIED MAYONNAISE DIP

Cook's Notes: We've never met a french fry we didn't like, and this recipe is a delicious twist on an old favorite. The exotically spiced dip would also go well with potato or plantain chips, or a platter of raw vegetables.

Serves 6 to 8

CURRIED MAYONNAISE DIP:
⅔ cup mayonnaise
⅓ cup plain low-fat yogurt
1 tablespoon curry powder
1 teaspoon ground ginger
½ teaspoon turmeric powder
½ teaspoon chili powder
½ teaspoon paprika, preferably sweet Hungarian
¼ teaspoon salt

SWEET POTATO FRIES:
3 medium sweet potatoes, "Louisiana yams," about 1½ pounds
Vegetable oil for deep-frying
1 teaspoon salt
¼ teaspoon freshly ground black pepper

1. Make the dip: In a small bowl, stir together the mayonnaise and yogurt. (Do not whisk, as the yogurt will thin out.) Stir in the curry, ginger, turmeric, chili powder, paprika, and salt. Cover, and refrigerate for at least 1 hour or overnight.
2. Preheat the oven to 200°.

3. Using a large sharp knife, cut the sweet potatoes into strips 3 inches long and ⅛ inch thick. Pat dry with paper towels.

4. In a deep medium saucepan, heat the oil over high heat until a deep-fry thermometer reads 375°. In batches, deep-fry the sweet potato sticks until golden brown, 3 to 4 minutes. Using kitchen tongs, transfer the sweet potato sticks to a paper towel–lined baking sheet to drain. Keep the sticks warm in the oven while frying the remaining sweet potatoes. Sprinkle with the salt and pepper, and serve warm, with the curried mayonnaise alongside for dipping.

CHARLESTON CRAB SPREAD WITH BENNE CRACKERS
(UNITED STATES)

The roots of black Southern seafood are hinted at in this great party snack.

CHARLESTON CRAB SPREAD WITH BENNE CRACKERS

Cook's Notes: Chunky seafood spread slathered onto crisp sesame ("benne") crackers is a popular cocktail go-with down South Carolina way. Make the spread at least 8 hours ahead to allow the flavors to combine.

Makes about 2½ cups

1 (8-ounce) package cream cheese, at room temperature
½ cup mayonnaise
½ pound fresh crabmeat, picked over for cartilage, or imitation crab
2 tablespoons minced onion
1 garlic clove, crushed through a garlic press
1½ teaspoons Old Bay Seasoning
1 teaspoon fresh lemon juice
1 teaspoon Worcestershire sauce
2 tablespoons chopped fresh chives or parsley, for garnish
Sesame-topped crackers

1. In a medium bowl, cream the cream cheese and mayonnaise together with a wooden spoon until smooth. Stir in the crabmeat, onion, garlic, Old Bay Seasoning, lemon juice, and Worcestershire until mixed. Cover, and refrigerate for at least 8 hours or overnight.
2. Transfer the spread to a bowl, garnish with the chives or parsley, and serve with the sesame crackers.

CHICARRONES DE POLLO
Fried Chicken Dominican Style

Cook's Notes: Chicarrones de Pollo are great appetizers, but we often serve them as a main course at dinnertime with Arroz con Coco (page 195) and a green salad. For the most flavorful results, allow a full 24 hours for the chicken to marinate.

Makes 12 appetizers

6 chicken thighs (about 2 pounds)
¼ cup soy sauce
¼ cup fresh lime juice
¼ cup dark rum
1 tablespoon grated fresh ginger
2 tablespoons light brown sugar
¼ teaspoon hot red pepper flakes
Vegetable oil for deep-frying

1. Using a heavy cleaver, chop the chicken pieces in half vertically, through the thigh bone. (Or have the butcher do this for you.) In a large nonreactive bowl, combine the soy sauce, lime juice, rum, ginger, brown sugar, and red pepper flakes; mix thoroughly. Add the chicken pieces and coat well. Cover, and refrigerate for at least 8 hours or up to 24 hours.
2. Pour enough oil into a large skillet to reach ½ inch up the sides. Heat the oil over medium-high heat until very hot but not smoking. (An electric skillet set at 325° works well.) Drain the chicken pieces, and pat them dry on paper towels. Fry the chicken pieces, turning often, until they are deeply browned on all sides and show no sign of pink when pierced with the tip of a sharp knife, about 15 minutes. Drain the chicken briefly on paper towels before serving hot, warm, or at room temperature.

CHICARRONES DE POLLO
Fried Chicken Dominican Style
(DOMINICAN REPUBLIC)

These are the national snack of the Dominican Republic, and they will become one of your favorites too.

PICKLED WATERMELON RIND
(UNITED STATES)

Audie Odum-Stallato remembers that her mother would pickle cucumbers, green tomatoes, and various vegetables every year. Audie's mother had heard about pickling watermelon rinds and asked a relative who lived in the South how it was done. "We used pickled watermelon rinds as a relish with a main dish," Audie remembers. "It's also really nice to use it in a potato salad instead of gherkins." And what does pickled watermelon taste like to the novitiate? "Sort of like a pickled cucumber, but watermelon has a more delicate flavor," Audie says.

PICKLED WATERMELON RIND

Cook's Notes: You may not be able to find watermelon in the winter in your town, so keep this recipe in mind for summertime. You can put up the watermelon pickles then and let them ripen to perfection, to enjoy during the holidays on your buffet table. If you can't find pickling salt, use plain noniodized salt.

Makes about 2 quarts

2 quarts cut-up watermelon rind, in 1-inch squares
3 tablespoons plain noniodized salt
Cold water
2 tablespoons pickling spices
1 quart cider vinegar
3 cups granulated sugar
¼ cup fresh lemon juice
2 (1-quart) canning jars with brand-new lids and rings (see "Notes on Canning and Preserving," page 205)

1. Using a small sharp knife, pare away all of the green rind and any remaining pulp from each rind square.
2. In a large bowl, combine the salt and 1 quart cold water, stirring to dissolve the salt. Add the watermelon rinds and enough cold water to cover the rinds completely. Cover with a plate to keep the rinds submerged, and let stand at room temperature at least 8 hours or overnight. Drain well.
3. In a large saucepan, bring the watermelon rinds and cold water to cover to a boil over high heat. Reduce the heat to medium, and cook until the rinds are crisp-tender, about 10 minutes. Drain well.

4. Place the pickling spices in a cheesecloth square, and tie it into a bundle. In a large saucepan, combine the vinegar, sugar, lemon juice, and pickling spices. Bring to a boil over high heat, stirring to dissolve the sugar. Reduce the heat to low, and simmer for 10 minutes. Add the watermelon rinds, return to simmer, and cook until the rinds are translucent, about 30 minutes.

5. Using a slotted spoon, transfer the watermelon rinds to two hot sterilized canning jars. Ladle the hot syrup into the jars. Wipe the rims clean with a hot wet cloth. Screw on the jars' lids and rings, and let cool completely. Let the watermelon pickles stand for at least 1 month before serving.

Nguzo Saba

Umoja (Unity)
Kujichagulia (Self-determination)
Ujima (Collective Work and Responsibility)
Ujamaa (Cooperative Economics)
Nia (Purpose)
Kuumba (Creativity)
Imani (Faith)

CARRINGTON

Before he was Malcolm X—black revolutionary—Malcolm X was Malcolm Little, one of five children born to Rev. Earl Little and his wife, Louise, in Omaha, Nebraska. Malcolm's early awareness of his responsibility as a black person came first from his parents, both of whom were members of Marcus Garvey's Universal Negro Improvement Association. The goals of the UNIA were to promote unity among blacks of the world by instilling racial pride, to acquire economic independence, and to build a black government in Africa. (Remember that from about the turn of the century until 1957, all of sub-Saharan Africa had been colonized and was run by whites.) But when Malcolm was six and living in Lansing, Michigan, where his family had moved after a group of Ku Klux Klansmen had attacked their house, his father was murdered by the Lansing version of the Klan. Shortly afterward his mother was committed to a mental hospital, and Malcolm and his siblings were parceled out to different foster homes. Malcolm later became a hustler and drug dealer in Detroit, Boston, and New York until he was arrested for burglary and sentenced to prison. It was in prison that he converted to Islam and became a member of the Nation of Islam. When he was released, he became the Nation of Islam's most charismatic spokesman. He was assassinated at the Audubon Ballroom in Harlem in 1965.

In this excerpt adapted from *The Autobiography of Malcolm X*, written with Alex Haley, Malcolm X is in prison, waking up to the effects of his illiteracy. While there are many instances in black history where education is emphasized, I chose Malcolm for a couple of reasons: First, because he was undeniably a "tough guy." He was a man who would put to rest any thought that learning and education were worthless or weak. Malcolm exhibited Creativity (Kuumba) and Purpose (Nia) when he set about learning how to articulate his pride in his race and his faith in his people. Second, because literacy was the vehicle for Malcolm's finding out about African and African-American history. When I see young African-Americans discovering Malcolm X, I hope they realize just how much he valued education.

I became increasingly frustrated at not being able to express what I wanted to convey in letters that I wrote. In the street, I had been the most articulate hustler out there. But now, trying to write simple English, I not only wasn't articulate, I wasn't even functional.

Many who today hear me somewhere in person, or on television, or those who read something I've said, will think I went to school far beyond the eighth grade. This impression is due entirely to my prison studies.

It had really begun back in the Charlestown Prison, when Bimbi [a fellow inmate] made me feel envious of his stock of knowledge. I had tried to emulate him. But I understood so few words of every book I picked up that these books might as well have been written in Chinese.

I saw that the best thing I could do was get hold of a dictionary—to study, to learn some words. I spent two days just riffling uncertainly through the dictionary's pages. I'd never realized so many words existed! I didn't know *which* words I needed to learn. Finally, just to start some kind of action, I began copying.

CARRINGTON

In my slow, painstaking, ragged handwriting, I copied into my tablet everything printed on that first page, down to the punctuation marks. I woke up the next morning, thinking about those words—immensely proud to realize that not only had I written so much at one time, but I'd written words that I never knew were in the world. Moreover, with a little effort, I also could remember what many of these words meant. I reviewed the words whose meanings I didn't remember.

I was so fascinated that I went on—I copied the dictionary's next page. With every succeeding page, I also learned of people and places and events from history. Actually the dictionary is like a miniature encyclopedia. That was the way I started copying what eventually became the entire dictionary.

I suppose it was inevitable that as my word-base broadened, I could for the first time pick up a book and read and now begin to understand what the book was saying. Anyone who has read a great deal can imagine the new world that opened. Let me tell you something: from then until I left that prison, in every free moment I had, if I was not reading in the library, I was reading on my bunk. You couldn't have gotten me out of books with a wedge. In fact, up to then, I never had been so truly free.

Joel Chandler Harris was a white newspaper reporter in the nineteenth century who, as a sideline, traveled around the South and compiled what remains the largest single collection of black American folktales. To give the collection unity, he created a character, Uncle Remus, who told these tales to a white child.

For the longest time, I'd heard how engaging these Uncle Remus tales were, but every time I tried to read one I was put off by the dialect. I'd read that Harris took great care to record them just the way they were told to him, but to my ears they sounded false. Or perhaps they were that "deep." Regardless, I couldn't make his stories sing in my head.

But then I came across the tales as retold by the poet and novelist Julius Lester. They have a loose bluesy quality that I found irresistible. In the foreword to *The Tales of Uncle Remus: The Adventures of Brer Rabbit*, from which this story comes, Lester admits that his first, most important, and most delicate decision in retelling the story was in deciding on a voice: Should he use straight English or some variety of black English? In the end, Lester opted for what he calls "a modified contemporary southern black English, which is a combination of standard English and black English."

"Sometimes *kind of* is used," he writes, "and other times *kinna*. How a word is pronounced depends on where it is in a sentence and whether the sentence requires the harder sound of *kind of* or the softer sound of *kinna*. In black English sound is as important as meaning." Anyway, after reading Lester's versions, suddenly I knew why there was all the fuss about this black folklore. Lester's versions are warm, readable, and speakable. They are a joy and a fun way to get the whole family talking about Creativity (Kuumba).

One year Brer Tiger moved into the community. None of the animals wanted to have a thing to do with him. . . . He was big, looked like he didn't have no friends, and didn't want none. Everybody kept their distance, everybody except Brer Rabbit.

Brer Tiger was hardly moved into his house good when Brer Rabbit invited him to go for a walk so they could get acquainted.

They were strolling along chatting with one another when they came to a creek. Neither one wanted to wade across and get his feet wet. Brer Rabbit saw a vine hanging from a tree and he swung across to the other side. Brer Tiger thought that looked easy enough, so he grabbed the vine and started to swing across. But he's such a heavy creature that the vine broke and he landed smack dab in the middle of the creek—KERSPLASH!

CARRINGTON

When he drug himself out and saw Brer Rabbit sitting on the bank laughing, he growled. Brer Rabbit laughed again.

"How come you ain't scared of me like all the other animals?" Brer Tiger wanted to know. "Everybody else run when my shadow hits the ground."

"How come the fleas ain't scared of you?" Brer Rabbit asked. "They littler than me."

Brer Tiger didn't like that kind of sass. "You best be glad I had my breakfast, 'cause if I was hungry you'd be in my stomach now."

Brer Rabbit looked at him. "Brer Tiger, I'm gon' tell you something. If you'd done that, you'd have more sense in you than you got now."

Brer Tiger growled louder. "I'm going to let you off this time, but next time I see you, you mine."

Brer Rabbit laughed. "If you so much as dream about messing with me, I want you to get up the next morning and come apologize."

Brer Rabbit hopped away. Brer Tiger got so mad he grabbed a tree and clawed all the bark off it.

Brer Rabbit was angry too. He shook his fist at the tree stumps and carried on like he was quarreling with his shadow because it was following after him.

He hadn't gone far when he heard a terrible noise. It was Brer Elephant tromping through the woods, eating off the tops of trees. Brer Rabbit marched up to him.

"Brer Elephant, how would you like to help me run Brer Tiger back where he came from?"

"Well, having him in the community sho' has lowered property values, Brer Rabbit, but I don't know. If I help you, I won't get hurt, will I?"

"What can hurt something as big as you?"

"Brer Tiger got sharp claws and big teeth. He might bite and scratch me."

Brer Rabbit said, "Don't worry about that. Just do what I say and we'll run Brer Tiger away from here."

Early the next morning Brer Rabbit was up and moving about. When he saw Brer Tiger coming, he ran to where he'd told Brer Elephant to wait. Brer Rabbit tied a long vine around one of Brer Elephant's hind legs and tied the other end to a big tree. Then Brer Elephant kneeled down and Brer Rabbit hopped on.

A couple of minutes later Brer Tiger came up and saw Brer Rabbit on Brer Elephant's back. He smiled. He thought Brer Rabbit was caught up there and couldn't get down. Brer Elephant started swinging backward and forward and rocking from side to side.

"Well, Brer Rabbit. I ain't had my breakfast this morning and I sho' am hungry," said Brer Tiger.

"That so?" Brer Rabbit returned. "Well, you just wait till I get through skinning this here elephant I caught this morning and I'll be down to take care of you."

Brer Rabbit whispered in Brer Elephant's ear: "When I put my nose on your neck, scream loud as you can. Don't be scared. Just scream!"

Brer Elephant screamed so loud he knocked over a couple of trees.

"You wait right there, Brer Tiger. I be done skinning this elephant in a few minutes."

Brer Rabbit bent over and made like he was nibbling behind Brer Elephant's ear. Brer Elephant screamed again. A couple of more trees fell.

Brer Tiger started inching backward.

"Where you going, Brer Tiger? I'm almost done. Be down to get you shortly. Just hold on."

Brer Rabbit bent over; Brer Elephant screamed; some more trees fell, and Brer Tiger began putting himself into serious reverse.

"I'm all done now. Elephant blood is all right, but ain't as good as tiger blood from what I hear."

CARRINGTON

Brer Rabbit made like he was about to get off the elephant, but Brer Tiger wasn't around to see if he did or not. He lit off from there and before noontime had moved out of his house and left the community.

You won't find this story in history books. It's not a "big" story. But thousands of incidents like this—some person or group fighting an injustice at personal risk—occurred during slavery times. And they happen to this day, but in a contemporary context. This story about a young African-American in Amherst, Massachusetts, was written by storyteller Eshu Bumpus and was researched by his brother, Djata. Eshu is one of hundreds of black storytellers throughout the United States who carry on the tradition of African *griots*, itinerant storyteller/musicians who sing songs and tell folktales and tales of the historic past to impart a moral.

For me there is a connection between the story of Angeline Palmer and the proverb that follows her story. They both emphasize Unity (Umoja) and Collective Work and Responsibility (Ujima). The story of Angeline also shows Self-Determination (Kujichagulia), in this case the determination as to whether you call yourself slave or free.

When I hear a story like this I am reminded how indebted we are to storytellers. The very act of storytelling exhibits all of the principles. Kwanzaa is a good time to thank storytellers—especially grandparents and teachers—for keeping our family and public history alive.

In 1840 Angeline Palmer was eleven years old. She was so poor that the people of Amherst decided to find a family that would care for her. She had a half-brother, Lewis B. Frazier, who lived in Amherst. But he was only twenty years old and couldn't take care of her by himself.

42

Mason and Susan Shaw, from Belchertown, about 10 miles from Amherst, offered to take Angeline to live with them. They seemed like a nice couple, so Amherst town officials were satisfied to have found a home for Angeline.

But things were not as pleasant as they seemed. The Shaws had a secret reason for taking Angeline. They had been planning to visit one of the southern states where many African-Americans were held in slavery. They decided to take Angeline with them and sell her to a slave dealer. Then, when the Shaws returned to Massachusetts, they would tell people that Angeline ran away.

Luckily, a woman overheard Mason Shaw telling some of his friends about the scheme. She didn't like what the Shaws were planning, so she made sure that Angeline's brother, Lewis, found out about it.

Lewis Frazier was a brave young man. He wasn't going to let anything happen to his sister. Lewis got two of his friends, Henry Jackson and William Jennings, to help him. The three young African-American men broke into the Shaws' house and rescued Angeline. They brought Angeline to Spencer and Sarah Church's farm in North Amherst. The Churches were European-Americans with eight children of their own. But Mrs. Church agreed to care for Angeline and hide her when necessary.

Of course, Lewis knew that his sister couldn't stay in Amherst. He and his two friends sought the advice of an African-American woman named Huldah Kiles, who also lived in North Amherst. She brought Lewis and Angeline to her brother, Charles Green, who lived in Colrain, a small town next to the Vermont border. At last Angeline had found a real home.

About two weeks later, Jennings, Jackson, and Frazier turned themselves in and were put in jail. When the trial came up, the judge offered to dismiss all charges if they would reveal Angeline's where-abouts. But the young men knew they were right and would not say a word. So they were sentenced to three months in jail.

Knowing their story, however, the jail keeper didn't take their

sentence seriously. He let them leave the jail during the day as long as they promised to return at night, which they did. They were also allowed plenty of visitors, who brought them food and clothes.

When finally the three returned home to Amherst, they were received as heroes by both whites and blacks of the town. Angeline Palmer continued to live a secure and happy life in Colrain.

If farmers do not cultivate their fields, the people in
the town will die of hunger.

Proverb, Guinea

SOUPS

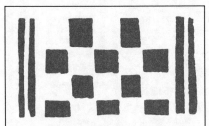

ANTIGUAN PEPPER POT
(ANTIGUA AND BARBUDA)

Pepper pot is an American Indian dish that originated in Guyana, where it is a national dish.

"I remember my grandmother would wrap a clean bleached flour sack around her waist so that it formed a bag, and she would go out into the garden to pick the vegetables for the pepper pot," recalls Gwendolyn Tonge, a home economist for the Antiguan government who contributed this recipe. "We had a lot of pepper pot. We had it nearly every Saturday, sometimes with little dumplings."

ANTIGUAN PEPPER POT

Cook's Notes: This hearty soup is almost a stew, so you may want to use it as a filling Sunday lunch rather than as a first course. In Antigua the soup would be made with salted beef and such exotic pig parts as snout or tail. We've altered the recipe to use more familiar meats, but the spirit is 100 percent Island. It is the Scotch bonnet pepper, an incendiary little devil that is at least ten times hotter than the jalapeño, that gives the dish its name.

Serves 6 to 8

1 cup (½ pound) dried pigeon peas (*gandules*), rinsed
      and picked over*
1 pound corned beef, cut into 1-inch pieces
1 smoked ham hock, cut in half crosswise
2 quarts water
2 tablespoons vegetable oil
1 large onion, chopped
4 scallions, chopped
3 garlic cloves, minced
1 fresh hot chile pepper, such as Scotch bonnet, seeded and minced
1 (14-ounce) can peeled tomatoes in juice, drained
¼ cup tomato paste
1 tablespoon chopped fresh chives, or 1 teaspoon dried
½ teaspoon dried thyme
1 medium eggplant, cut into 1-inch pieces
1 pound *calabaza* or acorn squash, peeled, seeded, and cut
      into 1-inch pieces

*One (16-ounce) can of pigeon peas or green peas, drained, may be substituted for the dried peas. Skip steps 1 and 2.

½ pound white yam (*name*), peeled and cut into 1-inch pieces

¾ pound fresh spinach, stemmed, well washed, and coarsely
    chopped

¼ teaspoon freshly ground black pepper, or to taste

1. In a medium saucepan, combine the pigeon peas and enough water to cover by 1 inch. Bring to a boil over high heat, and boil for 1 minute. Remove the pan from the heat, cover tightly, and let stand for 1 hour. (Or soak the beans overnight in a large bowl with enough cold water to cover by 1 inch.)

2. Drain the peas and return them to the medium saucepan with enough fresh water to cover by 1 inch. Bring to a boil over high heat, reduce the heat to low, and simmer until the peas are tender, about 1 hour. Drain again.

3. Meanwhile, in a 5-quart Dutch oven or soup kettle, bring the corned beef, ham hock, and water to a boil over high heat. Reduce the heat to low, and simmer until the meat is tender, about 1½ hours. Drain the meat, reserving both the meat and the cooking liquid. Remove the meat from the ham hock and chop it coarsely; discard the bones.

4. In a 5-quart Dutch oven or soup kettle, heat the oil over medium heat. Add the onion, scallions, garlic, and chile pepper. Cook, stirring often, until the onion has softened, about 4 minutes. Then stir in the tomatoes, tomato paste, chives, and thyme, breaking up the tomatoes with a spoon. Bring to a boil, reduce the heat to low, and simmer for 10 minutes.

5. Stir in the eggplant, *calabaza*, and white yam and cook for 5 minutes, stirring often. Stir in the reserved meat cooking liquid and the meat. Bring to a boil, reduce the heat to low, and simmer, stirring often, until the vegetables are tender, about 20 minutes. Stir in the cooked pigeon peas and the spinach, and cook until the spinach has wilted, about 5 minutes. Season with the pepper, depending on the hotness of the chile pepper. Serve immediately.

CARRINGTON

PAPAYA AND CHILE SOUP

PAPAYA AND CHILE SOUP
(SOUTH AFRICA)

Americans generally think of the papaya as a fruit, but among black South Africans, from whom this recipe was adapted by Audie Odum-Stallato, unripe papaya is frequently used as a vegetable. "We think of it as sweet, but it actually tastes almost like a squash," she explains. Audie emphasizes that after the milk is added, you should not cook the soup longer than three minutes more. "You just want to warm the milk, not curdle it," she cautions. Unlike much African food, this soup is not powerfully spicy. "It's a nice fireplace kind of soup," she adds.

Cook's Notes: Don't be dismayed by the combination of papaya, onion, garlic, and chile peppers in this soup—after all, they meet in chutneys, too.

4 to 6 servings

3 tablespoons unsalted butter
1 medium onion, chopped
1 green, unripe papaya, peeled, halved, seeded, and cut
    into 1-inch cubes
1 garlic clove, minced
1 fresh hot chile pepper such as serrano, seeded and minced
1½ cups papaya nectar (available at Latin American
    and Caribbean markets)
½ cup chicken broth, homemade or canned
2 tablespoons cornstarch
2 cups milk
½ teaspoon salt
¼ teaspoon grated nutmeg
¼ cup chopped fresh parsley or cilantro

1. In a 5-quart Dutch oven or soup kettle, melt the butter over medium heat. Add the onion and papaya. Cook, stirring often, until the onions are softened, about 3 minutes. Add the garlic and chile pepper and cook, stirring gently, for 1 minute. Stir in the papaya nectar and chicken broth, bring to a simmer, and cook until the papaya is tender, about 15 minutes.
2. In a small bowl, dissolve the cornstarch in ¼ cup of the milk. Add the cornstarch mixture, the remaining 1¾ cups milk, and the salt and nutmeg to the soup. Bring to a simmer. Serve immediately, sprinkling each serving with parsley or cilantro.

WINTER GARDEN VEGETARIAN CONSOMMÉ

Cook's Notes: This recipe was originally developed to use purely as a stock in our vegetarian dishes. But it was so tasty that we began sipping it on its own, and began to realize its possibilities as a light soup for those celebrations that are built around a rich main course.

Makes about 2 quarts

2 medium onions, chopped
2 medium celery ribs with leaves, chopped
2 medium carrots with leaves, chopped
2 medium Russet potatoes, scrubbed but unpeeled,
    cut into 2-inch pieces
1 medium turnip, scrubbed but unpeeled, cut into 2-inch pieces
1 whole head garlic, unpeeled, halved horizontally
2 sprigs parsley
½ teaspoon salt
⅛ teaspoon peppercorns
2½ quarts water

In a 5-quart Dutch oven or soup kettle, bring all of the ingredients just to a boil over high heat. Reduce the heat to low, and simmer gently for 2½ to 3 hours. (Don't boil, or the potato may fall apart and cloud the consommé.) Carefully spoon the consommé and its vegetables through a sieve set over a large bowl. Cool the broth completely; then cover and refrigerate for up to 4 days, or you can freeze it.

WINTER GARDEN VEGETARIAN CONSOMMÉ (UNITED STATES)

With this recipe, you'll be able to have a soup with a fresh, clean taste made with winter garden vegetables.

PEANUT BUTTER, SWEET POTATO, AND WINTER SQUASH SOUP
(UNITED STATES)

"There were always peanuts in our house," says Empress Akweke, a Brooklyn-based caterer, remembering her childhood in Alabama. ("Empress" is her given name.) "And around the holiday season my mother would buy pumpkin and squash and try to make unusual dishes out of them. One day she said, 'I'm going to marry the peanut butter with the pumpkin.' Then she added, 'And you're going to perform the ceremony. You're going to decide what ingredients will go into the soup.' We started with peanut butter, the pumpkin, then sweet potato to give it a foundation, and because it seemed natural to use it since the sweet potato is used so much in black cooking. I told my mother that I wanted to add something green like

PEANUT BUTTER, SWEET POTATO, AND WINTER SQUASH SOUP

Cook's Notes: Here's a gorgeous-looking, bright golden-yellow soup custom-made for guests who are increasing their vegetable consumption. Two of winter's favorite ingredients, sweet potatoes and pumpkin, join forces in this meatless soup, and peanut butter adds an African touch.

Serves 6 to 8

4 pounds sugar pumpkin, *calabaza*, or acorn squash, peeled, seeded, and cut into 1-inch pieces

1 pound sweet potatoes, "Louisiana yams," peeled and cut into 1-inch pieces

4 tablespoons (½ stick) unsalted butter or soy margarine (see Note)

5 cups Winter Garden Vegetarian Consommé (see page 49)

1 teaspoon Vege-Sal (see Note)

½ teaspoon freshly ground black pepper

½ cup unsalted sugarless peanut butter (see Note)

6 to 8 small jack-o'-lantern pumpkins, tops removed, insides hollowed out

½ cup sour cream, at room temperature (optional)

2 scallions, chopped

1. In a large saucepan of boiling salted water, boil the pumpkin and sweet potatoes over high heat until both are tender, about 15 minutes. Drain well. Using a potato masher or a food mill, purée the pumpkin and sweet potatoes together.
2. In a 5-quart Dutch oven or soup kettle, melt the butter over medium heat. Add the purée and stir until the butter is incorporated.

Gradually stir in the consommé, Vege-Sal, and pepper; bring to a simmer. Reduce the heat to low and simmer, stirring often, until the flavors are blended, about 15 minutes.

3. Whisk the peanut butter with 1 cup of the hot soup in a medium bowl until smooth. Stir the peanut butter mixture into the soup, and cook just until heated through. Serve immediately in the small pumpkins, topping each serving with a dollop of sour cream and a sprinkling of scallions.

NOTE: Soy margarine, Vege-Sal, and unsalted sugarless peanut butter are available in natural foods groceries. Vegans will opt to use the soy margarine and delete the sour cream.

spinach, but she said she wanted a creamy texture. So, I sprinkle scallions on top to get the green in there. Anyway, everybody who tasted it fell in love with it. As a finale, I hollowed out small pumpkins—the way you'd do with a jack-o'-lantern—and served the soup in the gourds. And that's how I serve it today."

BOUNTIFUL BLACK BEAN SOUP
(UNITED STATES)

"Black bean soup has become the most popular soup to welcome guests while we are waiting for the main feast," says Catherine Bailey, a teacher who lives in Boston. "As guests arrive, we offer them soup and tea and a starchy tidbit such as plantain chips, or homemade herb bread that has been thinly sliced, coated with a sheer mix of olive oil and crushed garlic, then toasted. One year I attempted a rather complex recipe for Ethiopian pancakes (Chechbsa). I tend to make less ambitious dishes for the hors d'oeuvres segment now."

BOUNTIFUL BLACK BEAN SOUP

Cook's Notes: A passel of vegetables gives this ebony-dark soup its sumptuous richness. Many black bean recipes call for a smoked ham hock, Madeira wine, or herbs for flavor. This soup doesn't need any frills, but you could experiment with your own ornamentations. But try it in all of its unadorned splendor first—you'll be pleasantly surprised.

Makes about 3 quarts, 10 to 12 servings

1 pound dried black beans, rinsed and picked over
4 quarts chicken broth, homemade or canned
1 bunch celery with leaves, chopped
1 pound carrots, chopped
2 large onions, chopped
Grated zest of 1 large lemon
¼ cup fresh lemon juice
1 teaspoon salt
¼ teaspoon freshly ground black pepper
1 large lemon, thinly sliced, then slices quartered

1. In a large saucepan, combine the beans with enough water to cover by 1 inch. Bring to a boil over high heat, and boil for 1 minute. Remove the pan from the heat, cover tightly, and let stand for 1 hour. (Or soak the beans overnight in a large bowl with enough cold water to cover by 1 inch.) Drain the beans.
2. In a 5-quart Dutch oven or soup kettle, combine the drained beans, chicken broth, celery, carrots, onions, and lemon zest. Bring to a boil over high heat. Reduce the heat to low, and simmer, uncovered, until

the liquid is just below the surface of the beans and the ingredients are very tender, 2½ to 3 hours.

3. Using a slotted spoon, transfer the soup solids, in batches, to a food processor, and purée. Transfer the purée to a large bowl, and add the cooking liquid. (Or purée the solids and liquid together in a blender. You may also force the soup through a coarse sieve or pass it through a food mill; discard the skins left in the sieve or mill.)

4. Return the soup to the Dutch oven. Stir in the lemon juice, salt, and pepper, and cook over medium heat, stirring constantly, until heated through. Place a lemon quarter in the bottom of each bowl, and serve immediately.

"This is another recipe from my grandmother," says Audie Odum-Stallato. "She grew up in the South, and she and her six brothers and sisters lived next to a large stream, so they frequently fished for their dinner. Every summer my grandmother would take me to where she grew up and we would fish. I'd never catch anything. So I would start exploring and looking at the old plantations, the old boats, talking with the sharecroppers.

"In the evening, the chowder made from my grandmother's catch would be served with fresh homemade bread to soak up the gravy. This dish reminds me of the outdoors and makes me think of summer, although you can serve it any time of the year. I've always found that nice small young fish are best for this dish because they are more flavorful. This makes a light but satisfying meal."

SOUTH CAROLINA TROUT AND BACON CHOWDER

Cook's Notes: Back when the trout were caught in the stream behind the smokehouse, this soup was a quick, delicious meal. Now it is a little pricier, but the rewards are great. Serve it with Grandma's Creamed Cornbread (page 236) for a real culinary journey to the Low Country.

Serves 4 to 6

½ pound sliced bacon
1 large onion, sliced
¼ cup all-purpose flour
3 rainbow trout (1 pound each), fileted
3 cups chicken broth, homemade or canned
½ teaspoon dried thyme
¼ teaspoon salt
⅛ teaspoon freshly ground black pepper
1 bay leaf

1. In a 5-quart Dutch oven or soup kettle, cook the bacon over medium heat, turning once, until crisp, about 4 minutes. Transfer the bacon to paper towels to drain, and set aside. Pour off all but 3 tablespoons bacon fat from the Dutch oven.

2. Add the onion and cook, stirring often, until softened, about 3 minutes. Add the flour and reduce the heat to low. Cook, whisking constantly, without browning the flour, for 2 minutes. Add the trout fillets and reserved bacon. Then add the chicken broth, thyme, salt, pepper, and bay leaf. Bring to a simmer and cook, uncovered, until the fish is opaque throughout, 10 to 15 minutes.

CALALOU CHEZ CLARA

Cook's Note: Callaloo greens, the leaves of the taro root plant (spelled differently from the name of the soup), are difficult to get in this country. Luckily spinach leaves are an excellent alternative.

Makes about 2 quarts

1 pound fresh spinach or callaloo greens, stemmed, well washed, and coarsely chopped
1 pound okra, stems and tips trimmed, cut into ¼-inch-thick slices
1 medium onion, chopped
1 scallion, chopped
1 garlic clove, minced
2 sprigs parsley
½ fresh hot chile pepper, such as Scotch bonnet, seeded and minced
1 teaspoon salt
¼ teaspoon dried thyme
¼ teaspoon freshly ground black pepper
6½ cups water
½ pound cooked smoked ham, chopped (about ¾ cup)
⅓ cup fresh lime juice

1. In a 5-quart Dutch oven or soup kettle, combine the spinach leaves, okra, onion, scallion, garlic, parsley, chile pepper, salt, thyme, and pepper. Add the water and bring to a boil over high heat. Reduce the heat to medium-low and simmer, covered, until the okra is very tender, about 30 minutes.
2. Purée the soup in a blender, food processor, or food mill. Return the soup to the Dutch oven, and stir in the ham and lime juice. Cook, stirring constantly, over medium heat just until the ham is heated through, about 5 minutes. Serve immediately.

CALALOU CHEZ CLARA (GUADELOUPE)

Calalou is another dish that changes from island to island, with shrimp, crab, chicken, and tomatoes all making guest appearances. Here's a straightforward but superlative rendition from *Sky Juice and Flying Fish* by Jessica B. Harris.

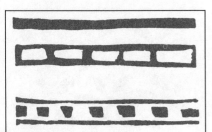

JAMAICAN PIG AND PEAS SOUP
(JAMAICA)

This ubiquitous Caribbean legume is called pigeon peas, Congo peas, Congo beans, gungo peas, goongoo peas, gandules, and gandures, depending on the island where it's served. It is a staple of the West Indian diet, but, as you can see here, may also play a part in holiday meals.

"Just after Christmas we'd always look forward to this dish, because we'd use the ham bone from Christmas, which gives the gungo peas a special flavor," remembers Georgia Dunn, a secretary with the Jamaican consulate and a part-time caterer. "The rest of the year we don't use the ham bone because it's usually not around."

JAMAICAN PIG AND PEAS SOUP

Cook's Notes: Another stew-soup that is a real rib-sticker. Jamaican cooks make this with whatever pork product is around, but we've settled for the foot and a ham hock. Once again, try to search out the Scotch bonnet chile pepper so it can lend its complex, almost vegetable-like flavor.

Serves 8 to 10

3 quarts water
1 pig's foot, split
1 smoked ham hock, cut in half crosswise
1 pound dried pigeon peas (*gandules*) or dried red beans, rinsed and
    picked over
3 scallions, chopped
1 fresh hot chile pepper, such as Scotch bonnet, seeded and minced
¼ teaspoon dried thyme
⅛ teaspoon ground allspice
1½ pounds *malanga* (*yautia*), pared and cut into 1-inch pieces
1 pound white yam (*name*), cut into 1-inch pieces
1 teaspoon salt
¼ teaspoon freshly ground black pepper

1. In a 5-quart Dutch oven, bring the water, pig's foot, and ham hock to a boil over high heat. Reduce the heat to medium-low and simmer, skimming often, for 1 hour.
2. Meanwhile, in a large saucepan, combine the peas with enough cold water to cover by 1 inch. Bring to a boil over high heat, and boil for 1 minute. Remove the pan from the heat, cover tightly, and let stand for 1 hour. Drain well.

3. Add the drained peas, scallions, chile pepper, thyme, and allspice to the meat. Simmer, partially covered, for about 45 minutes, until the beans are almost tender.

4. Stir in the *malanga* and *name*, and simmer until all the ingredients are tender, about 30 minutes. Season with the salt and pepper, tasting first to check the impact of the salt in the ham and the heat of the chile pepper.

5. Remove the ham hock and pig's foot. Remove and chop the meat from the ham hock, and stir it back into the soup. Discard the hock bones and the pig's foot. Serve the soup immediately.

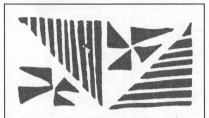

DUCK AND SMOKED SAUSAGE GUMBO
(UNITED STATES)

Here is a delicious variation of this all-time great meal-in-a-pot.

DUCK AND SMOKED SAUSAGE GUMBO

Cook's Notes: While gumbo can be made with any number of main ingredients, including crab, chicken, or beef, there is one constant factor: it gets its distinctive gelatinous texture from okra or filé powder (pulverized sassafras leaves). Andouille, a spicy Cajun sausage that is becoming increasingly available all over the country, is the sausage of choice here, but kielbasa will do in a pinch.

1 (5-pound) duck, cut into quarters

3 tablespoons vegetable oil

¾ pound andouille or kielbasa sausage, cut into ½-inch-thick slices

½ cup all-purpose flour

2 celery ribs with leaves, chopped

1 medium onion, chopped

2 medium green bell peppers, chopped

¾ pound okra, stems and tips trimmed, cut into ½-inch-thick slices

3 garlic cloves, minced

1 (35-ounce) can peeled tomatoes in juice, drained, seeded, and chopped

1½ quarts chicken broth, homemade or canned

¼ cup chopped fresh parsley

1 teaspoon dried thyme

½ teaspoon salt

½ teaspoon cayenne pepper

¼ teaspoon freshly ground black pepper

2 bay leaves

4 cups hot, freshly cooked long-grain rice

1. Using the upturned tines of a meat fork, pierce the skin of the duck all over, being careful not to go into the meat. In a 5-quart Dutch oven or soup kettle, heat the oil over medium heat. Add the duck quarters and cook, turning often, until lightly browned on all sides, about 10 minutes. Transfer the duck to a plate and set aside.

2. Add the andouille slices and cook, turning often, until lightly browned, about 5 minutes. Transfer the sausage to the plate with the duck pieces, and reserve. Pour off all but ½ cup of the fat in the Dutch oven.

3. Raise the heat to high. When the fat is very hot, gradually whisk in the flour. Then reduce the heat to medium and cook, whisking constantly, until the flour mixture is nutty brown, 3 to 4 minutes. Add the celery, onion, and bell peppers and cook, stirring often, until the vegetables have softened, about 5 minutes. Add the okra and garlic and cook for 2 minutes. Add the tomatoes and the reserved duck and sausage, and bring to a simmer. Stir in the broth and bring to a simmer, skimming often. Stir in the parsley, thyme, salt, cayenne, black pepper, and bay leaves. Reduce the heat to low and simmer, partially covered, until the duck is tender, about 1¼ hours.

4. Remove the duck pieces and let them cool slightly. Remove the meat from the bones and coarsely chop it, discarding the skin and bones. Stir the duck meat back into the gumbo and cook until heated through, about 5 minutes. Skim the fat off the surface of the soup.

5. To serve, place a large spoonful of rice in each soup bowl, and ladle the gumbo over the rice.

SALADS

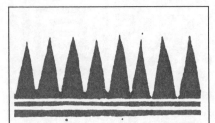

AVOCADO MOUSSE WITH SHRIMP SAUCE
(BRAZIL)

A Brazilian delight contributed by Yara Roberts, a Brazilian-born part-time caterer who lives in Boston.

AVOCADO MOUSSE WITH SHRIMP SAUCE

Cook's Notes: Hass avocados, with pebbly black skins, are worth searching out for this sophisticated first course. They have a much better flavor than the large smooth-skinned Florida varieties.

Serves 6

AVOCADO MOUSSE:

3 envelopes plain unflavored gelatin

2 cups cold water

1 (15-ounce) can tomato sauce

¼ cup mayonnaise

¼ cup fresh lemon juice

2 tablespoons olive oil

1 tablespoon white vinegar

1 teaspoon salt

¼ teaspoon freshly ground white pepper

2 ripe avocados, halved, pitted, peeled, and cut into ½-inch pieces

SHRIMP SAUCE:

2 pounds medium shrimp

1 cup mayonnaise

3 tablespoons fresh lemon juice

3 tablespoons milk

1 teaspoon sugar

¼ teaspoon salt

⅛ teaspoon freshly ground white pepper

1 ripe avocado, halved, pitted, peeled, and cut into ½-inch pieces

1. Make the avocado mousse: In a large glass measuring cup, sprinkle the gelatin over the water and let stand for 5 minutes. Set the cup in a medium saucepan filled with simmering water, and stir constantly until the gelatin has dissolved, about 3 minutes.

2. In a medium bowl, whisk together the tomato sauce, mayonnaise, lemon juice, olive oil, vinegar, salt, and white pepper until smooth. Whisk the gelatin mixture into the tomato mixture. Set the bowl in a larger bowl filled with iced water, and let it stand, stirring occasionally, until partially set, about 10 minutes. Fold in the avocado.

3. Lightly oil a 2-quart ring or tube mold. Pour in the mousse, cover tightly with plastic wrap, and refrigerate until firm, at least 3 hours or overnight.

4. Make the shrimp sauce: Bring a large saucepan of salted water to a boil over high heat. Add the shrimp, return to the boil, and cook just until the shrimp turn pink, about 3 minutes. Drain well. Peel, devein, and chop the shrimp coarsely, setting aside six whole shrimp for garnish. Place the chopped and the whole shrimp in bowls, cover, and refrigerate until ready to serve.

5. In a medium bowl, whisk together the mayonnaise, lemon juice, milk, sugar, salt, and white pepper. Fold in the chopped shrimp, cover, and refrigerate until ready to serve.

6. Invert the mold onto a serving platter. Pour the sauce into the center of the mold and around the sides. Top the mold with the six reserved shrimp, and serve immediately.

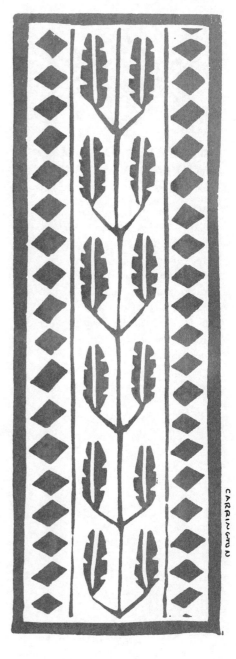

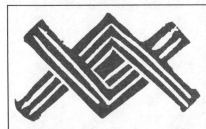

BLACK-EYED PEAS SALAD WITH BASIL VINAIGRETTE
(UNITED STATES)

"We grew lots of different kinds of peas in the garden on our farm, including crowder peas, chick-peas, and black-eyed peas," says Mavis Young. "In fact, black-eyed peas were a staple. In making this salad, make sure you don't overcook the peas. In other words, the peas should retain some firmness."

BLACK-EYED PEAS SALAD WITH BASIL VINAIGRETTE

Cook's Notes: While fresh herbs are nothing new to the African-American kitchen, fresh basil is a nontraditional addition to black-eyed peas salad. But no matter—it sure is good, especially when served with fried chicken. (Don't forget this recipe the next time you need a bean salad for a picnic.) You can use 2 (16-ounce) cans of black-eyed peas, well drained, if you don't cook up your own peas.

Serves 6

1 cup dried black-eyed peas, rinsed and picked over (about 8 ounces)
1 medium onion, halved
¾ teaspoon salt
3 tablespoons cider vinegar
2 tablespoons chopped fresh basil, or ¾ teaspoon dried
2 garlic cloves, crushed through a garlic press
1 teaspoon sugar
¼ teaspoon freshly ground black pepper
¾ cup olive oil
1 medium onion, finely chopped
2 celery ribs, finely chopped
1 small red bell pepper, seeded and finely chopped

1. In a medium saucepan, combine the peas and enough water to cover by 1 inch. Bring to a boil over high heat, and boil for 1 minute. Remove the pan from the heat, cover tightly, and let stand 1 hour. (Or soak the beans overnight in a large bowl with enough cold water to cover by 1 inch.)

2. Drain the peas and return them to the saucepan with enough fresh water to cover by 1 inch. Add the onion halves. Bring to a boil over high heat, reduce the heat to low, and simmer until the peas are tender, about 45 minutes. During the last 10 minutes of cooking, add ½ teaspoon of the salt. Drain the beans well, discarding the onion halves. Rinse the beans under cold running water, drain again, and let cool completely.

3. In a small bowl, whisk together the vinegar, basil, garlic, sugar, remaining ¼ teaspoon salt, and pepper. Gradually whisk in the oil until the basil vinaigrette is smooth.

4. In a medium bowl, combine the peas, the chopped onion, celery, bell pepper, and basil vinaigrette. Cover and refrigerate until chilled, at least 2 hours or overnight.

AMBROSIA
(UNITED STATES)

"My mother seldom cooked; my grandmother tended to that," says Audie Odum-Stallato. "But during the holidays, when we'd traditionally fix the ambrosia, we —my mother, me, and my aunt —would fight over who'd make it. Why? Because you could eat little bits of it while making it.

"Make sure that the ambrosia chills for the full time I mention before serving, because the marshmallows need to soak up the juices from the sour cream."

AMBROSIA

Cook's Notes: For many an African-American household, it just isn't a holiday without someone making a big bowl of Ambrosia. The secret of perfect Ambrosia is to drain the fruits well, then adjust the thickness of the salad with the reserved syrups after chilling it. Some people like theirs thick, some saucy. For novice cooks, here's the classic recipe.

Serves 6 to 8

1 (20-ounce) can pineapple chunks in light syrup
1 (17-ounce) can mixed fruit cocktail in light syrup
1 (11-ounce) can mandarin oranges
1 (10-ounce) jar maraschino cherries
3 cups miniature marshmallows
1 cup sour cream
⅓ cup sweetened coconut flakes

1. Drain the pineapple, fruit cocktail, mandarin oranges, and cherries in a large sieve set over a large bowl; save the combined syrups. Let the fruit stand in the sieve for 30 minutes; then transfer it to another large bowl. Pour the syrup into a small bowl, cover, and refrigerate.
2. Add the marshmallows and sour cream to the fruit, and toss to combine. Cover, and refrigerate until chilled, at least 1 hour or overnight. When ready to serve, add enough reserved syrup to reach the desired consistency.

TANZANIAN FRUIT AND CASHEW SALAD WITH RUM CREAM

Cook's Notes: Could this salad have been the forefather of Ambrosia? Make it well ahead of serving, since it only gets better as the fruit macerates in the rum cream. Here's how to choose a ripe pineapple: It should "give" slightly when squeezed and should smell sweet. The rind should have a golden cast, and a leaf should pull out easily with a gentle tug.

Serves 6 to 8

1 large ripe pineapple
½ cup heavy (whipping) cream
¼ cup dark rum
2 tablespoons honey
2 tangerines, peeled and sectioned
½ cup cashews, for garnish (about 2 ounces)
¼ cup shredded fresh coconut (or sweetened coconut flakes), for
    garnish

1. Using a large sharp knife, cut away the crown of leaves and the pineapple rind. If desired, remove the "eyes" with the tip of the knife. Quarter the pineapple, then remove the tough core from each quarter. Cut the pineapple into 1-inch pieces, and transfer them to a medium bowl.
2. In a small bowl, whisk together the cream, rum, and honey. Stir this into the pineapple. Cover, and refrigerate until well chilled, at least 2 hours or overnight.
3. Fold the tangerines into the pineapple mixture.
4. If the cashews are salted, place them in a sieve and rinse under cold running water to remove the salt; pat dry with paper towels. Chop the cashews coarsely. Sprinkle the top of the salad with the chopped cashews and the coconut, and serve.

TANZANIAN FRUIT AND CASHEW SALAD WITH RUM CREAM
(TANZANIA)

"I have always liked to have salads with my main meals," says Audie Odum-Stallato, "and when I was served this at an African restaurant in Harlem, I was attracted to it immediately. There aren't many uncooked foods in African cuisine. It's also a good palate cleanser after a meal."

CHILLED CARIBBEAN SHRIMP ON SEASONAL GREENS
(CARIBBEAN)

Dee Dee Dailey outdid herself with this West Indian–inspired first course.

CHILLED CARIBBEAN SHRIMP ON SEASONAL GREENS

Cook's Notes: When you need an eye-opening first course for a special holiday dinner, you can't do any better than these cold, zesty shrimp served on a bed of crisp greens. It is the ultimate "shrimp cocktail."

Serves 6

½ cup plus 2 tablespoons olive oil

1 medium onion, chopped

1 medium green bell pepper, seeded and chopped

4 scallions, chopped

4 garlic cloves, minced

2 pounds ripe plum tomatoes, peeled, seeded, and coarsely
        chopped, or 1 (35-ounce) can tomatoes in juice, drained and
        chopped

½ cup dry white wine

½ cup Fish Stock (see page 164), or bottled clam juice

⅓ cup chopped fresh cilantro

⅓ cup chopped fresh parsley

2 teaspoons dried thyme

½ teaspoon salt

⅛ teaspoon cayenne pepper, or to taste

2 pounds medium shrimp, peeled and deveined

2 tablespoons fresh lime juice

1 shallot, minced

⅛ teaspoon freshly ground black pepper

1 head red-leaf lettuce, separated into leaves

1 head green-leaf lettuce, separated into leaves

2 tablespoons minced fresh chives, for garnish

1. In a large skillet, heat 2 tablespoons of the oil over medium heat. Add the onion, bell pepper, and scallions and cook, stirring often, until the onion is softened, about 4 minutes. Add the garlic and stir for 1 minute. Then add the tomatoes, wine, and clam juice and bring to a boil. Stir in the cilantro, parsley, thyme, ¼ teaspoon of the salt, and cayenne. Reduce the heat to low and simmer, stirring often, until reduced to a thick sauce, about 20 minutes.

2. Stir in the shrimp and cook just until they turn pink, about 3 minutes. Remove the skillet from the heat and stir for 1 minute. Let the mixture cool completely, stirring often. Transfer the shrimp and sauce to a medium bowl, cover, and refrigerate until chilled, at least 1 hour or up to 8 hours.

3. In a small bowl, whisk together the lime juice, shallot, the remaining ¼ teaspoon salt, and the pepper. Gradually whisk in the remaining ½ cup olive oil until combined. Line six dinner plates with the red and green lettuce leaves. Drizzle the lettuce leaves with the lime dressing. Place a spoonful of marinated shrimp on each plate, and serve immediately.

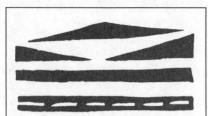

ANTIGUA FRUIT SALAD WITH LIME-NUTMEG DRESSING
(ANTIGUA AND BARBUDA)

Just a little something thrown together by Gwendolyn Tonge in her role as a home economist in Antigua. Tonge said she came up with this because, oddly enough, Antiguans were importing their fruit cocktail in cans from America and Britain. Now it has become popular to use fresh island fruits for salads and cocktails.

ANTIGUA FRUIT SALAD WITH LIME-NUTMEG DRESSING

Cook's Notes: Of course any collection of ripe tropical fruits can be used in this salad. Just be sure that your lime-nutmeg dressing is cooled completely before combining it with the fruits.

Serves 6 to 8

1 cup water
½ cup turbinado or raw sugar
¼ cup fresh lime juice
¼ teaspoon freshly grated nutmeg
1 large ripe pineapple
2 ripe bananas, peeled and cut into ½-inch-thick rounds
1 ugli fruit, peeled and sectioned
1 orange, peeled and sectioned
1 ripe papaya, halved, seeded, peeled, and cut into 1-inch pieces

1. In a small saucepan, bring the water, sugar, lime juice, and nutmeg to a boil over medium-high heat, stirring constantly until the mixture boils. Stop stirring, and cook 2 minutes, until syrupy. Cool the syrup completely.
2. Using a large sharp knife, cut away the crown of leaves and the pineapple rind. If desired, remove the "eyes" with the tip of the knife. Quarter the pineapple, then remove the tough core from each quarter. Cut the pineapple into 1-inch pieces and transfer them to a large bowl.
3. Add the banana, ugli fruit, orange, papaya, and cooled syrup and toss lightly. Cover, and refrigerate until chilled, at least 1 hour or up to 8 hours. Serve chilled.

ALICE'S POTATO SALAD

Cook's Notes: Alice Betsill's potato salad has something for everyone—hard-boiled eggs for added richness, celery for crunch, mustard for sharpness, and a dash of sweet pickle relish as her "secret ingredient." Choose waxy potatoes, such as the red-skinned variety, for potato salad, as they hold their shape best after boiling.

Serves 6 to 8

3 pounds red-skinned potatoes
1 cup mayonnaise
6 scallions, chopped
2 celery ribs, chopped
3 tablespoons sweet pickle relish
1 tablespoon prepared mustard
½ teaspoon salt
¼ teaspoon Worcestershire sauce
¼ teaspoon freshly ground black pepper
⅛ teaspoon hot pepper sauce
6 hard-boiled large eggs, sliced

1. In a large saucepan of boiling salted water, boil the potatoes over high heat just until they are tender when pierced with the tip of a sharp knife, about 15 minutes. Drain, rinse under cold running water, and drain again. Cool the potatoes completely. Cut them into ¾-inch-thick slices.
2. In a large bowl, whisk together the mayonnaise, scallions, celery, relish, mustard, salt, Worcestershire sauce, pepper, and hot pepper sauce. Add the potatoes and hard-boiled eggs, and toss gently. Cover, and refrigerate until chilled, at least 2 hours or overnight. Serve chilled.

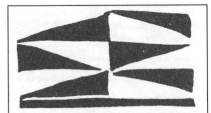

ALICE'S POTATO SALAD
(UNITED STATES)

"This is an old family recipe that my mother (Alice) got from her mother," says Roscoe Betsill, a food stylist and food writer who lives in New York. "My mother made it for all our picnics, whether they were in the park or the backyard. Whenever there was a cookout, there was her potato salad."

GARDEN PATCH MACARONI SALAD

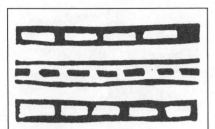

**GARDEN PATCH
MACARONI SALAD
(UNITED STATES)**

This colorful pasta salad will brighten up your Kwanzaa buffet table.

Cook's Notes: The vegetables in this salad will keep their fresh colors if you don't make it too far ahead (eventually the vinegar will dull the broccoli's bright green). As a concession to those who like their macaroni salad creamy, there is an optional dollop of mayonnaise. To turn this into a main-course salad, add 2 cups chopped cooked chicken or ham.

Makes 6 to 8 servings

8 ounces small tubular macaroni
1 small bunch broccoli, cut into florets
3 tablespoons red wine vinegar
1 teaspoon Italian seasoning
¼ teaspoon salt
⅛ teaspoon hot red pepper flakes
⅔ cup olive or vegetable oil
1 red bell pepper, seeded and chopped
1 medium celery rib with leaves, chopped
1 medium carrot, grated
1 cup cherry tomatoes, stemmed and halved
1 medium cucumber, halved, seeded, and chopped
⅓ cup mayonnaise
3 tablespoons chopped fresh parsley

1. In a large saucepan of boiling salted water, cook the macaroni over high heat until just tender, about 6 minutes. Drain, rinse under cold water, and drain well.
2. In another large saucepan of boiling salted water, cook the broccoli florets over high heat until crisp-tender, about 3 minutes. Drain, rinse

under cold water, and drain well.

3. In a small bowl, whisk together the vinegar, Italian seasoning, salt, and red pepper flakes. Gradually whisk in the oil until the dressing is smooth.

4. In a large bowl, combine the cooked macaroni and broccoli, bell pepper, celery, carrot, cherry tomatoes, and cucumber. Drizzle the dressing over the salad and toss again. Add the mayonnaise and toss until combined. Cover, and refrigerate until chilled, at least 1 hour or up to 8 hours.

5. Before serving, correct seasoning with additional vinegar, salt, and pepper. Sprinkle the salad with the parsley, and serve chilled.

**FRESH GREENS AND
APPLES WITH
CURRIED YOGURT
DRESSING**
(UNITED STATES)

The Indian influence in southern
Africa inspired this recipe.

FRESH GREENS AND APPLES WITH CURRIED YOGURT DRESSING

Cook's Notes: This salad utilizes crisp tart apples, one of the stars of winter's bounty.

Serves 6

2 tablespoons cider vinegar
1 teaspoon curry powder
¼ teaspoon salt
⅛ teaspoon freshly ground black pepper
6 tablespoons vegetable oil
6 tablespoons plain low-fat yogurt
2 teaspoons chopped fresh chives, or ¾ teaspoon dried
1 head red-leaf lettuce, rinsed, dried, and torn into pieces
1 bunch watercress, stemmed
2 medium tart apples, such as Granny Smith, cored and cut into
    ¼-inch-thick slices

1. In a small bowl, whisk the vinegar, curry powder, salt, and pepper until blended. Gradually whisk in the oil. Using a wooden spoon, stir in the yogurt and the chives. (Use the dressing immediately or it may curdle.)
2. In a large bowl, toss the lettuce, watercress, and apples together. Add the curry dressing, toss well, and serve immediately.

Nguzo Saba

Umoja (Unity)
Kujichagulia (Self-determination)
Ujima (Collective Work and Responsibility)
Ujamaa (Cooperative Economics)
Nia (Purpose)
Kuumba (Creativity)
Imani (Faith)

This story from the Wolof people comes from a collection called *The King's Drum and Other African Stories* by Harold Courlander. From the fourteenth through the sixteenth century, the Wolof empire consisted of four large kingdoms; today they live in what is now Senegal and the Gambia in West Africa. When I read this story to my son, I call the "harp" a kora. A kora is a twenty-one–string West African instrument that has a soft harplike sound. But European-style harps are not used in traditional African music or storytelling. In my oral rendition, I also call the "minstrel," which is a European term, a *griot*, the West African term for itinerant musicians who traditionally sing the praises or the history of a local personage or place, or folktales or about gossip, kind of like a singing newspaper. *Griots* frequently play koras. Last, I omit the reference to the king's slaves and instead say "the king and his court."

Because this story illustrates Collective Work and Responsibility (Ujima), it is a good one to read before some work needs to be done in the house: food preparation, dishes, cleanup. My son got the picture right away, and he finally cleaned up his room!

In the town of Sedo, it is said, there was a king named Sabar. Sabar's armies were powerful. They conquered many towns, and many people paid tribute to him. If a neighboring chief passed through Sedo, he came to Sabar's house, touched his forehead to the ground, and presented gifts to the king. As the king grew old, he grew proud. His word was law in Sedo. And if his word was heard in other places, it was law there too. Sabar said to himself: "I am indeed great, for who is there to contradict me? And who is my master?"

There came to Sedo one day a minstrel and he was called on to entertain the king. He sang a song of praise to Sabar, and to his ancestors. He danced. And then he sang:

> *The dog is great among dogs,*
> *Yet he serves man.*
> *The woman is great among women,*
> *Yet she waits upon her children.*
>
> *The hunter is great among hunters,*
> *Yet he serves the village.*
> *Minstrels are great among minstrels,*
> *Yet they sing for the king and his slaves.*

When the song was finished, Sabar said to the minstrel, "What is the meaning of this song?"

The minstrel replied, "The meaning is that all men serve, whatever their station."

And Sabar said to him, "Not all men. The king of Sedo does not serve. It is others who serve him. Is this not the truth?"

The minstrel was silent, and Sabar asked, "Is this not the truth?" The minstrel answered, "Who am I to say the king of Sedo speaks what is not true?"

At that moment a wandering holy man came through the crowd and asked for food. The minstrel said to the king, "Please allow me to give this unfortunate man a little of the food which you have not eaten."

Sabar said, "Give it, and let us get on with the discussion."

The minstrel said, "Here is my harp until I have finished feeding

77

him." He placed his harp in the king's hands, took a little food from the king's bowl, and gave it to the holy man. Then he came back and stood before Sabar.

"King of Sedo," he said, "you have said what I could not say, for who contradicts a king? You have said that all men serve the king of Sedo and that he does not serve. Yet you have given a wandering holy man food from your bowl, and you have held the harp for a mere minstrel while he served another. How then can one say a king does not serve? It is said 'The head and the body must serve each other.' "

And the minstrel picked up his harp from the hands of the king and sang:

> *The soldier is great among soldiers,*
> *Yet he serves the clan.*
> *The king is great among kings,*
> *Yet he serves his people.*

Scratch a black person and you're sure to find an entrepreneur. That is certainly the case now, but it was the case over two hundred years ago also. Paul Cuffee, who is best known for trying to colonize Sierra Leone with free blacks from America, was one of scores of fearless, persistent African-American entrepreneurs. His story illustrates the principles of Unity (Umoja), Self-determination (Kujichagulia), Collective Work and Responsibility (Ujima), and Purpose (Nia).

Paul Cuffee was born in 1759, the son of an ex-slave who had purchased his freedom. Raised on Cuttyhunk Island, near New Bedford, Massachusetts, Cuffee developed a love of the sea. Unable to attend school, Paul educated himself so that he could learn how to sail ships.

At sixteen Cuffee joined the crew of a whaling ship and was captured by the British during the Revolutionary War. After a three-month imprisonment in New York, Cuffee bought a farm with his savings, but he continued to study sailing. In time, with one small open boat, Cuffee began his own business, carrying goods from town to town along the coast near New Bedford. He was attacked by pirates five times, losing his freight and boats in every instance. Undeterred, Cuffee kept on building boats. Finally his business took root; he became a successful businessman and built a succession of bigger, better boats. In addition to his whaling and freighting enterprises, Cuffee invested in real estate. He had become wealthy. But the wealth, for him, was the means to an end. He took his money and built a schoolhouse on his farm and hired a teacher so that his children, and others in the area, could receive the education denied him.

By 1811 Cuffee was one of many Americans who were considering the notion of sending free blacks back to Africa. He sailed to the West African nation of Sierra Leone that year, and upon returning to America, financed a return trip for thirty-eight other blacks. But before he could fulfill his dream and take more people to Sierra Leone to live, Cuffee died. He left his family $20,000, farmland, houses, and the profitable sailing business he had built from nothing but vision and determination.

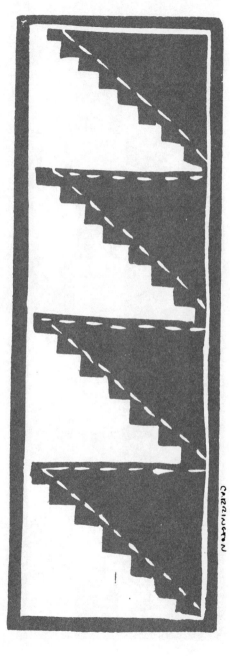

Anticipate the good so that you may enjoy it.
Proverb, Ethiopia

W hile the preceding proverb illustrates Faith (Imani) for me, the following excerpt from Fannie Lou Hamer's autobiography, *To Praise Our Bridges*, shows a commanding sense of Purpose (Nia) and Self-determination (Kujichagulia), especially in the last paragraphs.

Hamer was a civil rights leader who urged blacks to register to vote, join labor unions, and form agricultural cooperatives. She died in 1977 at the age of sixty. She is the reason I registered to vote on my eighteenth birthday and voted in every election for the next seventeen years. But when I moved out of New York City, I let my registration lapse. I don't know why. There never seemed to be enough time to find out where to register, or enough time to go to the place. And then I came across this excerpt from Hamer's autobiography, and I hurried to the registrar.

My parents were sharecroppers and they had a big family. Twenty children. Fourteen boys and six girls. I'm the twentieth child. All of us worked in the fields, of course, but we never did get anything out of sharecropping. We'd make fifty and sixty bales and end up with nothing.

I was about six years old when I first went to the fields to pick cotton. I can remember very well the landowner telling me one day that if I would pick thirty pounds he would give me something out of the commissary: some Cracker-Jacks, Daddy Wide-Legs, and some sardines. These were things that he knew I loved and never had a chance to have. So I picked thirty pounds that day. Well, the next week I had to pick sixty and by the time I was thirteen I was picking two and three hundred pounds. . . .

Well, after the white man killed off our mules, my parents never did get a chance to get up again. We went back to sharecropping, halving, it's called. You split the cotton half and half with the plantation owner. But the seed, fertilizer, cost of hired hands, everything is paid out of the cropper's half. My parents tried so hard to do what they could to keep us in school, but school didn't last but four months out of the year and most of the time we didn't have clothes to wear. I dropped out of school and cut corn stalks to help the family. . . .

I married in 1944 and stayed on the plantation until 1962, when I went down to the courthouse in Indianola to register to vote. That happened because I went to a mass meeting one night.

Until then I'd never heard of no mass meeting and I didn't know that a Negro could register and vote. Bob Moses, Reggie Robinson, Jim Bevel, and James Forman were some of the SNCC workers who ran that meeting. When they asked for those to raise their hands who'd go down to the courthouse the next day, I raised mine. Had it up high as I could get it. I guess if I'd had any sense I'd a-been a little scared, but what was the point of being scared. The only thing they could do to me was kill me and it seemed like they'd been trying to do that a little bit at a time every since I could remember. . . .

Well, there was eighteen of us who went down to the courthouse that day and all of us were arrested. Police said the bus was painted the wrong color—said it was too yellow. After I got bailed out I went back to the plantation where Pap [Hamer's husband] and I had lived for eighteen years. My oldest girl met me and told me that Mr. Marlow, the plantation owner, was mad and raising sand. He had heard that I had tried to register. That night he called on us and said, "We're not going to have this in Mississippi and you will have to withdraw. I am looking for your answer, yea or nay?" I just looked. He said, "I will give you until tomorrow morning. And if you don't withdraw, you will have to leave. If you do go withdraw, it's only how I feel, you might still have to leave." So I left that same night. Pap had to stay on till work on the plantation was through. Ten days later they fired into Mrs. Tucker's house where I was staying. They also shot two girls at Mr. Sissel's. . . .

What I really feel is necessary is that the black people in this country will have to upset this applecart. We can no longer ignore the fact that America is NOT the "land of the free and the home of the brave." I used to question this for years—what did our kids actually fight for? They would go in the service and go through all of that and come right out to be drowned in the river in Mississippi. . . .

I've worked on voter registration here ever since I went to that first mass meeting. In 1964, we registered 63,000 black people from

Mississippi into the Freedom Democratic Party. We formed our own party because the whites wouldn't even let us register. We decided to challenge the white Mississippi Democratic Party at the National Convention. We followed all the laws the white people themselves made. We tried to attend the precinct meetings and they locked the doors on us or moved the meetings and that's against the law they made for their own selves. So we were the ones that held the real precinct meetings. At all these meetings across the state we elected our representatives to go to the National Democratic Convention in Atlantic City. But we learned the hard way that even though we had all the law and all the righteousness on our side, that white man is not going to give up his power to us.

We have to build our own power. We have to win every single political office we can, where we have a majority of black people. . . . The question for black people is not, when is the white man going to give us our rights, or when is he going to give us a good education for our children, or when is he going to give us jobs—if the white man gives you anything—just remember when he gets ready he will take it right back. We have to take for ourselves.

MAIN DISHES

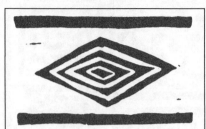

PORK BONES, FAMILY STYLE
(UNITED STATES)

"There is a saying in the South: 'We use everything on the pig except the oink.' In other words, we learned to be very creative," says Hiram Bonner, an institutional chef. "Pork bones, for instance, were very inexpensive and could be made to be very tasty.

"I grew up with this recipe," he continues. "I had it at least twice a month. Throughout my childhood I remember coming home and smelling the spicy aroma of pork bones mixed with candied yams and three mixed greens. And cornbread was always on the table.

"Pork bones are very messy to eat, because you have to use your fingers to hold on to the bone and suck the meat and juices from it. You'd probably only want to eat it alone, or with close friends and family."

PORK BONES, FAMILY STYLE

Cook's Notes: Pork neck is sold in many supermarkets as pork stew meat, so it shouldn't be too hard to find. There's not much meat on the bones, but what there is, is succulent. Since the nicest meat is next to the bone, food lovers don't much mind picking up the bones with their fingers and slurping in front of guests. These are so good, you won't mind who's around while you are digging in.

Makes 4 servings

2 tablespoons vegetable oil
4 pounds pork neck bones
2 medium onions, chopped
2 medium celery ribs, chopped
1 large green bell pepper, chopped
2 garlic cloves, minced
1 teaspoon salt
½ teaspoon crushed hot red pepper flakes
¼ teaspoon freshly ground black pepper
1½ cups water

1. Heat the oil in a 5-quart Dutch oven or soup kettle. In batches, cook the pork bones over medium-high heat, turning often until browned on all sides, about 6 minutes per batch. Set the browned pork neck bones aside.
2. Add the onions, celery, bell pepper, and garlic to the pot. Reduce the heat to medium and cook, stirring often, until the vegetables have softened, about 5 minutes. Return the bones to the pot, and sprinkle with the salt, red pepper flakes, and black pepper. Add the water and bring to a simmer.

3. Reduce the heat to medium-low and simmer, covered, until the meat on the bones is tender and the liquid has almost evaporated, about 45 minutes.

4. Ladle the bones into bowls and eat with your hands. Be sure to provide plenty of napkins.

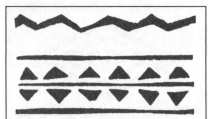

VENISON SAUSAGE WITH HONEY SAUCE
(UNITED STATES)

"This was a special treat," recalls Hiram Bonner, who grew up in Houston, Texas. "Every Christmas Eve my family would have a reunion at a different relative's house. There'd be cousins, uncles, aunts, and great-grandchildren. All the old-timers would get together and prepare a Christmas breakfast. My favorite item at these breakfasts was the venison sausage. It was the perfect mixture of venison, beef, pork, and sausage seasonings. They'd be served with breakfast standards of eggs, biscuits, a slab of bacon, and Virginia ham steaks."

VENISON SAUSAGE WITH HONEY SAUCE

Cook's Notes: Ground venison, if not acquired as a gift from a hunter, can be ordered from top-notch butchers. It will be pricey, since it is usually prepared from the high-quality lean haunch. The honey and red wine sauce complements the venison patties to a "T."

1½ teaspoons salt
½ teaspoon ground ginger
½ teaspoon freshly ground white pepper
⅛ teaspoon grated nutmeg
Pinch of cloves
1 bay leaf, finely crumbled
1½ pounds ground venison
¾ pound ground beef chuck
½ pound ground pork
2 tablespoons vegetable oil
½ cup dry red wine
½ cup honey

1. Position a rack in the top third of the oven, and preheat to 400°.
2. In a large bowl, combine the salt, ginger, white pepper, nutmeg, cloves, and bay leaf. Add the venison, chuck, and pork, and knead lightly with your clean hands until combined. Form the mixture into six patties, about 4 inches in diameter and 1 inch thick.
3. Heat the oil in a large skillet. Add the patties and cook over medium-high heat, turning once, until browned on both sides, about 4 minutes. (The patties will still be very rare.) Transfer the patties to a 9- by 13-inch baking dish.

4. Drain off all the fat from the skillet. Add the wine, bring to a boil, and cook until reduced by half, about 2 minutes. Remove the skillet from the heat, and stir in the honey until blended. Pour the honey mixture over the patties.

5. Bake until the patties are cooked as desired (cut into the center of one to check), about 10 minutes for medium-rare, longer if desired. Serve immediately, drizzled with the honey sauce.

ROAST LEG OF VENISON WITH VEGETABLE GRAVY
(UNITED STATES)

"At a family gathering, usually around Juneteenth (celebrated in Texas and other parts of the Deep South in memory of the day in 1865 when Union general Granger proclaimed the slaves of Texas free), we would have a get-together in one of the large parks in the city and barbecue game," says Hiram Bonner. "We'd soak the deer leg overnight in evaporated milk and then roast it indoors."

ROAST LEG OF VENISON WITH VEGETABLE GRAVY

Cook's Notes: An extravagant show-stopper, roast leg of venison is an entrée to be savored by your most favored guests. Leg of venison is a very lean meat and needs to have a little extra fat added to prevent its drying out. So Hiram recommends marinating it overnight in evaporated milk, which would also counteract the gaminess of bagged venison. The vegetables that surround the roast as it cooks are puréed to create a light, flourless gravy, which plays against the richness of the meat.

Serves 8 to 10

1 (12-ounce) can evaporated milk
1 (6-pound) leg of venison, bone in, tied
1 teaspoon salt
½ teaspoon dried thyme
½ teaspoon dried rosemary
¼ teaspoon freshly ground black pepper
⅛ teaspoon cayenne pepper
3 tablespoons vegetable oil, plus extra if needed
1 medium onion, chopped
1 medium carrot, chopped
1 medium celery rib, chopped
1 medium green bell pepper, seeded and chopped
2 garlic cloves, crushed through a garlic press
1 cup dry red wine
2 cups beef broth, homemade or canned

1. Pour the evaporated milk over the venison in a large bowl. Cover, and refrigerate for at least 8 hours or overnight, turning the meat three or four times.

2. Remove the meat from the evaporated milk; discard the milk. Pat the venison completely dry with paper towels. In a small bowl, combine the salt, thyme, rosemary, and black pepper and cayenne pepper. Rub the venison all over with the mixture.

3. Position a rack in the center of the oven, and preheat to 350°.

4. In a large flameproof roasting pan placed over two burners, heat the oil until very hot but not smoking. Add the venison and cook it over medium-high heat, turning often, until browned on all sides, about 10 minutes. Transfer the venison to a large platter and set it aside.

5. Add additional oil to the pan if necessary. Add the onion, carrot, celery, bell pepper, and garlic. Reduce the heat to medium and cook, stirring often, until the vegetables have softened, about 5 minutes.

6. Set a rack in the roasting pan, and place the venison on the rack. Transfer the pan to the oven and roast, basting occasionally with the red wine and the drippings in the bottom of the pan, until a meat thermometer inserted in the thickest part of the roast (not touching a bone) reads 135°, about 1 hour and 40 minutes for medium-rare meat, longer if desired. Transfer the roast to a serving platter, cover with foil, and let stand at least 15 minutes before carving.

7. While the roast is resting, use a slotted spoon to transfer the vegetables to a blender. Skim off any fat from the drippings in the pan. Place the pan over two burners on top of the stove, on medium-high heat. When the drippings are sizzling, pour in the broth and bring it to a simmer, scraping up the browned bits on the bottom of the pan with a wooden spoon. Pour the hot broth into the blender, and purée it with the vegetables until smooth. (Add more broth to make a thinner gravy if desired.)

8. Transfer the gravy to a medium saucepan. Cook, stirring constantly,

until simmering. Season to taste with additional salt and pepper if desired, and keep the gravy warm until ready to serve.

9. To carve the venison, hold the meat steady with a carving fork, and then slice the meat horizontally, parallel to the bone. When you reach the bone, turn the roast over and repeat the procedure. Serve the venison immediately, with the warm gravy.

SAUTÉED CALVES' LIVER SMOTHERED IN ONIONS
(UNITED STATES)

Hiram Bonner's recipe for calves' liver comes from his Aunt Janie Ward. Hiram warns, "If you cook the liver for too long, you will toughen it, so watch out! We always had this with milk, iced tea, or Kool-Aid."

SAUTÉED CALVES' LIVER SMOTHERED IN ONIONS

Cook's Notes: There are few people who will argue against the fact that the best way to enjoy calves' liver is medium-rare and covered with tender cooked onions. This recipe is a fine example of this conviction. As the smothered onions are on the soupy side, Hiram recommends serving this with hot rice to sop up the savory juices.

Makes 4 servings

½ cup all-purpose flour
½ teaspoon salt
½ teaspoon freshly ground black pepper
2 pounds calves' liver, sliced about ¾ inch thick, cut into 4 pieces
2 tablespoons vegetable oil, plus extra if needed
2 tablespoons unsalted butter, plus extra if needed
3 medium onions, thinly sliced
1½ cups beef broth, homemade or canned
Hot cooked rice

1. Preheat the oven to 200°.

2. Combine the flour, salt, and pepper on a plate. Dredge the calves' liver in the flour mixture, shaking off any excess.

3. Heat the oil and butter together in a large skillet until very hot but not smoking. In batches, add the calves' liver and cook over medium-high heat, turning once, until browned on both sides, about 1 minute per side for medium-rare, or longer if desired. Transfer the browned calves' liver to a heatproof serving platter, cover with foil, and keep it warm in the oven while cooking the onions.

4. Add additional butter and oil to the pan if necessary. Add the onions and stir until just softened, about 1 minute. Add about 2 tablespoons of the broth to the skillet, and scrape up the browned bits on the bottom of the skillet with a wooden spoon. Add the rest of the broth, bring to a boil, and cook until the onions are very tender, about 3 minutes.

5. Pour the onions over the calves' liver, and serve immediately with hot cooked rice.

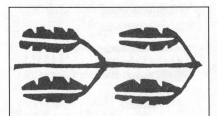

CHILI TEXAS STYLE
(UNITED STATES)

No self-respecting Texan would be caught dead serving chili with all ground beef. And Hiram Bonner, who contributed this recipe, is no exception. He also hand-cuts beef chuck steaks into cubes to give his chili some texture. "The recipe was given to me by my Aunt Janie, whose husband was the first black district attorney in Houston. Because she did a lot of entertaining, she learned to be creative and came up with this recipe.

"It's extremely spicy—almost three alarm," cautions Bonner. "The fumes alone from this chili will make your eyes water."

CHILI TEXAS STYLE

Cook's Notes: Chili is like spaghetti sauce—ask ten different cooks and you get ten different recipes. Everyone has at least one hint on how to make the ultimate chili, but Hiram has two. The first is to melt a full pound of Monterey Jack cheese into the simmering chili at the end, adding a creamy smoothness to the gravy that your guests will love. Second, he purées simmered jalapeño peppers to create a seasoning "sauce," so you can turn up your chili's heat at will. If you can, make the chili a day ahead so the spices can mellow.

Serves 4 to 6

5 fresh jalapeño peppers
2 tablespoons olive oil
1 pound ground beef round
1 pound boneless beef chuck, cut into ½-inch cubes
2 medium onions, chopped
3 garlic cloves, minced
½ cup chili powder
1 teaspoon cumin seeds, crushed
1 quart beef broth, homemade or canned
2 tablespoons tomato paste
2 tablespoons Worcestershire sauce
1 teaspoon salt
½ teaspoon crushed hot red pepper flakes
1 pound shredded Monterey Jack cheese
Hot cooked rice or kidney beans

1. In a small saucepan of simmering water, cook the jalapeños just until tender when pierced with the tip of a small knife, about 10

minutes. Drain and cool slightly. Cut open the jalapeños, remove the seeds, and chop fine. Scrape the chiles into a small bowl and set aside.

2. Heat the oil in a large saucepan. Add the ground round and cubed chuck, and cook over medium-high heat, stirring often, until the meat loses its pink color, about 6 minutes. Add the onions, garlic, and half the chopped jalapeños. Cook, stirring often, until the onions have softened, about 5 minutes. Add the chili powder and cumin seeds and stir for 1 minute.

3. Stir in the beef broth, tomato paste, Worcestershire sauce, salt, and red pepper flakes. Bring to a boil. Reduce the heat to low, and cook until slightly thickened, about 45 minutes.

4. Gradually stir in the shredded cheese. Taste, and season with additional chopped jalapeños, salt, and red pepper flakes, if desired. Serve with hot cooked rice or kidney beans on the side.

SPICY MATOKE
Beef and Plantain "Cake"
(KENYA)

Maggie Marenga, a tourist assistant at the Kenya Tourist Office in New York, remembers eating this dish just about every other day while she was growing up in Kenya. "This is a common dish in the western part of Kenya," says Maggie. "We'd eat it with chicken stew, beef stew, or vegetables.

"Make sure the plantains are well mashed," she advises. "I grew up on the farm where my parents grew plantains, which we called 'bananas.' In this dish, you have to eat the meal hot or the plantains get hard. My advice is to use green plantains, because they keep their texture and won't get mushy."

SPICY MATOKE
Beef and Plantain "Cake"

Cook's Notes: Intriguingly spiced beef cubes are folded into an unusual plantain and spinach purée, then baked into a casserole-like main course. Green, unripe plantains and bananas (which haven't developed their fruity sweetness yet) are used in many countries in ways similar to our potato, so the combination is more familiar than you'd imagine.

Serves 4

2 tablespoons vegetable oil
2 pounds beef chuck, cut into 1½-inch pieces
½ teaspoon salt
¼ teaspoon freshly ground black pepper
1 small onion, coarsely chopped
1 fresh hot chile pepper, such as jalapeño, seeded and chopped
1 teaspoon curry powder
1 teaspoon ground coriander seeds
½ cup water
4 medium green plantains, or 8 small green (unripe) bananas, peeled and cut into ½-inch-thick slices (see page 230)
3 tablespoons fresh lemon juice
1 cup well-washed chopped spinach leaves (about 5 ounces)
2 tablespoons unsalted butter, softened
½ cup freshly grated coconut (optional; see Note, page 196)

1. In a 5-quart Dutch oven, heat the oil over medium-high heat. Sprinkle the beef with the salt and pepper. In batches, add the beef and cook, turning occasionally, until browned on all sides, 8 to 10

minutes. Using a slotted spoon, transfer the browned beef to a plate and set it aside.

2. Add the onion and chile pepper to the Dutch oven. Reduce the heat to medium and cook, stirring often, until the onion has softened, about 3 minutes. Add the curry powder and coriander, and stir for 1 minute. Return the beef to the Dutch oven, and stir in the water. Reduce the heat to low and cook, covered, until the meat is tender and the liquid has almost completely evaporated, about 1 hour. (If the stew looks as if it's drying out, add a little more water.)

3. Preheat the oven to 350°. Lightly butter a 9-inch square baking dish.

4. In a large bowl, combine the green plantain slices and lemon juice. Add enough lukewarm water to cover, and let stand for 3 minutes; drain well.

5. In a medium bowl, combine the plantains and spinach, and mash together with a fork until fairly smooth. Stir in the beef stew. Spread the mixture evenly in the prepared baking dish, and dot the top with the butter.

6. Bake until the top is golden brown, about 30 minutes. Sprinkle with the grated coconut if desired, and serve immediately.

CACHUPA
Cape Verdian Sausage and Vegetable Stew
(CAPE VERDE)

Cape Verde, which is comprised of ten islands off the west coast of Africa, has been called the Brazil of West Africa, probably because of the racial mixture of the island, which was a stop during the slave trade. Although the country has a population of only 300,000, there are flourishing communities in the northeastern United States. This meal is so popular, according to Steven Barboza, a New York–based writer of Cape Verdian descent, that it is virtually the nation's national dish.

CACHUPA
Cape Verdian Sausage and Vegetable Stew

Cook's Notes: A rib-sticking stew for your heartiest-eating guests, with an abundance of ethnic vegetables. We give instructions for both the time-saving pressure cooker and the traditional stewpot.

Serves 8 to 10

1 pound slab bacon, rind removed

¼ cup olive oil

2 medium onions, coarsely chopped

2 garlic cloves, minced

2 bay leaves

1 pound dried cracked corn (available in Latin American markets)

1 pig's foot, split

6 cups cold water

½ medium head green cabbage (about ¾ pound), cored and cut into wedges

⅓ cup dried kidney beans

⅓ cup dried lima beans

1 pound kale

4 small green (unripe) bananas, peeled and cut into 1-inch chunks (see page 229)

1 pound white yam (*name*), pared and cut into 1-inch chunks

1 pound *boniatos* (*batatas*), peeled and cut into 1-inch chunks

½ pound *calabaza* or acorn squash, pared, seeded, and cut into 1-inch chunks

1 pound chourico, linguica, or chorizo sausage, cut into 1-inch slices

1 (15-ounce) can peeled plum tomatoes, drained and chopped

Pressure Cooker Method

1. Place the slab bacon in a large saucepan, and add enough cold water to cover by 1 inch. Bring to a simmer over medium heat, and cook for 5 minutes. Drain, rinse well under cold running water, and drain again. Cut the bacon across the grain into strips about 3½ inches long and ¾ inch wide. Set aside.

2. In a 5-quart pressure cooker, heat 2 tablespoons of the oil over medium heat. Add half the onions, and the garlic and bay leaves. Cook, stirring often, until the onions have softened, about 5 minutes.

3. Add the corn and pig's foot. Stir in 4 cups of the water. Engage the pressure cooker lid and bring to full pressure over high heat. Reduce the heat to low, and cook for 15 minutes. To quickly drop the pressure, place the edge of the pressure cooker lid under cold running water. Or remove the cooker from the heat and let it stand until the pressure drops naturally.

4. Remove the lid and add the cabbage wedges, kidney and lima beans, and the reserved bacon. Stir in the remaining 2 cups cold water. Replace the lid and bring to full pressure over high heat. Reduce the heat to low, and cook for 10 minutes.

5. While the beans are cooking, place the kale in a large sink of lukewarm water. Remove and discard any woody stems. Agitate the kale well to remove any hidden grit. Carefully lift the leaves floating on the water, and transfer them to a colander, leaving the sand and grit on the bottom of the sink. Drain the kale well, then cut it crosswise into ½-inch-wide strips.

6. Again let the pressure in the cooker drop, by the quick method or naturally. Remove the lid and discard the pig's foot. Stir in the kale and bring it to a simmer over medium heat. Cook, uncovered (without pressure), stirring often, until the kale has wilted, about 5 minutes. Then stir in the green bananas, white yam, *boniato*, and *calabaza*. Bring to a boil. Reduce the heat to low and cook, uncovered (without pressure), stirring the stew often and carefully to avoid breaking up the

CARRINGTON

vegetables, until the ingredients are almost tender, about 15 minutes.

7. Meanwhile, heat the remaining 2 tablespoons oil in a large skillet over medium heat. Add the sausage and cook, turning often, until lightly browned on all sides, about 5 minutes. Using a slotted spoon, transfer the sausage to paper towels to drain. Add the remaining onion and cook, stirring often, until softened, about 5 minutes. Stir in the tomatoes and bring to a simmer. Reduce the heat to low and simmer for 5 minutes. Stir in the reserved sausage.

8. Stir the sausage mixture into the stew. Cook, stirring carefully and often, until the ingredients are tender, about 15 minutes.

Traditional Cooking Method

Refer to the pressure cooker instructions above for cooking procedure details.

1. Place the corn, kidney beans, and lima beans in separate bowls. Add enough water to each bowl to cover by 1 inch, and soak overnight. Drain well.

2. Blanch the bacon and cut it into strips.

3. Heat 2 tablespoons of the oil in a 6-quart Dutch oven. Add half the onions, and the garlic and bay leaves, and cook over medium heat until softened, about 5 minutes. Add the corn and the pig's foot. Add enough cold water to cover by 1 inch, and bring to a boil over high heat. Reduce the heat and simmer for 1 hour.

4. Stir in the bacon strips and kidney and lima beans. Simmer until the corn and beans are tender, about 1½ hours, adding more boiling water if necessary.

5. Clean the kale and stir it into the stew along with the cabbage wedges. Add enough water to cover by 1 inch, and simmer for 10 minutes.

6. Stir in the bananas, white yam, *boniato*, and *calabaza*. Add enough water to cover by 1 inch, and simmer until the ingredients are almost tender, 15 minutes.

7. Heat the remaining 2 tablespoons oil in a large skillet, and cook the sausage. Remove the sausage and drain on paper towels. Cook the remaining onions until softened. Add the tomatoes and cook 5 minutes. Stir in the sausage.

8. Stir the sausage mixture into the stew, and simmer until all the ingredients are tender, about 10 minutes.

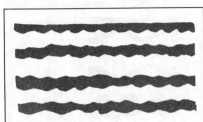

GARLICKY PORK ROAST
(UNITED STATES)

"When I was growing up, my mother used onion a lot," says Cynthia Lewis, co-owner of Mavis' and Cyn's Restaurant and Catering. I started using garlic instead."

GARLICKY PORK ROAST

Cook's Notes: Cynthia Lewis's trick of basting with gravy ensures a fabulous crust. This pork roast is cooked just to juicy, barely pink perfection—155°. Beware of overcooking, or it will be tough and dry. Cynthia doesn't normally serve gravy with the roast, as it's all used up during the basting, so you might want to offer Kahlúa-Soaked Dried Fruit Compote (page 192) or homemade applesauce alongside.

Serves 6

1 (3-pound) center-cut boneless pork loin roast, tied
1 large garlic clove, cut into 8 slivers
½ teaspoon salt
½ teaspoon freshly ground black pepper
1 cup dry white wine
1 tablespoon cornstarch
½ cup cold water

1. Preheat the oven to 350°.
2. Using the tip of a small sharp knife, pierce the pork roast with eight deep slits. Stuff each slit with a garlic sliver. Season the roast with the salt and pepper, and place it on a rack in an aluminum foil–lined roasting pan.
3. Bake, basting often with the wine, for 1 hour. Remove the pan from the oven, and remove the roast and the rack. In a small bowl, whisk the cornstarch into the water until dissolved. Pour the cornstarch mixture into the drippings, return the roast on the rack to the roasting pan, and return the pan to the oven.
4. Continue baking, basting often with the mixture in the bottom of the pan, until a meat thermometer inserted in the center of the roast reads 155° for medium-well, about 20 minutes, or longer if desired. Let the roast stand for 10 minutes before slicing.

BAKED HAM WITH A SECRET GLAZE

Cook's Notes: Mavis and Cyn used to keep the recipe for their out-of-this-world baked ham close to their vests. It's not a secret anymore. We prefer using a bone-in ham, but this punchlike blend of wine, honey, and pineapple juice is also just the thing to gussy up a canned ham. If you cook a larger ham, allow 10 minutes per pound to heat the ham through, but baste only during the last hour of cooking, or the glaze may scorch.

Serves 8 to 10

½ cup packed light brown sugar
½ cup honey
½ cup dry red wine
½ cup pineapple juice
1 garlic clove, minced
1 (6-pound) bone-in smoked precooked ham

1. In a large bowl, whisk together the brown sugar, honey, red wine, pineapple juice, and garlic. Place the ham in the marinade, turn to coat it, and let it stand at room temperature for at least 1 or up to 4 hours, or cover and refrigerate overnight. Turn the ham in the marinade as many times as you remember to do so.
2. Preheat the oven to 350°.
3. Place the ham on a rack in an aluminum foil–lined roasting pan, reserving the marinade. Bake the ham, basting often with the reserved marinade, until a meat thermometer inserted in the thickest part of the ham (not touching the bone) reads 120°, about 1 hour.
4. To carve the ham, hold the meat steady with a carving fork and slice the meat horizontally, parallel to the bone. When you reach the bone, turn the ham over and repeat the procedure on the other side.

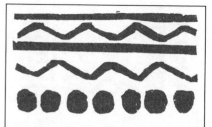

BAKED HAM WITH A SECRET GLAZE (UNITED STATES)

"This is mostly a holiday kind of dish—a holiday ham," says Mavis Young, the other half of Mavis' and Cyn's Restaurant and Catering. "I usually make it for a large gathering of family or friends so that not much will be left over. Otherwise I might try to finish it all up myself!"

ALL-IN-ONE MEAT LOAF
(UNITED STATES)

"Back when I was a full-time nurse, I'd try to do as much as I could in my spare time," says Mavis Young. "On the weekend, I'd do the meat loaf. I'd just put it in the oven early in the day and let it cook slowly. I could wash and clean the house, and by the time I was finished with those chores, an entire dinner would be ready."

ALL-IN-ONE MEAT LOAF

Cook's Notes: What an ingenious idea! Chop your vegetables and place them in the bottom of a loaf pan, then top with a meat loaf mixture. You'll have a great one-dish meal, needing only a green salad to round out your dinner. If you use ground sirloin instead of the ground round suggested here, you'll have a drier, more compact loaf.

Serves 4 to 6

1 large onion, chopped
1 medium carrot, chopped
1 medium celery rib, chopped
1 medium Russet potato, peeled and cut into 1-inch cubes
1 teaspoon salt
¼ teaspoon freshly ground black pepper
1 cup Saltine cracker crumbs
1 (8-ounce) can tomato sauce
¼ cup milk
1 large egg
1 small red bell pepper, seeded and finely chopped
2 garlic cloves, minced
¼ teaspoon Italian seasoning
¼ teaspoon Worcestershire sauce
1½ pounds ground beef round
3 tablespoons ketchup (optional)

1. Preheat the oven to 350°. Lightly butter a 9- by 5-inch loaf pan. Set aside ½ cup of the chopped onion.
2. In the bottom of the prepared loaf pan, toss the remaining onion,

the carrot, celery, potato, ¼ teaspoon of the salt, and ⅛ teaspoon of the pepper; set the pan aside.

3. In a medium bowl, combine the cracker crumbs, tomato sauce, milk, egg, bell pepper, garlic, Italian seasoning, Worcestershire sauce, and the remaining ½ cup onion, ¾ teaspoon salt, and ⅛ teaspoon pepper. Add the ground round and knead the mixture lightly with your clean hands until combined. Transfer it to the loaf pan, pressing the meat lightly so it adheres to the vegetables. Place the loaf pan on a baking sheet.

4. Bake until a meat thermometer inserted in the center of the loaf reads 160°, about 1¼ hours. (If desired, spread the top of the loaf with ketchup during the last 10 minutes of baking.) Let the loaf stand 10 minutes. Drain off excess fat, invert the meat loaf onto a platter, and slice.

GRILLED RABBIT WITH TANGY SPICY MARINADE
(UNITED STATES)

Hiram Bonner, a chef in New York City, says his family would use versions of this marinade with any of the game they might have hunted that day: rabbit, of course, but also venison, raccoon, doves, and armadillo—yes, armadillo!

GRILLED RABBIT WITH TANGY SPICY MARINADE

Cook's Notes: Hiram Bonner's family in Texas usually bag their own game and marinate it overnight in a tenderizing mixture of 6 cups water, 2 cups cider vinegar, 1 tablespoon hot red pepper flakes, and 2 crushed garlic cloves. We assume you will be buying your rabbit at the butcher's, so our baste, although similar, is gentler, and intended for flavoring only. To avoid drying out tender meats like rabbit and poultry, grill them until browned over hot coals (in the center of the fire), then move them to the cooler areas (the outside edges of the fire) to finish cooking.

Serves 6 to 8

2 (3-pound) fresh rabbits, dressed
½ cup olive oil
2 garlic cloves, crushed through a garlic press
2 tablespoons fresh lemon juice
1 tablespoon Dijon mustard
¼ teaspoon liquid smoke (optional)
¼ teaspoon salt
⅛ teaspoon crushed hot red pepper flakes
Hiram's Barbecue Sauce (optional, page 106)

1. Using a sharp knife and a cleaver, cut up each rabbit into eight pieces as follows: Cut off the two forequarter sections where the rib cage begins. Cut off the two hindquarter sections where the rib cage ends. Chop the long center section in half vertically. Chop each rib section in half crosswise.

2. In a large bowl, whisk together the oil, garlic, lemon juice, mustard, liquid smoke, salt, and red pepper flakes. Add the rabbit pieces, cover, and refrigerate for at least 2 hours or up to 6 hours. Do not overmarinate rabbit, or the texture will become rubbery.

3. Prepare a hot fire in an outdoor grill. (When it is ready, the charcoal will be covered with white ash.) Remove the rabbit from the marinade, and pat the pieces dry with paper towels. Grill the rabbit in the hot center area of the grill, basting it with the marinade and turning often, until browned, about 10 minutes. Then move the rabbit pieces to the cooler outside edges of the grill, and cover with the lid. Grill, basting and turning occasionally, until the rabbit shows no sign of pink at the bone when prodded with the tip of a sharp knife, about 30 minutes. The center sections of the rabbit will be done before the meatier portions, so remove them when done and keep warm. If desired, baste the rabbit with Hiram's Barbecue Sauce during the last 10 minutes of grilling.

105

**REAL TEXAN BARBECUED
SPARERIBS AND SAUCE**
(UNITED STATES)

"This barbecue sauce, one of my Aunt Clara's recipes, was used at all the family gatherings," Hiram Bonner remembers.

REAL TEXAN BARBECUED SPARERIBS AND SAUCE

Cook's Notes: *Real* barbecue is slow-cooked over smoldering hardwood coals, and in Texas that wood is almost always mesquite. Use readily available mesquite chips to add that smoky flavor that makes barbecue so special. Spareribs take a long time to barbecue to finger-licking tenderness, and cooks are always trying to devise a way to precook them before placing them on the grill. Solve the problem by first rubbing the ribs with spices, wrapping them in foil, and cooking them in their own simmering juices over hot coals. Then unwrap and finish with a delectable glazing of Hiram Bonner's Barbecue Sauce.

Serves 4 to 6; makes about 1½ quarts sauce

HIRAM BONNER'S BARBECUE SAUCE:
4 slices bacon, coarsely chopped
1 large onion, chopped
2 garlic cloves, minced
2 large lemons, halved
1 (12-ounce) bottle chili sauce (such as Heinz 57 Variety)
1 (12-ounce) bottle beer
1 (8-ounce) can tomato sauce
1 cup ketchup
½ cup dry red wine
½ cup packed light brown sugar
2 tablespoons strong brewed coffee
2 tablespoons peppercorns
1 tablespoon prepared horseradish
1 bay leaf
½ teaspoon hot pepper sauce, or to taste

2 teaspoons garlic salt

1 teaspoon paprika

½ teaspoon freshly ground black pepper

¼ teaspoon cayenne pepper

4 pounds pork spareribs

Mesquite wood chips, soaked at least 1 hour in water to cover

1. Make the sauce: In a large saucepan, cook the bacon over medium heat, stirring often, until crisp and brown, about 3 minutes. Using a slotted spoon, transfer the bacon to paper towels to drain, and set aside, leaving the fat in the pan.

2. Add the onion and garlic to the pan and cook, stirring often, until the onion has softened, about 5 minutes. Using your hands, squeeze the lemons of their juice right into the saucepan, and drop in the lemon halves. Stir in the reserved bacon and the chili sauce, beer, tomato sauce, ketchup, wine, brown sugar, brewed coffee, peppercorns, horseradish, and bay leaf; bring to a simmer. Reduce the heat to low and simmer, stirring often, until slightly thickened, about 1 hour. Season with the hot sauce.

3. Strain the sauce through a sieve set over a large bowl, pressing hard on the solids. Discard the solids and cool the sauce completely. The sauce can be made up to 1 week ahead; keep it covered and refrigerated.

4. Prepare the ribs: In a small bowl, combine the garlic salt, paprika, black pepper, and cayenne. Rub the spareribs all over with the spice mixture. Wrap each slab of ribs separately in a double thickness of aluminum foil. Let the foil packets stand at room temperature for 1 hour, or refrigerate for at least 2 hours or overnight (the longer the better).

5. Prepare a hot charcoal fire in an outdoor grill. (It is ready when the charcoal is covered with white ash.) Place the foil packets on the grill, cover with the lid and grill, turning occasionally, until the

spareribs are almost tender, about 1 hour. (Open up a packet to be sure.) Set the wrapped spareribs aside.

6. Add more fresh charcoal to the fire and wait until it has burned down to medium-hot. (You should be able to hold your hand 6 inches above the coals for a count of 3. If you can count only to 1 or 2, the coals are too hot, so wait a minute. Any longer than 3 and the coals are cooling off, so proceed immediately.)

7. Drain the mesquite chips and sprinkle them over the coals. Unwrap the ribs, arrange them on the grill, and cover with the lid. Grill, turning occasionally, until tender, about 30 minutes. (Add more drained wood chips occasionally to keep the grill smoking.) During the last 10 minutes, baste often with the barbecue sauce.

KIDDIE (GOAT) STEW

Cook's Notes: Ask at Italian or Latin American meat markets if they can order goat for you. It is delicious, with a taste (not surprisingly) similar to lamb. Goat stew meat is almost always sold cut into pieces with plenty of bone still attached, but those bones make a sensational sauce. If you have to make a substitute, use 4 pounds bone-in lamb stew (such as neck) or 3 pounds boneless lamb shoulder.

Serves 4 to 6

3 tablespoons vegetable oil
4 pounds goat stew meat, cut into 2-inch pieces
3 large onions, sliced
3 garlic cloves, minced
⅓ cup all-purpose flour
4 cups beef broth, homemade or canned
2 tablespoons tomato paste
2 tablespoons chopped fresh chives, or 2 teaspoons dried
½ teaspoon salt
¼ teaspoon freshly ground black pepper
Dash of ground cloves

1. Heat the oil in a 5-quart Dutch oven or soup kettle. In batches, add the meat and cook over medium-high heat, turning often, until browned on all sides, about 6 minutes per batch. Set the browned meat aside.
2. Add the onions and garlic to the Dutch oven and cook, stirring often, until the onions are lightly browned, about 6 minutes. Stir in the flour and cook, stirring constantly, until the flour is lightly

KIDDIE (GOAT) STEW
(ANTIGUA AND BARBUDA)

"Nowadays they call it Goat Water, but in my day we called it Kiddie Stew," says Gwendolyn Tonge. "When I was growing up it was a meal that was used mainly for celebrations: weddings, the completion of building a house, the end of cutting the sugarcane. It would be served with plenty of wine and bread. Now it's not used so much at weddings but at parties and for holidays."

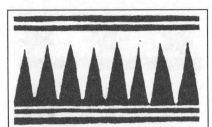

SEASONED RICE WITH PORK, CHICKEN, AND VEGETABLES
(ANTIGUA AND BARBUDA)

"This is a meal that can stretch," says Gwendolyn Tonge, "because you can put in bits of chicken and meats with the squash and beans, which, coupled with the rice, could serve a large family. I remember from my childhood that most children enjoyed the seasoned rice, so you found that your family cooked it. Even now I'd say that families in Antigua eat it at least once a week, but now they add a salad. In the early days, farmers would put the rice in a tin, and during their lunch break would build a little fire and heat it up. Many people use pepper sauce with their seasoned rice. In days gone by they used pepper vinegar: onion, thyme, garlic, and hot fresh pepper put into a bottle of vinegar—it keeps for weeks."

browned, about 2 minutes. Then stir in the broth, tomato paste, chives, salt, pepper, and cloves.

3. Return the meat to the pot and bring to a simmer. Reduce the heat to medium-low and simmer, stirring often, until the meat is tender, about 1½ hours. Serve immediately.

SEASONED RICE WITH PORK, CHICKEN, AND VEGETABLES

Cook's Notes: Kind of an Island-style paella, this hearty dish is jammed with lots of inexpensive, but good, things. It seems to be a close relation to West African Jolof Rice (see page 128).

Serves 8

3 quarts water
1 pig's foot, split
2 fresh ham hocks, cut in half crosswise
2 medium onions, chopped
4 garlic cloves, minced
3 sprigs parsley
1 teaspoon salt
½ teaspoon freshly ground black pepper
½ pound salt pork, rind removed
2 tablespoons vegetable oil
1 pound chicken wings
1 medium green bell pepper, seeded and chopped
2 cups long-grain rice

1 pound *calabaza* or acorn squash, pared, seeded, and cut into
    1-inch pieces
2 tablespoons tomato paste
2 tablespoons chopped fresh chives, or 2 teaspoons dried
1 tablespoon soy sauce
½ teaspoon dried thyme
1 (16-ounce) can pigeon peas (*gandules*), drained
1 cup well-washed chopped spinach leaves (about 5 ounces)

1. In a 5-quart Dutch oven or soup kettle, combine the water, pig's foot, ham hocks, half the onion, half the garlic, parsley, salt, and ¼ teaspoon of the pepper. Bring to a boil over high heat. Reduce the heat to low and simmer until the meat is tender, about 1½ hours. Remove the ham hocks and pig's foot from the broth, reserving the broth. Let the meat cool slightly. Cut off all usable meat and chop it coarsely, discarding the bones; set the chopped meat aside.

2. Place the salt pork in a medium saucepan and add enough cold water to cover. Bring to a simmer over medium heat and cook for 5 minutes. Drain well and rinse under cold water. Cut the salt pork across the grain into 1- by 3-inch strips.

3. Heat the oil in a 5-quart Dutch oven or soup kettle. Add the salt pork strips and cook over medium heat, turning often, until lightly browned, about 5 minutes. Transfer the salt pork to paper towels to drain, leaving the fat in the Dutch oven.

4. Add the chicken wings to the Dutch oven and cook, turning often, until browned on all sides and partially cooked, about 15 minutes. Remove the chicken wings and set aside. Add the bell pepper, remaining chopped onion and minced garlic, and cook, stirring often, until the onion has softened, about 5 minutes.

5. Add the rice and stir until opaque, about 1 minute. Return the reserved chopped meat, chicken wings, and salt pork to the pot. Stir in the *calabaza*, tomato paste, chives, soy sauce, thyme, and remaining

BOBOTIE
Curried Beef Casserole
(SOUTH AFRICA)

This famous South African dish was introduced to that cuisine via Indonesia, which was also a Dutch colony.

¼ teaspoon pepper. Add the reserved broth and bring to a boil over high heat. Reduce the heat to low, cover tightly, and simmer until the rice is tender, about 20 minutes. Remove from the heat.

6. Stir in the drained pigeon peas and spinach, cover, and let stand 5 minutes to heat the peas and wilt the spinach. Serve immediately.

BOBOTIE
Curried Beef Casserole

Cook's Notes: This meal is easy to make ahead and reheat, and so it is a popular buffet dish.

Serves 6 to 8

1 cup fresh bread cumbs
1 cup milk
5 large eggs
2 tablespoons unsalted butter
2 pounds ground beef round
1 large onion, chopped
1 medium pear, cored and chopped
2 garlic cloves, minced
2 tablespoons curry powder
Grated zest of 1 large lemon
3 tablespoons fresh lemon juice
½ cup blanched slivered almonds
½ cup chopped dried apricots
1 teaspoon salt
¼ teaspoon cayenne pepper

¾ cup heavy (whipping) cream
4 bay leaves
Chutney, for garnish

1. Position a rack in the top third of the oven, and preheat to 325°.
Lightly butter a 9- by 13-inch baking dish.
2. In a medium bowl, mix together the bread crumbs, milk, and 1
of the eggs. Set aside.
3. Heat the butter in a large skillet. Add the ground round, onion,
and pear, and cook over high heat, stirring often, until the meat has
lost its pink color, about 5 minutes. Add the garlic, curry powder,
lemon zest, and lemon juice, and stir for 1 minute. Stir in the almonds,
apricots, salt, and cayenne. Remove the skillet from the heat and allow
the mixture to cool slightly.
4. Stir the meat mixture into the bread crumbs, and combine well.
Transfer to the prepared baking dish, smooth the top, and place on a
baking sheet.
5. In a medium bowl, whisk the heavy cream with the remaining 4
eggs until smooth. Press the bay leaves into the top of the meat, and
then pour the cream mixture over it.
6. Bake until the custard is set and lightly browned, about 45 minutes.
Serve, with a bowl of chutney passed alongside.

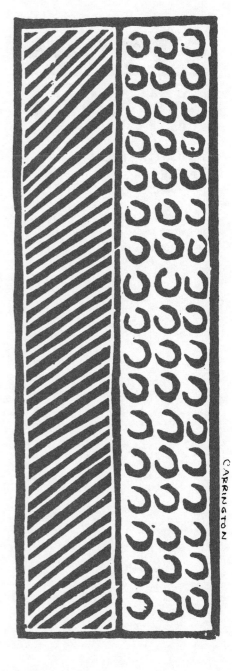

CARRINGTON

KINGSTON MEAT PATTIES
(JAMAICA)

Like Samoosas (page 16), these Jamaican treats are a popular snack food.

KINGSTON MEAT PATTIES

Cook's Notes: Spicy meat-stuffed pastries with a distinctive yellow crust are sold by street vendors all over Jamaica. You can make these with any ground meat you fancy—lamb, pork, or even turkey.

PASTRY:

2¼ cups all-purpose flour

1 teaspoon curry powder, preferably Jamaican

½ teaspoon salt

⅛ teaspoon cayenne pepper

¾ cup vegetable shortening, chilled

⅓ cup ice water

FILLING:

2 tablespoons unsalted butter

1 pound ground beef round

1 medium onion, chopped

½ fresh hot chile pepper, preferably Scotch bonnet, seeded and
　　minced

1 garlic clove, minced

1 tablespoon all-purpose flour

2 teaspoons curry powder, preferably Jamaican

½ teaspoon salt

½ teaspoon dried thyme

¼ teaspoon ground allspice

2 tablespoons tomato paste

2 tablespoons water

1 large egg, well beaten

1. Make the pastry dough: In a medium bowl, stir together the flour, curry powder, salt, and cayenne. Using a pastry blender or two knives, cut in the shortening until it resembles coarse meal. Tossing with a fork, gradually sprinkle in the ice water, mixing just until the mixture is moist enough to hold together when pinched between your thumb and forefinger. (You may need to add more water.) Gather the dough and form it into a flat disk, wrap it in waxed paper, and refrigerate at least 1 hour or overnight.

2. Make the filling: Heat the butter in a large skillet. Add the ground beef, onion, chile pepper, and garlic. Cook over medium-high heat, stirring often, until the meat is no longer pink, about 5 minutes. Then add the flour, curry powder, salt, thyme, and allspice, and stir for 1 minute. Stir in the tomato paste and water and cook until thickened, about 1 minute. Remove the skillet from the heat and allow the filling to cool completely.

3. Position a rack in the top third of the oven, and preheat to 400°. Lightly grease a baking sheet.

4. On a lightly floured work surface, roll out the dough to form a 12- by 14-inch rectangle about ⅛ inch thick. Cut it into eight 6- by 3-inch rectangles. Place about ¼ cup of the filling in the center of each rectangle, fold it over to enclose the filling, and press the edges with a fork to seal them. Transfer the patties to the prepared baking sheet, and brush them lightly with the beaten egg.

5. Bake until golden brown, 25 to 30 minutes. Serve hot, warm, or at room temperature.

CARRINGTON

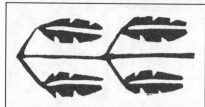

FRESH PORK ROAST ADOBO (CARIBBEAN)

Pork is the most reviled, and yet the most praised, food there is. If you like it, this subtly spiced dish will hit the spot.

FRESH PORK ROAST ADOBO

Cook's Notes: *Adobo* is a spice mixture found in the Spanish-speaking islands of the Caribbean. It can be just about any combination of herbs and spices, and is used to marinate or season just about anything. To feed a crowd, nothing beats a huge fresh ham (unsmoked leg of pork) rubbed with *adobo* and roasted.

Serves 10 to 12

ADOBO:

2 garlic cloves, crushed through a garlic press

1 tablespoon coarse (kosher) salt

¼ cup olive oil

2 tablespoons fresh lime juice

1 teaspoon dried oregano

1 teaspoon dried rosemary

1 teaspoon dried thyme

1 teaspoon freshly ground black pepper

1 (11-pound) bone-in fresh leg of pork ("fresh ham")

PORK STOCK:

1 tablespoon vegetable oil

2 pounds pork neck bones

1 small onion, chopped

1 small carrot, chopped

1 small celery rib with leaves, chopped

1½ quarts water

1 parsley sprig

⅛ teaspoon dried thyme

⅛ teaspoon peppercorns

2 tablespoons olive oil

1. Make the *adobo*: On a work surface, sprinkle the garlic with the salt. Using a large knife, chop and smear them together until the mixture forms a paste. Scrape up the garlic-salt paste and place it in a small bowl. Add the ¼ cup olive oil, lime juice, oregano, rosemary, thyme, and pepper, and whisk until smooth.

2. Using a sharp knife, score the ham skin in a diamond pattern, being sure not to cut into the meat itself. Rub the ham all over with the *adobo*. Place the ham in a large plastic bag (such as a plastic grocery bag or an unscented garbage bag), close tightly, and refrigerate for at least 8 hours or up to 24 hours.

3. Meanwhile, make the pork stock: Heat the oil in a medium saucepan. Add the pork bones and cook over medium-high heat, turning often, until browned, about 6 minutes. Add the onion, carrot, and celery, and cook, stirring often, until the vegetables have softened, about 5 minutes. Add the water and bring to a boil, skimming off any foam that rises to the top. Add the parsley, thyme, and peppercorns, reduce the heat to low, and simmer for 3 to 4 hours. Strain the pork broth, discarding the solids. Add water if necessary to make 5 cups total liquid. (The pork stock can be made up to 3 days ahead; allow it to cool, then cover and refrigerate.)

4. Position a rack in the center of the oven, and preheat to 400°.

5. Scrape off any excess *adobo* from the ham. Place the ham on a rack in a large flameproof roasting pan, and drizzle with the 2 tablespoons oil.

6. Bake the ham, basting it often with 1 cup of the pork broth and the drippings on the bottom of the pan. Allowing about 22 minutes per pound, until a meat thermometer inserted in the thickest part of the ham (not touching a bone) reads 155°, this will take about 4 hours and 20 minutes. Transfer the ham to a serving platter, and let it stand, loosely covered with aluminum foil, for at least 20 minutes before carving.

7. While the ham is resting, place the roasting pan over two burners on high heat. When the drippings are sizzling, pour in the remaining

4 cups pork stock and bring to a boil, scraping up the browned bits on the bottom of the pan with a wooden spoon. Boil until the stock is syrupy and reduced to about 1½ cups, about 10 minutes. Pour the sauce into a warmed sauceboat.

8. Carve the ham, and serve it with the sauce.

JERKED PORK CHOPS WITH FRESH PAPAYA CHUTNEY
(JAMAICA)

Time was when you could find "jerked" meats only in Jamaica, but now trendy eateries all over America do their own versions of the famous Caribbean barbecue.

JERKED PORK CHOPS WITH FRESH PAPAYA CHUTNEY

Cook's Notes: The most popular meats to "jerk" (that is, marinate in a scallion-chile-allspice paste and slow-cook over smoking coals) are chicken and pork, and these thick-cut pork chops take well to the jerk treatment. On the side, the fresh papaya chutney is a winner. You'll use it all year long to add interest to simply grilled meats—it's great with chicken breasts.

Serves 6

JERK SEASONING:

2 tablespoons whole allspice

4 scallions, finely chopped

2 garlic cloves, minced

1 fresh hot chile pepper, preferably Scotch bonnet, seeded and minced

2 tablespoons fresh lime juice

1 teaspoon dried thyme

½ teaspoon salt

¼ teaspoon grated nutmeg

¼ cup olive oil

6 pork loin chops (¾ pound each), about 1 inch thick

PAPAYA CHUTNEY:

1 ripe papaya, halved, seeded, peeled, and cut into ¼-inch cubes

2 tablespoons minced red onion

1 small fresh hot red chile pepper, such as serrano, seeded and
    minced

1 small garlic clove, minced

Grated zest of 1 lime

2 tablespoons fresh lime juice

1 tablespoon minced fresh cilantro

1. Finely crush the allspice with a mortar and pestle or in a spice grinder. (You can also crush them on a work surface, using the bottom of a heavy saucepan.)

2. In a large bowl, combine the crushed allspice, scallions, garlic, chile pepper, lime juice, thyme, salt, and nutmeg. Gradually stir in the oil to make a paste.

3. Add the pork chops and mix well to coat them with the paste. Cover, and refrigerate for at least 4 hours or overnight.

4. Build a hot charcoal fire on one side of an outdoor grill. (When they are ready, the coals will be covered with white ash.) Place a 9- by 13-inch disposable aluminum foil pan on the bottom of the other side of the grill. Lightly oil the grill rack and arrange the pork chops on it, directly over the aluminum pan. Cover with the lid and cook, turning occasionally, until the pork chops are no longer pink at the bone when prodded with a knife, about 1¼ hours. (Add additional charcoal to the fire if necessary to keep it alive.)

5. Meanwhile, make the papaya chutney: In a medium bowl, combine the papaya, red onion, chile pepper, garlic, lime zest and juice, and cilantro. Cover and refrigerate until ready to serve, but only up to 2 hours ahead. (This chutney is best if the flavors are fresh and distinct, and not blended.)

6. Serve the jerked pork chops with the papaya chutney.

**CHICKEN AND
GROUNDNUT STEW
(AFRICA AND CARIBBEAN)**

When you think of African food, one of the first dishes you think of is Peanut Stew. It is a well-known dish throughout not only Africa but also the Caribbean. There seem to be as many different recipes for this dish as there are names for the main ingredient, which include groundnut, earthnut, and goober. Some more unusual recipes call for a jigger of sherry or white wine, or a piece of rib for flavoring. Some of the more arcane measurements from older cookbooks will tell you to grind a "cigarette tin" of roasted nuts. This recipe was adapted from one given to us by Paula Yaa Johnson, a dancer who specializes in African dance.

CHICKEN AND GROUNDNUT STEW

Cook's Notes: Peanut butter stews abound all over the African continent. Their spiciness ranges from five-alarm to a warm glow, and this one falls in between. Arroz con Coco would be a fine side dish (see page 195).

Serves 6 to 8

2 tablespoons olive oil
9 chicken thighs (about 3 pounds)
2 medium onions, chopped
2 garlic cloves, minced
1 teaspoon curry powder
½ teaspoon dried thyme
2 bay leaves
½ teaspoon salt
¼ teaspoon cayenne pepper, or to taste
3 cups chicken broth, homemade or canned
2 (8-ounce) cans tomato sauce
¾ cup unsalted sugarless peanut butter (available at natural foods
     markets)

1. Heat the oil in a 5-quart Dutch oven. In batches, add the chicken and cook over medium-high heat, turning often, until browned on all sides, about 6 minutes per batch. Transfer the chicken to a plate and set aside.
2. Add the onions to the Dutch oven and cook, stirring, until lightly browned, about 5 minutes. Then add the garlic, curry powder, thyme, bay leaves, salt, and cayenne. Stir for 1 minute, and then stir in the chicken broth and tomato sauce.

3. Return the chicken thighs to the Dutch oven and bring to a simmer. Reduce the heat to medium-low, cover tightly, and simmer until the chicken shows no sign of pink at the bone when prodded with the tip of a sharp knife, about 45 minutes.

4. In a small bowl, blend the peanut butter with about 1 cup of the cooking liquid. Stir this mixture back into the sauce, and cook until heated through, about 2 minutes. Serve immediately.

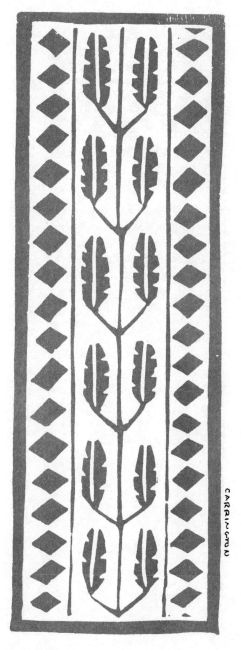

NEW-FASHIONED FRIED CHICKEN
(UNITED STATES)

"This is sort of my recipe and my cousin Kim's recipe, but it's my standard now," says Sheila Johnson. "It's a little spicier than your traditional southern fried chicken recipe, but that's simply because I like spicy food, especially after being exposed to other cuisines. This dish can stand alone or can serve as an appetizer."

NEW-FASHIONED FRIED CHICKEN

Cook's Notes: The old-fashioned classic fried chicken used rendered lard, something not found in a lot of households these days. Olive oil works very well, especially with high-powered seasonings. Here are a couple of hints for perfecting your fried chicken technique:

Try to use a heavy skillet, such as well-seasoned cast iron, to hold the oil's heat and prevent the chicken crust from burning on the bottom.

Be sure to use enough oil to reach halfway up the sides of the skillet, and heat the oil until it is very, very hot—but not smoking. This will ensure a crisp coating and discourage the chicken from becoming greasy.

Be sure the oil is hot before you dredge the chicken in the seasoned flour. If the flour sits too long on the chicken, it will become gummy and the coating will be substandard.

White meat cooks faster than dark meat. So everything will be finished at the same time, give the dark meat a head start by frying it for about 7 minutes before adding the breasts.

Fresh chicken is far superior to frozen. If the bones are black inside after cooking, your butcher is using frozen chickens.

Serves 3 or 4

1½ cups vegetable oil
1½ cups olive oil
1 (3¾-pound) chicken, cut into 8 pieces
2 tablespoons Old Bay Seasoning
2 teaspoons hot pepper sauce, or to taste
2 cups all-purpose flour

2 teaspoons poultry seasoning

1 teaspoon paprika

1 teaspoon freshly ground black pepper

¾ teaspoon salt

1. In a large heavy skillet, heat the vegetable and olive oils over medium-high heat until very hot but not smoking.

2. Combine the Old Bay Seasoning with the hot pepper sauce in a large bowl, and toss the chicken well to coat it with the seasoning.

3. Place the flour, poultry seasoning, paprika, pepper, and salt in a heavy paper grocery bag. A couple of pieces at a time, shake the dark meat in the seasoned flour and place in the hot oil. Cook, turning once, for 7 minutes. (Adjust the heat so the oil stays hot but doesn't begin to smoke.)

4. Shake the breast pieces in the seasoned flour, and add them to the oil. Cook all the chicken together for 5 minutes, turning once. Cover the skillet tightly, reduce the heat to medium-low, and cook for 15 minutes. Remove the cover and cook, turning occasionally, until the chicken is deeply browned and shows no sign of pink at the bone when prodded with the tip of a sharp knife.

5. Using kitchen tongs (not a meat fork, which will pierce the juicy chicken), transfer the chicken pieces to a paper bag or paper towels to drain. Serve the chicken hot, warm, or at room temperature.

YASSA
Spicy Marinated Chicken in Onion Sauce
(SENEGAL)

"The first time I had Yassa I was in Harlem," says Audie Odum-Stallato of this quintessentially Senegalese dish. "I was at a fast-food restaurant in an arcade that had only black proprietors. The people who owned the restaurant were from Africa. They gave me a heaping portion, not the skimpy portions you usually get at fast-food places. I asked African friends of mine about the dish, looked it up in recipe books, and eventually developed this variation. You can be very flexible with this dish. If you want to put something other than carrots and celery into the dish, go right ahead. I've done it with cassava leaves and foo foo (yam or cassava pounded into a paste) or yam dumplings, and eaten it with a bowl of rice or couscous." Other variations of Yassa use lamb, pork, or fish instead of chicken.

YASSA
Spicy Marinated Chicken in Onion Sauce

Cook's Notes: Yassa is normally served as the main attraction at a feast, in enormous proportions, heaped onto a mountain of rice. (The recipe is easy to multiply for your large-scale celebrations.) This is a version of manageable size, sure to become one of your favorite poultry dishes. As the marinated chicken simmers on the bed of onions, the onions cook down into a luscious sauce, a faultless topping for rice. To serve it African fashion, heap the chicken and onion sauce onto hot steaming rice or couscous and forgo forks and knives.

Serves 4

4 large onions, thinly sliced
½ cup fresh lime juice
1 teaspoon salt
½ teaspoon freshly ground black pepper
1 (3½-pound) chicken, cut into 8 pieces
3 tablespoons olive oil
1 medium carrot, chopped
1 medium celery rib, chopped
4 garlic cloves, minced
1 fresh hot chile pepper, such as jalapeño, seeded and minced
½ cup chicken broth, homemade or canned
Hot cooked rice or couscous

1. In a large bowl, combine the onions, lime juice, salt, and pepper. Add the chicken and toss to coat well. Cover, and refrigerate for at least 3 and up to 6 hours. Remove the chicken from the marinade and pat it dry with paper towels. Drain the marinade in a colander set

over a large bowl, and reserve both the liquid and the solids.

2. Heat the oil in a 5-quart Dutch oven. In batches, cook the chicken over medium-high heat, turning often, until browned on all sides, about 6 minutes per batch. Using tongs, transfer the chicken to a plate and set it aside.

3. Add the reserved marinated onions and the carrot, celery, garlic, and chile pepper to the Dutch oven. Cook over medium-high heat, stirring often, until the onions have softened, about 8 minutes. Stir in the chicken broth and the reserved marinade liquid; bring to a boil. Return the chicken to the Dutch oven, reduce the heat to medium-low, and simmer, covered, until the chicken shows no sign of pink at the bone when prodded with the tip of a sharp knife, 35 to 40 minutes.

4. Serve over hot rice or couscous.

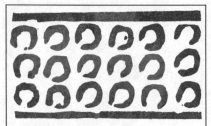

YOGURT-SAUCED CHICKEN CURRY (MOROCCO)

"This was one of the first African recipes I ever made," remembers Audie Odum-Stallato. "I have always been intrigued by North African foods. They often put fruit with their stews and couscous, and I always liked the contrast in flavors."

YOGURT-SAUCED CHICKEN CURRY

Cook's Notes: Curry is served throughout the African diaspora, from South African Bobotie, to the Country Captain (a curry-scented fricassee) of the Deep South, to the filling in a Jamaican meat patty. This time-honored recipe for chicken curry includes apples and bananas and is finished with a swirl of tangy yogurt, an excellent foil to the sweetness of the fruit. When cooking with yogurt, stir it in just at the last minute and cook just to heat through—boiling yogurt causes curdling.

Serves 4

4 chicken breast halves, bone in, skin on
2 tablespoons fresh lemon juice
½ cup all-purpose flour
½ teaspoon salt
¼ teaspoon freshly ground black pepper
2 tablespoons unsalted butter
2 tablespoons vegetable oil
1 medium onion, chopped
1 medium Granny Smith apple, cored and chopped
1 garlic clove, minced
1 tablespoon curry powder
¼ teaspoon ground cardamom
1 cup chicken broth, homemade or canned
⅓ cup dark raisins
1 ripe banana, peeled and sliced into ¼-inch-thick rounds
½ cup plain yogurt
½ cup chopped roasted cashews, rinsed to remove salt

1. In a medium bowl, sprinkle the chicken breast with the lemon juice; let stand at room temperature for 30 minutes. Combine the flour, salt, and pepper on a plate. Dredge the chicken breasts in the seasoned flour, shaking off any excess.

2. Heat the butter and oil in a large skillet over medium-high heat. Add the chicken breasts and cook, turning once, until browned on both sides, about 5 minutes. With tongs, transfer the chicken breasts to a plate and set aside.

3. Add the onion and apple to the skillet and cook, stirring often, until softened, about 3 minutes. Add the garlic, curry powder, and cardamom, reduce the heat to medium, and stir for 1 minute. Stir in the chicken broth and raisins. Return the chicken to the skillet and bring to a simmer.

3. Cook, covered, until the chicken breasts show no sign of pink at the bone when prodded with the tip of a sharp knife, about 20 minutes. Add the banana and yogurt, and stir constantly just until heated through, about 1 minute. Do not boil. Serve immediately, sprinkled with the cashews.

NEW TRADITION JOLOF RICE
(WEST AFRICA)

Jolof rice, basically an African pilaf, is so widespread throughout West Africa that it might qualify as a culinary lingua franca in that region. Variations, which depend as much on the individual cook as on the country of origin, include adding shrimp, beef, or vegetables, or any combination of them, to the rice. Dee Dee Dailey has created a chicken *jolof* rice because "so many African-Americans are beginning to eat less red meat, and are in general concerned with health and dietary habits."

NEW TRADITION JOLOF RICE

Cook's Notes: Dee Dee Dailey has updated this classic West African dish to reflect her approach to healthy, tasty eating. She prefers brown rice, uses chicken instead of pork, and stirs in carrots and green beans to add color.

Serves 8

1 cup dried black-eyed peas, rinsed and picked over
3 quarts water
⅓ cup vegetable oil
1 (3-pound) chicken, cut into 8 pieces
2 large onions, chopped
4 garlic cloves, minced
3 tablespoons grated fresh ginger
1 tablespoon curry powder
½ teaspoon cayenne pepper
1½ cups canned crushed tomatoes
2 tablespoons tomato paste
1 teaspoon salt
2½ cups long-grain brown rice
8 medium carrots, cut into ½-inch-thick rounds
½ pound green beans, trimmed, cut into 2-inch lengths

1. Combine the black-eyed peas with enough water to cover by 1 inch in a large saucepan. Bring to a boil over high heat, and cook for 1 minute. Then remove the pan from the heat, cover tightly, and let stand for 1 hour. (Or soak the peas overnight in a large bowl with enough cold water to cover by 1 inch.) Drain the peas well.
2. Place the black-eyed peas in a 5-quart Dutch oven and add the 3

quarts water. Bring to a boil over high heat, reduce the heat to medium, and cook for 15 minutes. Drain the peas in a colander set over a large bowl, reserving both the peas and 4 cups of the cooking liquid; discard the remaining cooking liquid.

3. Heat the oil in a 5-quart flameproof casserole. In batches, add the chicken and cook over medium-high heat, turning often, until browned on all sides, about 6 minutes per batch. Using tongs, transfer the chicken to a plate and set aside.

4. Add the onions, garlic, and ginger to the casserole and cook over medium-high heat, stirring often, until softened, about 4 minutes. Add the curry powder and cayenne, and stir for 1 minute. Stir in the reserved cooking liquid, crushed tomatoes, tomato paste, and salt; bring to a boil. Stir in the brown rice, reserved black-eyed peas, and carrots, and return to a boil. Reduce the heat to medium-low, cover, and cook 10 minutes. Return the chicken to the casserole, cover, and cook for 15 minutes.

5. Preheat the oven to 400°.

6. Stir the green beans into the rice mixture, cover, and transfer the casserole to the oven. Bake until the rice is tender and the chicken shows no sign of pink at the bone when prodded with the tip of a sharp knife, about 30 minutes. Remove the casserole from the oven and let stand 15 minutes before serving.

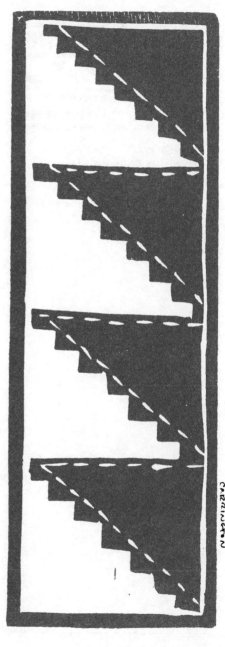

DORO WAT
Ethiopian Chicken Stew
(ETHIOPIA)

This spicy dish is a mainstay of
the Ethiopian dinner table.

DORO WAT
Ethiopian Chicken Stew

Cook's Notes: With one glance at the ingredients list, you can anticipate the exotic aromas that will fill your kitchen while making this incredible stew. To start, you prepare two of the staples of the Ethiopian kitchen: *niter kebbeh* (spiced butter) and *berbere* (an incendiary spice paste). This recipe will make more than you need here; store them in the refrigerator to use in other dishes. For example, replace plain butter with the spiced butter the next time you cook rice. Or in your next batch of chili, use the *berbere* instead of chili powder. They will both keep for about a month, but cover the top of the *berbere* with a film of oil to discourage a crust from forming.

Doro Wat can be served as a stew, still on the bone, with rice. But to serve it the Ethiopian way, remove and discard the bones and chop the meat coarsely. Return the meat to the sauce, and serve the stew spooned directly onto portions of crepe-like *Injera* bread (see page 241). Tearing off pieces of bread, use it to pick up chunks of stew, and pop both together into your mouth.

Makes 4 servings

NITER KEBBEH:
8 tablespoons (1 stick) unsalted butter
1 small onion, chopped
2 garlic cloves, minced
1 tablespoon grated fresh ginger
4 whole cloves

BERBERE:

1 teaspoon fenugreek seeds

1 teaspoon coriander seeds

1 teaspoon cumin seeds

1 teaspoon peppercorns

1 cup paprika, preferably sweet Hungarian

2 tablespoons salt

3 tablespoons crushed hot red pepper flakes

1 teaspoon ground ginger

½ teaspoon ground cardamom

¼ teaspoon grated nutmeg

¼ teaspoon ground cinnamon

½ cup dry red wine

¼ cup water

2 tablespoons minced onion

3 garlic cloves, minced

Olive oil

DORO WAT:

1 (3½-pound) chicken, cut into 8 pieces

3 tablespoons fresh lemon juice

1 teaspoon salt

¼ cup *niter kebbeh* (see above)

2 medium onions, chopped

2 garlic cloves, minced

½ cup *berbere* (see above)

½ cup dry red wine

½ cup water

2 tablespoons tomato paste

4 hard-boiled eggs

1. Make the *niter kebbeh*: In a small saucepan, bring the butter, onion, garlic, ginger, and cloves to a full boil over medium heat. Reduce the heat to very low and cook for 30 minutes. Strain the clear yellow top portion of butter into a small bowl through a sieve lined with squeezed-out rinsed cheesecloth, leaving the white solids in the bottom of the saucepan. Press hard on the solids, then discard. Cover and refrigerate the spiced butter until firm, at least 2 hours.

2. Make the *berbere*: Toast the fenugreek, coriander, cumin, and peppercorns together in a medium skillet over medium heat, stirring constantly until fragrant, about 1 minute. Transfer to a plate and cool completely. Crush the spices coarsely within a mortar and pestle or in a spice grinder.

3. In the same skillet over medium heat, combine the paprika, salt, red pepper flakes, ginger, cardamom, nutmeg, and cinnamon. Toast, stirring constantly until fragrant, about 1 minute. Immediately transfer to the container of a blender.

4. Add the crushed spices, wine, water, onion, and garlic to the blender. Process the mixture until completely smooth. Return it to the skillet and cook over low heat, stirring constantly, until the excess liquid has evaporated and the mixture forms a moist paste, about 3 minutes. Transfer the *berbere* to a small bowl, and cover the top with a thin film of olive oil. Cover tightly with plastic wrap and refrigerate until ready to use.

5. Make the *doro wat*: Combine the chicken, lemon juice, and salt in a large mixing bowl. Cover, and refrigerate for at least 2 hours or up to 8 hours.

6. Heat the *niter kebbeh* in a 5-quart Dutch oven. Pat the chicken dry with paper towels. In batches, add the chicken pieces and cook over medium-high heat, turning often, until browned on all sides, about 8 minutes per batch. Transfer the chicken to a plate and set aside.

7. Add the onions to the Dutch oven and cook, stirring often, until lightly browned, about 5 minutes. Add the garlic and cook for 1 minute. Stir in the *berbere*, wine, water, and tomato paste. Return the

chicken to the Dutch oven and bring to a simmer. Reduce the heat to low, cover, and simmer until the chicken shows no sign of pink when prodded with the tip of a sharp knife, about 45 minutes. During the last 10 minutes of cooking, add the hard-boiled eggs and stir to cover with the sauce. Serve immediately.

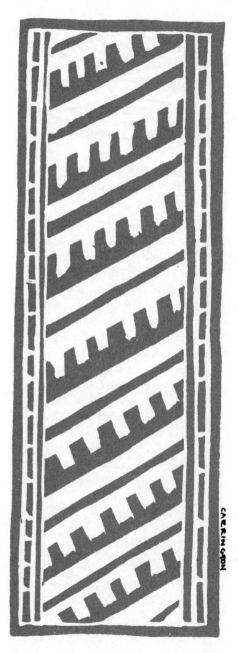

TAPO
Honduran Fish Stew with
Plantains and Yucca
(HONDURAS)

Frieda Jones got her Tapo recipe from a friend, Matilda Benedict. Benedict comes from the coastal city of La Ceiba, Honduras, where there is a large group of people of African descent.

"I've enjoyed Tapo many times," Jones says. "I have tasted this dish made by different people and each time it was a little different. I have tasted it without the coconut broth and with plain fish-flavored broth. I've had it with crabs in the shell and salted codfish. I have had it with large fish heads. But I like the variation I have given you the best."

TAPO
Honduran Fish Stew with Plantains and Yucca

Cook's Notes: Another variation on the fish stew theme, but this one is from Honduras and is less ornate than some others. The stew has a superior sauce, lightly thickened with the starches found in the plantains and *yucca*. Serve with Arroz con Coco (see page 195).

Serves 4 to 6

4 red snapper or red perch fillets (about 8 ounces each)
½ teaspoon salt
¼ teaspoon freshly ground black pepper
3 tablespoons vegetable oil
1 medium onion, chopped
2 garlic cloves, minced
1 fresh hot chile pepper, such as Scotch bonnet, seeded and minced
1 tablespoon chopped fresh cilantro
1 tablespoon chopped fresh *recato* or additional cilantro (see Note)
3 cups fresh unsweetened coconut milk, made from 1 coconut (see
    Note, page 196)
3 cups Fish Stock (see page 164), or 2 cups clam juice and 1 cup
    water
1½ pounds *yucca* (*cassava*), pared and cut into 1-inch chunks
2 green plantains, peeled, halved, and cut into 1-inch lengths (see
    page 230)
2 yellow-ripe plantains, peeled, halved, and cut into 1-inch lengths
1 pound medium shrimp, peeled and deveined
Chopped fresh cilantro, for garnish

1. Season the fish fillets with the salt and pepper. Heat the oil in a 5-quart Dutch oven. Add the fish fillets, and cook over medium-high heat, turning once, until lightly browned, about 3 minutes total. Using a slotted spatula, transfer the fillets to a plate, and set aside.

2. Add the onion, garlic, chile pepper, cilantro, and *recato* to the Dutch oven. Reduce the heat to medium and cook, stirring often, until softened, about 5 minutes. Stir in the coconut milk and fish stock, and bring to a simmer. Add the *yucca*, cover, and cook for 15 minutes.

3. Add the green plantains, cover, and cook for 10 minutes. Then add the yellow plantains, cover, and cook until the vegetables are tender, 10 to 15 minutes.

4. Stir in the shrimp. Arrange the fish fillets on top of the vegetables. Bring to a boil, cover, and cook for 3 minutes, until the fish is opaque throughout. Sprinkle with the cilantro, and serve directly from the Dutch oven.

NOTE: *Recato* is a cilantro with long spiky leaves, readily available in Latin American markets. It is slightly milder in flavor than the more familiar flat-leafed variety, but as far as a non-Latino cook is concerned, they are interchangeable.

CARRINGTON

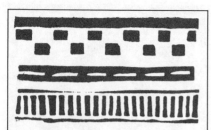

CYN'S ROASTED TURKEY
(UNITED STATES)

"Cyn, my younger sister, is an excellent cook," says Mavis Young. "She has a knack for seasoning so that everything comes out very tasty. Cyn never lets us throw away small pieces of vegetables, because that's what she uses to stuff the turkey." Cynthia Lewis adds, "I do a lot of experimental cooking, and I like to cook with herbs and spices. So one day it occurred to me to try putting foil over the turkey, instead of a lot of basting. And it turned out juicy, just how we like it."

CYN'S ROASTED TURKEY

Cook's Notes: A glorious, juicy turkey with a burnished skin is a holiday buffet centerpiece *par excellence*. Cyn stuffs her turkey with seasoning vegetables, and bakes the dressing on the side. (Stuffing the bird with a heavy bread dressing causes uneven roasting times.) Different sizes of birds have varying roasting times: hen turkeys (8 to 15 pounds) take approximately 22 minutes per pound; the larger toms (15 pounds and up) take only about 18 minutes per pound. If you insist on stuffing with dressing, add about 5 minutes per pound of turkey for either size bird. It goes without saying that Sausage and Cornbread Dressing (recipe follows) and Spiced Candied Sweet Potatoes (see page 223) are "musts" as side dishes. One last note: fresh turkeys are always better than frozen, so be sure to order one from your butcher.

Makes 15 to 20 servings

1 (18-pound) tom turkey, neck and giblets removed

VEGETABLE STUFFING:
1 medium onion, chopped
1 medium carrot, chopped
1 celery rib, chopped
2 garlic cloves, chopped
1 teaspoon salt
1 teaspoon dried thyme
1 teaspoon dried rosemary
1 teaspoon dried marjoram
½ teaspoon freshly ground black pepper

8 tablespoons (1 stick) unsalted butter, softened
1 teaspoon paprika

1 teaspoon salt
¼ freshly ground black pepper
2 cups dry white wine

TURKEY BROTH:
1 tablespoon vegetable oil
Reserved turkey neck and giblets
1 medium onion, chopped
1 medium carrot, chopped
1 medium celery rib, chopped
6 cups chicken broth, homemade or canned
2 parsley sprigs
¼ teaspoon dried thyme
⅛ teaspoon peppercorns
1 bay leaf

½ cup all-purpose flour

1. Preheat the oven to 325°. Rinse the turkey well, inside and out, under cold running water. Pat it dry with paper towels.
2. Make the vegetable stuffing: In a medium bowl, combine all the stuffing ingredients, and toss well to mix.
3. Stuff the neck cavity with some of the vegetable mixture; fold the neck skin over and skewer it to the back skin. Place the remaining vegetable mixture in the body cavity, and rub the cavity well with it. Skewer the body cavity closed. Using kitchen string, tie the wings close to the body, and tie the drumsticks together. Rub the turkey all over with the butter. Sprinkle with the paprika, salt, and pepper.
4. Place the turkey on a rack in a large flameproof roasting pan. Cover the *breast area only* with aluminum foil. Pour the wine in the bottom of the pan. Bake, uncovered, until a meat thermometer inserted in the meaty part of the thigh (but not touching a bone) reads 175°,

137

about 5 hours and 40 minutes. Three points to remember during roasting:

- Baste the turkey all over (including under the foil) every 20 minutes with the wine and drippings in the bottom of the pan.
- Remove the foil during the last hour to allow the skin to brown.
- Add ½ cup of water to the pan whenever the drippings threaten to burn.

Remove the turkey from the pan, and let it stand at room temperature for at least 20 minutes before carving.

5. While the turkey is roasting, prepare the broth: Heat the oil in a large saucepan. Add the giblets and neck (but not the liver, which you can reserve for another use), and cook over medium-high heat, turning often, until browned, about 10 minutes. Add the onion, carrot, and celery, and cook for 5 minutes. Pour in the chicken broth and bring to a simmer, skimming often. Add the parsley, thyme, peppercorns, and bay leaf, and simmer for 3 hours. Strain the broth, discarding the solids. (Reserve the giblets to chop and add to your gravy, if desired.) Add water to the broth if necessary to make 4 cups total.

6. While the turkey is standing, pour the drippings from the roasting pan into a glass bowl or measuring cup. Let it stand for 5 minutes; then skim off the clear yellow fat that has risen to the top. Place the roasting pan over two burners. Pour in the skimmed drippings, and bring to a boil over medium heat. Whisk in the flour and cook, whisking constantly, about 2 minutes. Then whisk in the strained turkey broth and bring to a simmer. Reduce the heat to low and simmer, whisking often, until the gravy has thickened, about 4 minutes. Season with additional salt and pepper, if desired.

7. Carve the turkey and serve the gravy alongside. (Do not serve the stuffing vegetables—they are only for seasoning.)

SAUSAGE AND CORNBREAD DRESSING

Cook's Notes: This dressing is supposed to be baked outside of the turkey, although it can be used as a stuffing if you wish.

If you have only one oven for both the turkey and the dressing, don't despair. Remove the turkey from the oven, tent it with foil, and let it stand at room temperature for up to 1 hour. (It won't get cold and will be much easier to slice, as the juices will retract back into the turkey while it stands.) Now the oven is empty, and you can use it to bake the dressing and whatever other side dishes you like. See how easy that was?

Serves 12 to 16

2 batches Grandma's Creamed Cornbread (see page 236)
2 tablespoons vegetable oil
1 pound spicy bulk pork sausage
2 medium onions, chopped
2 medium Granny Smith apples, unpeeled, cored and chopped
4 medium celery ribs, chopped
¾ cup chicken broth, homemade or canned
4 tablespoons (½ stick) unsalted butter, melted
¼ cup chopped fresh parsley
2 teaspoons crumbled dried sage
½ teaspoon dried thyme
½ teaspoon dried rosemary
½ teaspoon salt
¼ teaspoon freshly ground black pepper

SAUSAGE AND CORNBREAD DRESSING
(UNITED STATES)

A marvelous accompaniment for any turkey, but a special delight with Cyn's.

1. Crumble the cornbread into large pieces, spread them on baking sheets, and let stand overnight at room temperature to stale. Or bake in a preheated 300° oven until dried, about 30 minutes.

2. Preheat the oven to 375°.

3. Heat the oil in a large skillet. Add the sausage and cook over medium-high heat, stirring often to break it up, until it is firm and has lost its raw look, about 8 minutes. Using a slotted spoon, transfer the sausage to a plate and set it aside, leaving the fat in the skillet.

4. Add the onions, apples, and celery, to the skillet. Cook, stirring often, until softened, about 5 minutes. Transfer the mixture to a large bowl.

5. Add the reserved cornbread and sausage, and the chicken broth, melted butter, parsley, sage, thyme, rosemary, salt, and pepper. Toss well to mix. Transfer the dressing to a 9- by 13-inch baking dish, and cover with aluminum foil. The dressing can be prepared up to 8 hours ahead; keep refrigerated.

6. Bake until heated through, 35 to 45 minutes. If you like a crusty dressing, remove the foil during the last 20 minutes. If desired, baste the dressing occasionally with some of the turkey's pan juices.

NORTH AFRICAN CORNISH HENS

Cook's Notes: These Cornish hens are rubbed with a streamlined version of the Moroccan spice mixture *ras al hanout*, marinated, and roasted with lemons and oranges. (Don't serve the fruit with the chicken—they are there only for flavoring's sake.)

Serves 4

4 (1½-pound) Cornish game hens
2 lemons, halved
1 orange, quartered
5 garlic cloves, crushed through a garlic press
1½ teaspoons salt, preferably coarse (kosher)
2 tablespoons paprika, preferably hot Hungarian
2 teaspoons cumin seed
1 teaspoon ground ginger
¼ teaspoon cayenne pepper (optional)
¼ cup olive oil

1. Using a sharp knife or a cleaver, split each hen down its back and open it up flat, like a book. Arrange the hens, skin side up, on two large roasting pans. Squeeze the lemons and oranges over the hens, and then place the squeezed lemon and orange pieces underneath the hens.
2. On a work surface, sprinkle the garlic with the salt. Using a large knife, chop and smear them together to form a paste. Scrape the garlic paste into a small bowl, and stir in the paprika, cumin, ginger, and optional cayenne. Gradually stir in the oil to make a paste. Spread the paste on the hens' skin, and let them stand at room temperature, covered, for 1 hour before roasting.

NORTH AFRICAN CORNISH HENS (NORTH AFRICA)

Perhaps the most aromatic cuisine in the world comes from northern Africa, where every dish is a symphony of spices.

3. Position a rack in the top third of the oven, and preheat to 400°.
4. Roast the hens, basting often with the drippings, until the juices run yellow when the flesh is pierced with a fork, 50 to 60 minutes. Serve immediately, discarding the cooked fruits.

JAMBALAYA CLASSIQUE

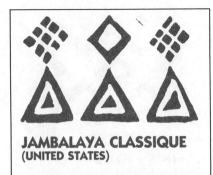

JAMBALAYA CLASSIQUE
(UNITED STATES)

Linguists claim that the word *jambalaya* comes from *jamon*, the Spanish word for ham, one of the main ingredients in the first jambalayas. But John F. Mariani in *The Dictionary of American Food and Drink* offers a more colorful possible origin: the owner of a New Orleans inn told his cook, whose name was Jean, to mix some things together— *balayez* in Creole dialect—when a late-night diner came to the inn. After devouring his food, the delighted guest dubbed his meal "Jean Balayez."

Cook's Notes: There's something about serving jambalaya at a party that almost guarantees the good times will roll. As it's difficult to decide just what *kind* of jambalaya to make (meat, shellfish, or poultry), we normally put a little bit of everything into the pot. (Not to complicate matters, but you can use 1 cup chopped smoked ham instead of the sausage. Or you could stir in ½ pound cooked crabmeat at the end to replace the shrimp.)

Serves 8

1 pound medium shrimp
2 chicken breast halves (about 1 pound total)
4 cups water
2 medium onions, chopped
2 medium celery ribs, chopped
3 garlic cloves, minced
2 teaspoons salt
1 tablespoon olive oil
½ pound andouille or kielbasa sausage, cut into ½-inch-thick rounds
1 medium green bell pepper, seeded and chopped
4 scallions, chopped
1 (15-ounce) can peeled plum tomatoes in juice
2 tablespoons Worcestershire sauce

¼ teaspoon dried thyme
¼ teaspoon cayenne pepper
2 cups long-grain rice
Chopped fresh parsley, for garnish

1. In a large saucepan of boiling salted water, cook the shrimp over high heat just until they turn pink, about 2 minutes. Cool, peel, and devein the shrimp, reserving the shrimp and their shells separately.

2. In a large saucepan, combine the chicken breasts, the reserved shrimp shells, the water, half the chopped onion, half the chopped celery, one third of the garlic, and 1 teaspoon salt. Bring to a simmer over medium-high heat. Reduce the heat to medium-low and cook, partially covered, until the chicken juices run clear yellow when pierced with a fork, 20 to 25 minutes. Remove the chicken breasts from the cooking liquid.

3. In a sieve set over a large bowl, drain and reserve the cooking liquid, discarding the solids. You should have about 4 cups of liquid; add water, if necessary. Remove and discard the chicken bones. Chop the breast meat coarsely and set it aside.

4. Heat the oil in a 5-quart Dutch oven. Add the sausage and cook over medium heat, stirring often, until lightly browned, about 5 minutes. Add the bell pepper, scallions, and the remaining onion, celery, and garlic. Cook, stirring, until the vegetables have softened, about 7 minutes. Then stir in the reserved cooking liquid, the remaining teaspoon of salt, the tomatoes with their juice, Worcestershire sauce, thyme, and cayenne. Bring to a simmer, breaking up the tomatoes with a spoon. Stir in the rice and return to the simmer. Cook over medium-low heat, tightly covered, until the rice has absorbed all the liquid, about 25 minutes.

5. Remove the Dutch oven from the heat, stir in the reserved shrimp and chicken, cover, and let stand for 5 minutes. Transfer the jambalaya to a warmed serving bowl, sprinkle with parsley, and serve immediately.

CARRINGTON

143

"In the '50s and '60s fish was very inexpensive," says Enoch Thompson, who immigrated to the United States from the Bahamas twenty years ago. "You just took a line and threw it in the water for the fish.

"We normally had this dish for big Sunday dinners and during the holidays," Thompson says, referring to his grandmother's recipe. "The grown-ups would drink wine. Lemonade was also popular. We'd squeeze it from fresh lemons, which grew like grass right outside.

"If you liked your meal spicy, you would add Bahamian goat pepper, which is very small and hot, on the side. You wouldn't want to put it in the stew because not everyone likes the same amount of hot pepper, especially the children. I had one uncle who liked it so spicy that he'd have to wipe the sweat off.

"Today I fix this dish for special occasions. For instance, my wife and I have created a naming ceremony for our children—we have five of them —and we have it after the ceremony."

PATIENCE DEVAUX'S BAHAMIAN GROUPER WITH TOMATO-THYME GRAVY

Cook's Notes: Here's another quick main course that can give you an instant taste of the Islands. Once the fish is marinated, the whole process goes rather quickly. In the Bahamas this would be served with Pigeon Peas and Rice (see page 178).

Serves 6

2 grouper filets (about 1½ pounds each), about 1 inch thick
3 tablespoons fresh lemon juice
½ teaspoon salt
¼ teaspoon freshly ground black pepper
½ cup vegetable oil
½ cup all-purpose flour
1 medium onion, chopped
1 garlic clove, minced
1 fresh hot chile pepper, such as serrano, seeded and minced
3 cups water
1 (6-ounce) can tomato paste
1 tablespoon fresh thyme leaves, or 1 teaspoon dried

1. Cut the grouper filets vertically into six pieces about 3 inches wide and 5 inches long. In a medium bowl, mix the lemon juice, salt, and pepper. Add the grouper and toss to mix. Let it stand at room temperature for 30 minutes. Then remove the grouper from the marinade and pat it dry with paper towels.
2. Heat the oil in a large skillet. Dredge the grouper in the flour, shaking off any excess. Cook the grouper over medium-high heat,

turning once, until lightly browned on both sides, about 5 minutes total. Transfer the grouper to paper towels to drain, and set aside.

3. Pour off all but 1 tablespoon of the oil in the skillet. Add the onion, garlic, and chile pepper, reduce the heat to medium, and cook, stirring often, until softened, about 5 minutes. Then stir in the water, tomato paste, and thyme, bring to a simmer, and cook for 5 minutes.

4. Return the fish to the skillet, reduce the heat to medium-low, and simmer until the sauce is slightly thickened, about 2 minutes. Serve immediately.

145

RED SNAPPER EN PAPILLOTE CARIBBEAN
(ANTIGUA AND BARBUDA)

"This is a recent recipe, say from the 1960s," says Gwendolyn Tonge. "Before that we never baked fish, but rather boiled or stewed them."

RED SNAPPER
EN PAPILLOTE CARIBBEAN

Cook's Notes: Cooking *en papillote* is always impressive, but presenting a huge whole red snapper surrounded by colorful vegetables will really make a splash.

Serves 4 to 6

1 (3-pound) whole red snapper, scaled and gutted
1 medium onion, chopped
1 medium celery rib with leaves, chopped
2 plum tomatoes, quartered
1 fresh hot chile pepper, such as serrano, seeded and chopped
2 garlic cloves, crushed through a garlic press
¼ cup chopped fresh parsley
2 tablespoons fresh lime juice
4 medium carrots, cut into 1-inch lengths
2 medium Russet potatoes, peeled and cut into 1-inch cubes
1 medium onion, thinly sliced
1 medium red bell pepper, seeded and cut into 1-inch-wide strips
¾ teaspoon salt
¼ teaspoon freshly ground black pepper
2 tablespoons unsalted butter, cut into pieces
1 lime, cut into wedges

1. Position a rack in the center of the oven, and preheat to 400°.
2. Rinse the fish, inside and out, under cold running water, and pat it dry with paper towels. Using a sharp thin knife, make two diagonal slashes about ½ inch deep on each side of the fish. Place the fish in a large roasting pan or a deep ovenproof baking dish.

3. Combine the chopped onion, celery, tomatoes, chile pepper, garlic, parsley, and lime juice in a food processor, and purée. Rub the purée all over the fish, especially into the slashes. Let the fish stand 30 minutes at room temperature.

4. Meanwhile, blanch the carrots and potatoes in a large pot of boiling salted water for 5 minutes. Drain well, rinse under cold water, and set aside.

5. Scrape the excess marinade off the fish. Rinse out the roasting pan, and line it with two overlapping sheets of aluminum foil, letting the excess foil hang over the edges. Return the fish to the roasting pan, and surround it with the blanched carrots and potatoes, and the sliced onion and bell pepper. Season the fish and the vegetables with the salt and pepper, and dot with the butter. Place a large piece of aluminum foil over the fish and vegetables, and crimp the foil on all sides to seal completely.

6. Bake until the fish is opaque in the center when prodded with the tip of a sharp knife, about 35 minutes. (Open up the foil and check to be sure.) Bring the *papillote* to the table, cut it open down the center, and serve directly from the foil wrapping. Pass the lime wedges.

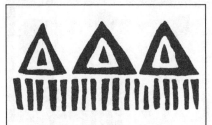

STUFFED CRAB BACKS WITH CHILE MAYONNAISE
(ANTIGUA AND BARBUDA)

"When I was a child, we'd go crabbing in mangrove swamps," recalls Gwendolyn Tonge. "We'd usually go on moonlit nights with hurricane lamps so that we could see, bring them home in sacks, and put them in barrels filled with water to keep them alive. We'd feed them greens and fungi (cornmeal mush) for a week or two to purge them of what they had been eating. Now we just go to the supermarket, which is not as much of an adventure."

STUFFED CRAB BACKS WITH CHILE MAYONNAISE

Cook's Notes: Be careful if you make the mayonnaise with Scotch bonnet chiles, as they are the hottest chile in the world! (All chiles are not created equal.) Start with a mere eighth of a whole minced chile, and add more to taste. You can be bolder with other varieties, such as serrano or jalapeño. Blue crabs run around ½ pound each, so you may need to serve more than one crab per serving.

Serves 2

1 cup mayonnaise
1 fresh hot chile pepper, such as Scotch bonnet, seeded and minced, slowly added to taste (see Cook's Notes)
4 large blue crabs
2 tablespoons Old Bay Seasoning
5 tablespoons unsalted butter
1 small onion, minced
1 small celery rib, minced
¼ cup minced red bell pepper
1 garlic clove, minced
2 cups fresh bread crumbs
2 tablespoons bottled clam juice or white wine
1 tablespoon chopped fresh chives, or 1 teaspoon dried
Grated zest of 1 lime
½ teaspoon salt
¼ teaspoon freshly ground black pepper

1. In a small bowl, mix the mayonnaise with chile pepper to taste until blended. Cover and refrigerate until ready to serve.

2. Position a rack in the top third of the oven, and preheat to 400°.

3. In a large pot of boiling water, cook the crabs with the Old Bay Seasoning just until they turn red, about 5 minutes. Drain the crabs and let them cool.

4. Break off the crabs' legs, crack the shells, and remove and reserve all usable meat. Remove the underside of the crab in one piece by digging your thumb into the triangle-shaped "apron" in the center of the crab, and lifting. Scrape out all of the orange fat, yellowish tomalley, and usable meat, avoiding the feathery gray gills, and reserve. Discard all of the shells except the large crab backs.

5. Heat 4 tablespoons of the butter in a medium skillet. Add the onion, celery, bell pepper, and garlic. Cook over medium heat, stirring often, until softened, about 5 minutes. Stir in the reserved crabmeat and the bread crumbs, clam juice, chives, lime zest, salt, and pepper. Cook until dried slightly, about 2 minutes. Stuff the dressing into the crab backs, pressing it with your hand to form a dome. Cut the remaining 1 tablespoon butter into small pieces, and dot the tops of the crabs with it.

6. Bake until the stuffing is lightly browned, about 15 minutes. Serve hot on individual plates, with a dollop of chile mayonnaise spooned on the side.

PIRI PIRI SHRIMP WITH LEMON BUTTER
(ANGOLA)

"I always try to include a seafood dish in my Kwanzaa menu because of my personal and cultural connection with fish and fishing," explains Sheila Johnson. "There is a long and little-known history of African-Americans on Long Island, which is where I grew up. There used to be black fishermen who would go out on boats. My grandmother and grandfather fished, although it was for recreation, not as a profession. They would go out every weekend. And my mother, who is Catholic, would serve fish on Fridays.

"I selected this dish because there is a certain area of Angola that is famous throughout the world for the richness and taste of its prawns. Also, my family likes to barbecue year-round. In the winter we barbecue on the porch on our Weber grill.

"I've never traveled to Africa; I got this recipe from a friend who lived in Angola for a while. I serve this dish with plain green salad and beer."

PIRI PIRI SHRIMP WITH LEMON BUTTER

Cook's Notes: In just a few minutes, you can be serving one of the classics of African cooking. *Piri piri* is a chameleon-like spice mixture, changing from country to country, with the recipe (and name) slightly altered in each location. It can be a wet marinade, a fiery dipping sauce or condiment, or, as in this case, a dry rub. And it may be called *piri-piri, pilli-pilli*, or *peri-peri*. This shrimp dish is as versatile as its namesake, being equally welcome as an entrée and as an appetizer (in which case it would serve about 8 people).

Serves 3 to 4

½ teaspoon salt, preferably coarse (kosher)
½ teaspoon ground cardamom
½ teaspoon ground ginger
½ teaspoon dried basil
½ teaspoon garlic powder
½ teaspoon onion powder
¼ teaspoon cayenne pepper, or to taste
1 pound large shrimp, peeled and deveined
8 tablespoons (1 stick) unsalted butter
3 tablespoons fresh lemon juice

1. In a medium bowl, combine the salt, cardamom, ginger, basil, garlic and onion powders, and cayenne. Add the shrimp and toss until well coated. Let the shrimp stand at room temperature for 15 to 30 minutes.
2. Meanwhile, position a lightly oiled broiler rack 6 inches from the heat, and preheat the broiler.

3. Combine the butter and lemon juice in a small saucepan, and heat until melted. Keep warm.

4. Broil the shrimp, basting them occasionally with some of the lemon butter and turning them once, just until they turn pink, about 4 minutes total. Serve immediately, with the remaining lemon butter poured into a small bowl and offered as a dip.

151

TIEBOU DIENNE
Senegalese Herb-Stuffed Fish Steaks with Seasoned Rice
(SENEGAL)

Tiebou Dienne (pronounced "che-boo jenn") is the national dish of Senegal. It's common to serve this dish with pickles on the side. Empress Akweke, who contributed this recipe, was introduced to Tiebou Dienne by Senegalese friends.

TIEBOU DIENNE
Senegalese Herb-Stuffed Fish Steaks with Seasoned Rice

Cook's Notes: Thick fresh fish steaks are given a pocket and stuffed with an aromatic parsley-chile "pesto." Simmered with a host of vegetables, the fish is briefly set aside while rice is cooked in the same liquid. The result is a winning meal-in-a-pot. Have your fishmonger create 1-inch-thick fillets from roundfish such as grouper, monkfish, swordfish, or tuna. Or alter the recipe by using 3 pounds of 1-inch-thick cross-cut fish steaks, such as cod or mako shark, or even bluefish.

Serves 6

6 fish fillets (about 8 ounces each; see Cook's Notes), cut 1 inch thick
1 cup coarsely chopped fresh parsley
1 large onion, chopped
4 garlic cloves, crushed through a garlic press
2 fresh hot chile peppers, such as jalapeño, seeded and minced
4 tablespoons vegetable oil
1¼ teaspoons salt
6 cups Fish Stock (see page 164), or 4 cups water and 2 cups bottled clam juice
1 (6-ounce) can tomato paste
½ teaspoon freshly ground black pepper
1 small head cauliflower (about 1½ pounds), cut into florets
1 small head cabbage (about 1 pound), cut into wedges and cored
1 pound *yucca (cassava)*, pared and cut into 1-inch chunks, or 2 medium potatoes, peeled
4 medium carrots, cut into 1-inch lengths

1 medium turnip, peeled and cut into 1-inch pieces

1 medium eggplant, cut into 1-inch pieces

¼ pound okra, stems and tips trimmed, cut into ½-inch-thick
   rounds

2 cups long-grain rice

Chopped fresh parsley, for garnish

Lime wedges, for garnish

1. Using a small sharp knife, cut deep horizontal pockets into one side of each fish fillet, being sure not to cut through to the other side.

2. In a blender or mini food processor, purée the parsley, ¼ cup of the onion, half of the garlic, half of the chile pepper, 1 tablespoon of the oil, and ¼ teaspoon of the salt. Divide the parsley purée among the fish fillets, stuffing it into the pockets. Pat the fillets dry with paper towels.

3. Preheat the oven to 200°.

4. In a 6- to 8-quart Dutch oven, heat the remaining 3 tablespoons oil. Add the fish fillets and cook over medium-high heat, turning once, until partially cooked and lightly browned, about 3 minutes total. Using a spatula, transfer the fish to a plate, and set aside.

5. Add the remaining onion to the Dutch oven, reduce the heat to medium, and cook, stirring often, until lightly browned, about 5 minutes. Then add the remaining garlic and chile pepper, and stir for 1 minute. Stir in the fish stock, tomato paste, remaining 1 teaspoon salt, and pepper; bring to a boil. Add the cauliflower, cabbage, *yucca*, carrots, and turnip. Reduce the heat to medium-low and simmer, covered, for 15 minutes. Add the eggplant and okra, cover, and cook 10 minutes.

6. Return the fish to the Dutch oven, cover, and cook until it is opaque throughout and the vegetables are tender, about 10 minutes. Using a slotted spoon, transfer the fish, vegetables, and about ½ cup of the cooking liquid to a large baking dish. Cover the dish tightly

KOTOKYIM
Ghanese Crab Gratin
(GHANA)

"This is another seafood dish that is meant to reflect my Long Island background," says Sheila Johnson. "It also reflects my desire to incorporate dishes that reflect the different places where Africans and those of African heritage live."

Johnson adapted this recipe from the Kotokyim recipe in *A West African Cookbook* by Ellen Gibson Wilson.

with aluminum foil and keep it warm in the oven while cooking the rice.

7. Stir the rice into the Dutch oven and bring to a simmer. Cook, covered, until the liquid is absorbed and the rice is tender, about 20 minutes.

8. Spread the rice in a thick layer on a large warmed platter, and arrange the fish on top. Spoon the vegetables around the fish, and drizzle with any collected juices in the baking dish. Sprinkle with the parsley, and serve with the lime wedges.

KOTOKYIM
Ghanese Crab Gratin

Cook's Notes: This is an exquisite dish to have on file when you are short on time (but long on cash). Made in a snap but bursting with flavor, it can be prepared well ahead and only needs a quick visit to the oven before serving.

Serves 4

2 tablespoons olive oil
1 medium onion, chopped
4 scallions, chopped
1 fresh hot chile pepper, such as serrano, seeded and minced
1 garlic clove, minced
3 plum tomatoes (about ½ pound), peeled, seeded, and chopped or 1 (15-ounce) can peeled plum tomatoes in juice, drained and chopped
1 cup Fish Stock (see page 164) or tomato juice
¼ teaspoon salt

⅛ teaspoon freshly ground black pepper

1½ pounds fresh crabmeat, picked over to remove cartilage

Salt and freshly ground black pepper, to taste

1 cup fresh bread crumbs

2 tablespoons unsalted butter, cut into pieces

Chopped fresh parsley, for garnish

1. Heat the oil in a large skillet. Add the onion, scallions, chile pepper, and garlic, and cook over medium heat, stirring often, until softened, about 5 minutes. Add the tomatoes and cook, stirring often, until softened, about 5 minutes.

2. Stir in the fish stock, salt, and pepper. Bring to a simmer and cook until the liquid is reduced by half, about 6 minutes. Stir in the crabmeat and cook just until heated through, about 2 minutes. Season the crab with salt and pepper to taste. The recipe can be prepared up to this point 2 hours ahead; cover and set aside at room temperature.

3. Preheat the oven to 400°. Lightly butter shallow 1½-quart casserole.

4. Spread the crab in the prepared baking dish, sprinkle it with the bread crumbs, and dot with the butter. Bake until the top of the casserole is golden brown, 20 to 25 minutes. Sprinkle with the parsley, and serve immediately.

SHRIMP CREOLE FETTUCINE
(UNITED STATES)

Although there are no official Kwanzaa dishes, Karen Grigsby Bates, a journalist who lives in Los Angeles, thinks her Shrimp Creole is appropriate because it tastes as if it could have come from Africa. "Perhaps it did," says Bates, who serves her Creole over rice. "I remember making a big pot of it in college and inviting a young man from the Cameroons, who was visiting one of my roommates, to stay and have dinner with us. He ate with great seriousness, and I wondered whether he was just being heroically polite. When he was done, he looked up and spoke: 'It's very good,' he said solemnly. 'It tastes like home.' It's one of the nicest things anyone has ever said to me, before or since."

SHRIMP CREOLE FETTUCINE

Cook's Notes: Shrimp Creole is normally served on white rice. It is equally mouth watering on pasta, creating a contemporary, quick, and easy entrée.

Makes 4 servings

2 tablespoons olive oil
1 medium onion, chopped
1 medium green bell pepper, seeded and chopped
3 medium celery ribs, chopped
3 garlic cloves, minced
1 fresh hot chile pepper, such as jalapeño, seeded and minced
1 (35-ounce) can peeled plum tomatoes in juice
2 tablespoons tomato paste
½ cup dry white wine
½ teaspoon dried basil
½ teaspoon dried oregano
¼ teaspoon dried thyme
⅛ teaspoon crushed hot red pepper flakes
2 pounds medium shrimp, peeled and deveined
1 pound fettucine, preferably fresh

1. Heat the oil in a large skillet. Add the onion, bell pepper, celery, garlic, and chile pepper. Cook over medium heat, stirring often, until softened, about 5 minutes.
2. Add the tomatoes with their juice, tomato paste, wine, basil, oregano, thyme, and red pepper flakes. Bring to a simmer, breaking up the tomatoes with a spoon. Reduce the heat to low and simmer, stirring often, until slightly thickened, about 20 minutes.

3. Stir in the shrimp and cook just until they turn pink, about 3 minutes.

4. Meanwhile, cook the fettucine in a large pot of boiling salted water until just tender, about 3 minutes. (If using dried fettucine, cook about 8 minutes.) Drain well, and transfer to a warmed deep serving bowl. Add the shrimp creole, toss well, and serve immediately.

CAMARAO À BAHIANA, FAROFA, MOLHO À BAHIANA
Bahian Shrimp Ragout with Toasted Manioc and Hot Peppers Sauce
(BRAZIL)

"Brazilian food is spicy, but not hot like Mexican or Indian food," says Isabella Bravim, a freelance gourmet cook who lives in Miami and is a native of Brazil.

The trio of recipes Bravim has contributed come from Bahia, the most African of Brazil's states. "Bahia is the place where the majority of the population of African descent comes from," says Bravim, who comes from the state of Minas Gerais. "Everything they do is influenced by African culture. For instance, Capoeira, a marshal art that looks like a dance, was originated by Africans who were brought to Brazil as slaves. The religion, although on the surface it seems Christian, is in fact a carryover of African religions. And the music! The root of Samba, for instance, is in Bahia. As for the food of Bahia, the general way of cooking it, the ingredients such as palm oil, and many of the spices are African or derived from Africa."

CAMARAO À BAHIANA, FAROFA, MOLHO À BAHIANA
Bahian Shrimp Ragout with Toasted Manioc and Hot Peppers Sauce

Cook's Notes: This trio of delightful dishes must be served in tandem to fully appreciate their Brazilian gusto. The fragrant shrimp ragout (*camarao*) could be served over rice, but do search out the manioc meal to make *farofa*. The dry and sandy *farofa* will seem odd at first, but reserve judgment until you moisten it with the ragout's fabulous juices. The palm oil used in these dishes adds a rich orange color and a subtle taste, but it's not vital.

Makes 6 servings

MOLHO DE BAHIA:
1 large onion, chopped
4 garlic cloves, minced
3 fresh hot red chile peppers, such as serrano, seeded and minced
1 teaspoon salt
½ teaspoon freshly ground black pepper
2 tablespoons palm oil (see Note) plus 1 tablespoon olive oil, or 3 tablespoons olive oil
1 large green bell pepper, seeded and chopped
4 plum tomatoes, (about ¾ pound), peeled, seeded, and chopped, or ¾ cup chopped drained canned peeled plum tomatoes in juice
2 tablespoons fresh lime juice
2 tablespoons water

CAMARAO À BAHIANA:

2 tablespoons fresh lemon juice

1½ teaspoons salt

¾ teaspoons freshly ground black pepper

3 pounds medium shrimp, peeled and deveined

3 tablespoons olive oil

2 medium onions, chopped

12 plum tomatoes (about 2¼ pounds), peeled, seeded, and
       chopped, or 3 (14-ounce) cans peeled plum tomatoes in
       juice, drained and chopped

3 garlic cloves, minced

3 small whole dried chile peppers, crumbled

3 bay leaves

1½ cups coconut milk (see page 197)

3 tablespoons palm oil (optional)

2 tablespoons chopped fresh parsley, for garnish

2 tablespoons unsweetened grated coconut (reserved from coconut
       milk), for garnish

FAROFA:

3 tablespoons olive oil

2 medium onions, finely chopped

4 garlic cloves, minced

2 whole dried chile peppers, crumbled

¼ cup palm oil, or 4 tablespoons (½ stick) unsalted butter, softened

3 cups manioc flour (see Note)

1 teaspoon salt

¼ teaspoon freshly ground black pepper

2 tablespoons chopped fresh parsley

NOTE: Palm oil and manioc flour (*farinha de mandioca*) are available in
Latin American and Brazilian markets.

1. Make the *Molho à Bahiana:* Combine the onion, garlic, chile peppers, salt, and pepper in a blender, and purée.

2. In a medium skillet, heat the palm oil and olive oil (or the 3 tablespoons olive oil). Add the vegetable purée and cook over medium heat, stirring constantly, until the excess moisture has evaporated and the mixture is quite dry, about 7 minutes. Stir in the bell pepper and tomatoes, and cook, stirring often, until the tomatoes have softened and formed a sauce, about 10 minutes. Stir in the lime juice and water. Let the sauce cool completely, and set aside.

3. Make the *Camarao à Bahiana:* In a large bowl, combine the lemon juice, ½ teaspoon of the salt, and ¼ teaspoon of the pepper. Add the shrimp, toss to combine, and cover; refrigerate for 30 minutes. (Do not marinate longer than 1 hour.)

4. Heat the oil in a large skillet. Add the onions and cook over medium-high heat, stirring often, until lightly browned, about 5 minutes. Add the tomatoes, garlic, dried peppers, bay leaves, and remaining 1 teaspoon salt and ½ teaspoon pepper. Bring to a simmer; then reduce the heat to medium-low and cook, stirring often, until the tomatoes have softened, about 7 minutes. Stir in the shrimp and their marinade, and cook just until the shrimp turn pink, about 2 minutes.

5. Stir in the coconut milk and optional palm oil, and bring just to a simmer. Cover tightly to keep warm while making the *farofa.*

6. Make the *Farofa:* Heat the olive oil in a medium skillet. Add the onions, garlic, and dried peppers. Cook over medium-high heat, stirring often, until softened, about 5 minutes.

7. Stir in the palm oil or butter. Add the manioc flour, salt, and pepper, and stir until heated through, about 2 minutes. Transfer to a serving bowl and sprinkle with the parsley.

8. To serve, spoon the *farofa* into individual soup bowls. Sprinkle the ragout with the parsley and coconut, and ladle the ragout over the *farofa.* Pass the hot peppers sauce separately.

FRIED CATFISH WITH ZIPPY CORNMEAL CRUST AND RÉMOULADE SAUCE

Cook's Notes: To simulate a Deep South fish fry in your own dining room, serve these gratifying golden brown fillets with Margaretta's Hush Puppies (page 234), Alice's Potato Salad (page 71), and Real Lemonade (page 264.)

Serves 4

RÉMOULADE SAUCE:

1 cup mayonnaise

Grated zest of 1 lemon

2 tablespoons chopped fresh parsley

2 tablespoons chopped dill pickle

1 tablespoon prepared mustard, preferably spicy Creole

1 tablespoon drained capers (optional)

1 teaspoon Worcestershire sauce

¼ teaspoon hot pepper sauce

CATFISH:

1 cup all-purpose flour

4 large eggs

1 cup yellow cornmeal

3 tablespoons Old Bay Seasoning

½ teaspoon salt

½ teaspoon garlic powder

½ cup vegetable oil

2 pounds catfish filets

Lemon wedges, for garnish

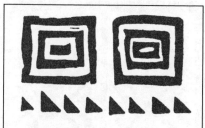

FRIED CATFISH WITH ZIPPY CORNMEAL CRUST AND RÉMOULADE SAUCE
(UNITED STATES)

This popular southern dish will get mouths watering from coast to coast.

1. Make the rémoulade sauce: In a small bowl, stir together all the sauce ingredients until well mixed. Cover, and refrigerate for at least 1 hour or overnight.

2. Prepare the catfish: Get everything ready before starting your fish fry: Place the flour on a plate. Beat the eggs well in a medium bowl. In a large bowl, whisk the cornmeal, Old Bay Seasoning, salt, and garlic powder to combine. Heat the oil in a large skillet over medium heat until very hot but not smoking. Preheat the oven to 200°.

3. The procedure will go smoothest if you reserve one hand for dredging the catfish in the flour and dipping it in the eggs, and the other for coating in the seasoned cornmeal. In batches, dredge the catfish in flour, shaking off any excess. Dip the catfish in the eggs, coating on both sides. Then dredge the dipped catfish in the seasoned cornmeal, patting the coating so it will adhere. Slip the coated catfish into the oil, and cook over medium heat, turning once, until golden brown on both sides, about 5 minutes total. Using a slotted spatula, transfer the browned catfish to a paper towel–lined baking sheet to drain, and keep warm in the oven while continuing with the remaining catfish.

4. Serve the catfish as soon as possible, with the rémoulade sauce on the side. Garnish with the lemon wedges.

MOQUECA, PIRAO, MOLHO DE PIMENTA
Brazilian Fish Stew with Manioc Polenta and Preserved Peppers Sauce

Cook's Notes: Another extraordinary Brazilian fish stew, this one uses a whole netful of fish. The manioc flour is cooked into a savory mush with the fish cooking liquid. You have some leeway in choosing what kind of fish you'd like to cook up (the Brazilians prefer the cheaper, oilier varieties like bluefish and mackerel), but pick varieties of approximately equal size so they'll all be done at the same time. Any good fishmonger will sell you the fish parts for the stock, but order ahead to be sure. *Moqueca* is definitely party fare, as it cannot be made for fewer than eight hungry people.

MOQUECA, PIRAO, MOLHO DE PIMENTA
Brazilian Fish Stew with Manioc Polenta and Preserved Peppers Sauce
(BRAZIL)

This quintessentially Bahian meal was contributed by Yara Roberts.

FISH STOCK:

5 pounds fish heads, scraps, or bones (non-oily varieties such as cod, snapper, or scrod), in any combination

Shrimp shells from 1½ pounds medium shrimp (see *Moqueca*, below)

1 medium onion, quartered

1 garlic clove, crushed through a garlic press

4 scallions, chopped

1 bay leaf

3 parsley sprigs

1½ quarts water

MOLHO DE PIMENTA:

2 tablespoons fresh lime juice

1 tablespoon chopped hot red peppers preserved in vinegar (see Note)

3 tablespoons minced onion

2 tablespoons olive oil

MOQUECA:

3 tablespoons fresh lemon juice

1 tablespoon fresh lime juice

6 garlic cloves, minced

½ teaspoon salt

¼ teaspoon freshly ground black pepper

3 pounds fish steaks, (such as cod, kingfish, bluefish, or mackerel), cut 1 inch thick

1½ pounds medium shrimp, shelled and deveined, shells reserved for stock (see above)

1 pound large sea scallops

¼ cup olive oil

1 large onion, chopped

1 medium green bell pepper, seeded and chopped

4 scallions, chopped

2 cups Fish Stock (see above)

6 plum tomatoes (about 1 pound), peeled, seeded, and
 chopped, or 1 (14-ounce) can peeled plum tomatoes in
 juice, drained and chopped

½ cup chopped fresh cilantro

1 cup coconut milk (see page 197)

2 tablespoons palm oil (optional; see Note)

¼ teaspoon cayenne pepper

12 mussels, well scrubbed and debearded

½ pound fresh crabmeat, picked over to remove cartilage

PIRAO:

2½ cups Fish Stock (see above)

1 tablespoon tomato paste

½ teaspoon salt

⅛ teaspoon freshly ground black pepper

1½ cups manioc flour (see Note)

NOTE: Preserved peppers in vinegar, palm oil, and manioc flour are
available at Latin American and Brazilian markets.

1. Make the fish stock: In a 5-quart Dutch oven or soup kettle,
combine the fish parts, shrimp shells, onion, garlic, scallions, bay leaf,
and parsley. Add the water and bring to a boil over high heat, skimming off any foam that rises to the top. Reduce the heat to low, and
simmer until reduced to about 5 cups, about 2 hours. Strain the stock
and discard the solids. Set aside.

2. Make the *molho de pimenta:* In a small bowl, combine the lime juice,
peppers, and onion. Let stand for at least 1 hour, then mash to a paste.
Whisk in the olive oil, and set aside.

3. Make the *moqueca:* In a large mixing bowl, combine the lemon and
lime juices, two thirds of the garlic (4 cloves), salt, and pepper. Add

the fish steaks, shrimp, and scallops, toss to combine, and cover. Refrigerate for at least 1 hour, but not more than 2 hours.

4. Meanwhile, heat the olive oil in a large stockpot. Add the onion, bell pepper, scallions, and the remaining 2 cloves of garlic. Cook over medium heat, stirring often, until well softened, about 10 minutes. Stir in the 2 cups fish stock, tomatoes, and cilantro, and bring to a boil. Reduce the heat to low, cover, and simmer for 1 hour.

5. Purée the vegetable–fish stock mixture in a food processor or blender. Return the sauce to the stockpot and stir in the coconut milk, optional palm oil, and cayenne. Bring to a simmer over medium heat.

6. Place the fish steaks, shrimp, and scallops in the sauce, along with their marinade, and arrange the mussels on top; bring to a simmer. Cover, and simmer until the mussels have opened and the fish is cooked through, 10 to 15 minutes. Stir in the crabmeat, remove from the heat, and cover tightly to keep warm while making the *pirao*.

7. Make the *pirao:* Bring the 2½ cups fish stock, tomato paste, salt, and pepper to a boil in a medium saucepan over medium-high heat, stirring to blend in the tomato paste. Gradually sprinkle in the manioc flour, stirring constantly until the mixture has the consistency of soft ice cream, about 2 minutes. Immediately transfer the *pirao* to a warmed serving dish.

8. To serve, spoon the *pirao* into deep soup bowls and ladle the stew over it. Pass the preserved peppers sauce on the side.

Nguzo Saba

Umoja (Unity)
Kujichagulia (Self-determination)
Ujima (Collective Work and Responsibility)
Ujamaa (Cooperative Economics)
Nia (Purpose)
Kuumba (Creativity)
Imani (Faith)

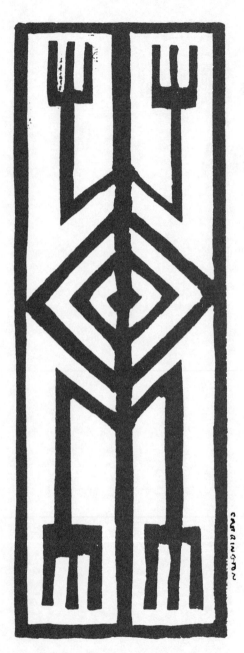

ately, amidst discussions with friends about black leadership—the lack or need of it—I have found myself wondering if it is even necessary for African-Americans to have a figure to rally around. Have we reached a point where we have a consensus on what black Americans need to accomplish through their individual efforts? Might a central figure actually be detrimental at this point? Well, the jury's still out on that question. However, while reading about the Haitian revolution—especially the excellent book *The Black Jacobins* by C.L.R. James—I began to see that the story of Haiti's independence is not just an instance of a few extraordinary individuals galvanizing a nation. On some level—as in the civil rights movement at critical points—it was accomplished by everybody simply doing his or her own part. When I summarize the story of Haitian independence to my family, I like to tell it as a story of Collective Work and Responsibility (Ujima), Creativity (Kuumba), and Unity (Umoja)—on a national scale.

Haiti (then called Saint Dominique) was the second colony in the Americas to become independent (the first was the United States), and the person generally considered the hero of that revolution is Toussaint L'Ouverture. Ironically, however, the revolution began and ended without Toussaint. It began in 1791 after a sudden slave revolt led by Boukman, an African who worked on one of the plantations, and ended in 1804, seven months after Toussaint L'Ouverture's death in a French prison.

Sometimes there is a collective will that is stronger than the directives of any individual leader. Upon Toussaint's death the revolution did not explode, nor did it expire. It percolated. Tribal leaders in the island's hinterlands successfully resisted the French. These chiefs, through their guerrilla tactics, kept the French army constantly off balance. In one such instance, a group of farmers pretended to be a large regiment of soldiers. They marched all night within hearing distance of a detachment of French soldiers, keeping them awake and their nerves on edge. The French captain later wrote to Napoleon that those kind of tricks played havoc with his troops' morale.

Who were the mountain people who toyed with the great French army? Only a few names have survived. But even those names are unimportant. What is important is that a collection of individuals—each like a single drop of rain falling on a dry field—combined with others to great effect, in this case moistening the earth from which sprang an independent Haiti.

And what were the Haitian generals, the people who had been part of Toussaint's inner circle, doing? At first, to a man, they refused to join in the growing uprising. In fact, some of these generals fought with the French in trying to quash the revolt. But slowly, very slowly—indeed only after the French made it clear that they intended to reinstitute slavery—did the members of Toussaint's circle begin to come around and join in the fight for independence.

The final battle was filled with ferocious fighting, the melodies of Haitian war songs as they advanced upon the French fortifications, and even grim humor, as the French cried, "Bravo! Bravo!" and held their fire while one of the bravest of the Haitian captains continued his advance on foot after his horse was shot out from under him. (Both sides held their fire while a French emissary rode out to congratulate the man on his bravery. Then the fighting began again.) By the end of the day, Haiti had won its freedom.

What does all this have to do with Kwanzaa? Two things: (1) The present state of Haiti shows that one never finishes applying the principles of Kwanzaa. (2) The story of the struggle for Haitian independence is inspiring. And although we are engaged in a different war today, one whose weapons are education and an economic base, in its way the battle is just as fierce.

Before shooting, one must aim.
Proverb, Nigeria

The proverb above speaks to the principle of Purpose (Nia), which is what Jake Simmons, Jr., was all about. Simmons was a multi-millionaire oilman from Oklahoma and an international tycoon. He, like so many successful black businessmen and -women, used his money and his political clout to advance the cause of equality and justice for the common good of African-Americans. Some other recent examples of Cooperative Economics (Ujamaa) at work include the writer Nelson George, who took money he made from his best-selling biography of Michael Jackson and invested in Spike Lee's *She's Gotta Have It*. Spike Lee grabbed the baton after he made it big. Using his clout in the film world, Lee makes sure that blacks are fairly represented on his film crews.

The following narrative is adapted from *Staking a Claim: Jake Simmons, Jr., and the Making of an African-American Oil Dynasty* by Jonathan Greenberg.

President Johnson delivered for the African-Americans by successfully pushing through both the Civil Rights Act of 1964 and the Voting

Rights Act of 1965. A "War on Poverty" had begun. Public expenditures would check the economic crisis that created ghettos. In their place would come "the Great Society." Money would placate the destructive rage that was beginning to explode in open conflict, such as the August 1965 Watts riot.

Jake Simmons had his own solution. The capitalist system he so enthusiastically embraced allowed all people a piece of the pie if they had a way to pay for it. Without jobs, all a people could ever hope for was the crumbs their government chose to give them. School desegregation, residential integration, even legislative equality, were less important to him than securing jobs for blacks. Simmons railed against every aspect of the system that limited black access to jobs. In the summer of 1967 he was appointed to a special Employment Opportunity Committee created by Muskogee's mayor. At the first meeting Simmons appealed to the city's employers to create jobs for blacks and train them. Mayor Jim Egan responded that it was "the general consensus of the committee that sufficiently trained Negroes were not available to fill Muskogee job vacancies when needed."

Simmons did his best to challenge this claim. After losing his regular secretary during the early 1960s he used the position in his office as a training ground for black women. He would hire an inexperienced person, then train her to answer phones and handle office machinery. Once she had acquired basic skills, he would lobby people he knew at businesses in town to interview her for a job vacancy. If he was doing business with that office, he used that leverage as a pressure point, saying things like, "I've got deposits in your bank and you don't have any blacks working for you." His recommendation went a long way toward establishing a potential employee's credentials.

Simmons also believed that the qualifications issue was often a cover for employment discrimination. When he came across an unintegrated workplace in Muskogee, he pulled whatever strings he could find to convince the business to hire black employees. If the estab-

lishment repeatedly turned down black applicants, he would unleash his secret weapon: Almetta Carter, a strong, well-trained, ebony-skinned woman, attractive and articulate. She had no trouble letting people know when they were stepping on her toes. Carter, a Muskogee native, was in her early twenties when she went to work for Simmons in 1966. She had recently graduated from business college and was trained to type, take shorthand, do bookkeeping, and manage office machinery. Her first attempt to obtain employment through a local job agency resulted in an offer to be a chicken plucker. Jake Simmons tested Carter's skills; interviewed her, then hired her as a full-time secretary. She impressed him with her powerful backbone: a divorced single mother who refused to allow anyone to push her around.

Simmons decided that she was just the person to test the hiring policies of unintegrated businesses, like manufacturing companies or a large department store that had never hired a black salesperson. He would wait until they advertised for workers, then send his secretary to apply for a job. Carter would arrive, qualifications in hand. Out would come the written tests for prospective employees. Carter passed with flying colors. Next would come the personal interview—although in some respects it was really she who did the interviewing. "He sent me to have interviews with employers to see exactly how they were treating people," she recalls, "whether they were accepting people on their level of education and qualifications as opposed to their color. Then I would report back to him the same day."

In every instance but one, Carter, who probably was known to have Simmons's backing, was given the job. She would work for a while at the new position, proving that business did not come to a standstill because of a black worker. Occasionally she would have to weather snide remarks and even attempts to sabotage her work, but she never had trouble standing up for herself. Once their point had been made, Simmons would help find another black person for the job, and Carter would return to his office. After a few years there weren't many large workplaces in Muskogee that hadn't been integrated.

This story was originally published in *Suriname Folk-lore* by Melville J. Herskovits and Frances S. Herskovits, but it is more readily available where I found it, in *Afro-American Folktales*, edited and selected by Roger D. Abrahams. One of the most intriguing facets of this small nation, which is located on the north central coast of South America, is its varied population. People of Native American, Chinese, European, Javanese, Indian, and African descent live together with no apparent friction. Surinam also has a population of "Bush Negroes," who inhabit the jungles and still use permutations of African languages. These "Bush Negroes" are the descendants of the Maroons, bands of African captives who fled to the forest. They survived by raiding plantations for provisions. Numerous efforts were made to re-enslave these fugitives, but nothing worked. Finally the Dutch, who controlled what is now Surinam, began bringing in Asian workers. The Africans were left alone.

The smallest bird in this story is the one that interests me because she, like the "Bush Negroes," shows that if you are Creative and Purposeful enough, you can overcome your disadvantage.

One day all the birds got together and decided that they needed a leader. They went to Lion to have him call a council of birds, as Lion was king of all the animals.

When the meeting was called, all the birds came together. Kunibre was the smallest, but she was smart! She thought about the subject, and finally announced that, despite her size, she would be the leader. The others wondered about this, but they didn't really know what to do.

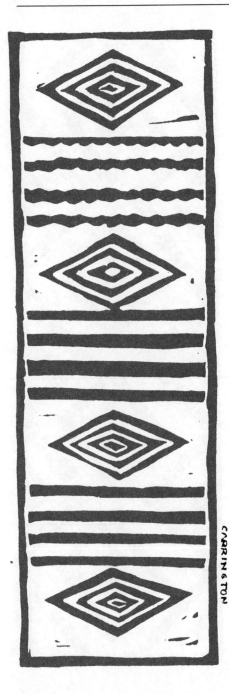

Lion thought about it and asked the birds how they thought it should be settled. They all talked, and Falcon, who knew he could fly high, hoped that they would decide by having a contest to see who could fly highest. But he couldn't suggest this because the other birds would know what he was up to. Luckily Nightingale said, "I want to say something. I won't suggest that you should choose by who sings most sweetly, because I know that if I raise a note, I should win. But let me say that God gave us all one thing and that is wings. So whoever can fly the highest, he or she should be made our leader." Falcon was pleased when he heard this as it had been on his mind for such a long time. He jumped up and said, "I think that is the best plan," and all the others agreed, even Kunibre. What no one knew was that Kunibre had her own plan in mind.

When they began the contest Kunibre sat right down in the middle of Falcon's back. Now Kunibre was so small that Falcon didn't even know she was up there. So they started out, and after a while, when they looked and saw how high Falcon had flown, they said, "Falcon takes first prize and he shall be our leader." But when he landed, they saw that Kunibre was there on top. So they had to say, "Well, no, Kunibre was even higher than Falcon, and she shall be our leader."

SIDE DISHES

DIRTY RICE
(UNITED STATES)

"Watching Aunt Janie, Aunt Clara, Aunt Elizabeth, and Mom cook when I was a child sparked my interest in cooking," Hiram Bonner recalls. "I was fascinated with the wonderful creations they were making. This, one of Aunt Clara's recipes, would go with barbecues and is one of my old favorites."

DIRTY RICE

Cook's Notes: So-called dirty rice gets its name from the chicken livers, which give it a brownish cast. In the Bayou, dirty rice is served as a side dish, but it's robust enough to be enjoyed as an entrée, too.

Serves 4 as a main course, 8 as a side dish

4 strips bacon, cut into 1-inch pieces
1 medium onion, chopped
1 medium green bell pepper, chopped
1 medium celery rib, chopped
1 garlic clove, minced
2 tablespoons all-purpose flour
1 pound chicken livers, trimmed, puréed in a food processor
2½ cups water
½ teaspoon salt
½ teaspoon poultry seasoning
¼ teaspoon dried thyme
¼ teaspoon freshly ground black pepper
⅛ teaspoon cayenne pepper
1¼ cups long-grain rice

1. Cook the bacon in a large saucepan over medium heat, stirring often, until crisp and brown, about 5 minutes. Using a slotted spoon, transfer the bacon to paper towels to drain, and set aside.
2. Add the onion, bell pepper, celery, and garlic to the pan. Cook, stirring often, until softened, about 5 minutes. Add the flour and stir for 1 minute. Stir in the chicken liver purée and cook, stirring often, until the purée loses its red look and is semi-solid, about 3 minutes.

3. Add the water, salt, poultry seasoning, thyme, and black and cayenne peppers. Bring to a boil. Stir in the rice and return to a boil. Reduce the heat to medium-low, cover, and cook until the rice is tender and the liquid has been absorbed, about 20 minutes.

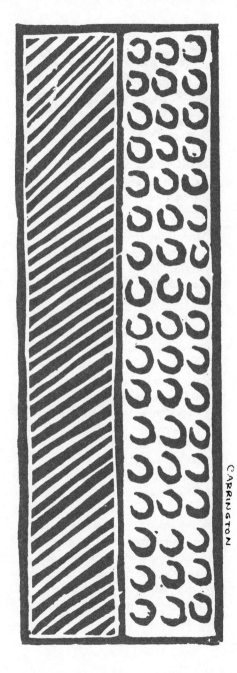

ARROZ CON GANDULES SAN JUAN
Pigeon Peas and Rice
(CARIBBEAN)

"This is the traditional main dish in Puerto Rico," says Saalik Cuevas. "If you don't have it at your birthday, your wedding, or as part of a holiday meal, it seems as if something is missing from the celebration. It's difficult to find these peas fresh in the United States, but you can find them canned. But in Puerto Rico you don't even have to buy them. You just go in your backyard and pick them."

SOFRITO

"You cannot cook Puerto Rican food without sofrito," says Saalik Cuevas. "It is the base of the whole cuisine, kind of like the roux in gumbo. Likewise, you judge the quality of the Puerto Rican meal by the quality of the sofrito. When we were having pork chops or fried chicken, my mother would make very colorful

ARROZ CON GANDULES SAN JUAN
Pigeon Peas and Rice

Cook's Notes: Rice and pigeon peas, separately and together, are omnipresent in Caribbean cookery. But they reach their peak in Puerto Rican cuisine, colored with achiote oil and seasoned with *sofrito*, both of which are available commercially in Latin American communities, although particular cooks insist on making it homemade. Achiote oil gets its deep orange color from a steeping of annatto seeds and gives many Latin American foods an exuberant yellow color. You may get in the Latino habit of always using achiote oil in place of butter when you make rice.

Sofrito is an all-purpose seasoning mixture of cooked savory vegetables that has many uses beyond this dish. Try stirring some into scrambled eggs, or simmering some with a can of herbed tomato sauce as a quick topping for pasta. So, while this recipe for unassuming "rice and pigeon peas" may seem complicated, it surely isn't—and you'll get many meals' worth of seasoning from making the achiote oil and *sofrito* as described here.

Serves 6

ACHIOTE OIL:
1 cup olive oil
3 tablespoons annatto seeds (available in Latin American groceries)

SOFRITO:
⅓ cup achiote oil (see above)
1 medium onion, chopped
1 head garlic, cloves crushed and peeled
1 medium green bell pepper, seeded and chopped

1 teaspoon dried oregano or 1 tablespoon chopped fresh oregano

½ teaspoon ground cumin

½ teaspoon salt

1 bay leaf, finely crumbled

½ cup chopped fresh parsley

1 cup (½ pound) dried pigeon peas (*gandules*), rinsed and picked over (see Note)

8 cups water

3 tablespoons achiote oil (see above)

⅓ cup *sofrito* (see above)

2 cups long-grain rice

1 teaspoon salt

¼ teaspoon freshly ground black pepper

2 tablespoons chopped parsley

1. Make the achiote oil: In a small saucepan, cook the oil and annatto seeds over low heat just until the mixture turns bright red, about 4 minutes. Do not let the mixture get too hot and overcook—it will go past the dark red stage and lighten in color and decrease in flavor. Longer steeping does not mean better flavor in this case, so it is best to underestimate your cooking time. Strain the achiote oil into a small jar, discarding the seeds. Cool completely, cover, and store indefinitely in the refrigerator.

2. Make the *sofrito*: Heat the ⅓ cup achiote oil in a medium skillet. Add the onion, garlic, bell pepper, oregano, cumin, salt, and bay leaf. Cook over medium-low heat, stirring often, until well softened, about 10 minutes. Stir in the parsley. Cool completely, transfer to a small jar or bowl, cover, and store for up to 2 weeks in the refrigerator.

3. In a large saucepan, combine the pigeon peas with enough water to cover by 1 inch; bring to a boil over high heat. Boil for 1 minute. Remove the pan from the heat, cover tightly, and let stand for 1 hour.

yellow rice, which she, like all Puerto Ricans, would turn yellow by adding sofrito. In Ghana they use a palm oil to get that color, as they do in Brazil. But of course sofrito is not all color; it's the spices that go into it. When I visited my mother after she moved back to Puerto Rico, I'd go into the garden to get the oregano and other spices used in it."

(Or soak the peas overnight in a large bowl with enough cold water to cover by 3 inches.) Drain well.

4. In a large saucepan, bring the drained peas and 4 cups of the water to a boil over high heat. Reduce the heat to low, and cook until the peas are almost tender, about 45 minutes. Drain the peas and set them aside.

5. Heat the 3 tablespoons achiote oil in a large saucepan. Add the ⅓ cup *sofrito* and cook over medium heat until very hot, about 2 minutes. Add the rice and stir until well coated and yellow, about 1 minute. Add the remaining 4 cups water, the drained peas, salt, and pepper, and bring to a boil. Reduce the heat to medium-low, and cook until the rice and peas are tender, about 20 minutes. Stir in the parsley and serve immediately.

NOTE: One (16-ounce) can pigeon peas, drained, can be substituted for the cooked peas; skip Steps 3 and 4.

SHEILA'S BLACK BEANS

Cook's Notes: Another outstanding recipe from Sheila Johnson. The black beans acquire a remarkable complexity from being simmered in beef broth. The secret is in the vinegar and red wine, as their acidity helps to break down the beans to ultimate smoothness. Sheila prefers to serve her black beans with popcorn rice (see page 335 for mail-order sources), but regular rice works well too. Sheila's Black Beans is superb served in a soup bowl as a light supper entrée. Pass the cornbread, please.

Serves 4 to 6

½ pound dried black beans, rinsed and picked over
4 cups cold water
4 cups beef broth, homemade or canned
¼ cup olive oil
1 large onion, chopped
1 medium red bell pepper, seeded and chopped
2 garlic cloves, minced
1 tablespoon red wine vinegar
1 tablespoon dry red wine
1 teaspoon granulated sugar
½ teaspoon dried oregano
3 bay leaves
½ teaspoon salt
¼ teaspoon freshly ground black pepper
2 cups chicken broth, homemade or canned
1 tablespoon unsalted butter
1 cup popcorn rice or long-grain rice

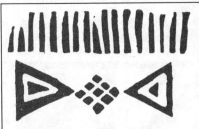

SHEILA'S BLACK BEANS
(UNITED STATES)

"I like my Kwanzaa menu to reflect the various places where those of African descent live," says Sheila Johnson. "This black bean dish is meant to introduce some Caribbean flavor to the meal. I started out making it for parties when I attended Spelman College. I noticed that people would stick their fingers in the pot to dig out every last bit."

1. In a medium saucepan, bring the black beans and water to a boil over high heat. Boil for 1 minute. Remove the pan from the heat, cover tightly, and let stand for 1 hour. Drain the beans well.

2. In a large saucepan, bring the drained beans and the beef broth to a boil over high heat. Reduce the heat to low, cover, and simmer for 1 hour.

3. Meanwhile, heat the oil in a medium skillet. Add the onion, bell pepper, and garlic. Cook over medium heat, stirring often, until tender, about 5 minutes. Remove the skillet from the heat, and stir in the vinegar, red wine, sugar, oregano, and bay leaves; set aside.

4. When the beans have cooked for 1 hour, stir in the vegetable mixture. Simmer, covered, until the beans are very tender, about 45 minutes. Stir in ¼ teaspoon of the salt and the pepper.

5. Meanwhile, bring the chicken broth, butter, and the remaining ¼ teaspoon salt to a boil in a medium saucepan over high heat. Stir in the rice, reduce the heat to medium-low, and cook, covered, until the rice is tender and has absorbed all the liquid, about 20 minutes.

6. To serve, spoon up a serving of rice and top it with the beans.

CRISTIANOS Y MOROS
"Christians and Moors"—Black Beans and Rice

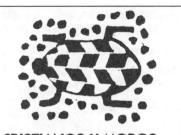

CRISTIANOS Y MOROS
"Christians and Moors"—
Black Beans and Rice
(CARIBBEAN)

"Cristianos y Moros" refers to the white and black colors of the dish, which relate to the skin colors of the Christians and Moors in history and legend.

Cook's Notes: Like *arroz con gandules*, black beans and rice abound in Latin American kitchens. The eating of legumes and rice together is nutritious whether or not you eat meat, as the bean/rice combination replaces the complete protein missing in diets with little or no meat. How fortunate that beans and rice are so great together, as well as being so healthy!

Serves 4 to 6

1 pound dried black beans, rinsed and picked over

½ cup *sofrito* (see page 178)

2 quarts plus 2½ cups water

2 medium Russet potatoes (about 10 ounces), peeled and cut into 1-inch pieces

1 teaspoon salt

¼ teaspoon freshly ground black pepper

1 cup long-grain rice

2 tablespoons unsalted butter or achiote oil

1. In a large saucepan, combine the black beans with enough water to cover by 1 inch; bring to a boil over high heat. Boil for 1 minute. Remove the pan from the heat, cover tightly, and let stand for 1 hour. (Or soak the beans overnight in a large bowl with enough cold water to cover by 3 inches.) Drain well.

2. In a large saucepan, cook the *sofrito* over medium-high heat, stirring often, until sizzling, about 1 minute. Add the drained beans, 2 quarts water, and potatoes, and bring to a boil. Reduce the heat to medium-

GARRINGTON

low, cover tightly, and cook until the beans are tender, about 45 minutes. (If the beans are soupy, increase the heat to medium-high and uncover the pan. Cook, stirring often, until the liquid has reduced to the desired consistency.) Stir in ½ teaspoon of the salt and the pepper.

3. Meanwhile, bring the remaining 2½ cups water and ½ teaspoon salt to a boil in a medium saucepan. Add the rice and butter, reduce the heat to medium-low, and cook, covered tightly, until the rice is tender and the liquid is absorbed, about 20 minutes.

4. Serve the black beans and rice together as a side dish. Spoon out each serving of rice and top it with black beans.

JUG JUG
Meat-Seasoned Millet Polenta

Cook's Notes: The recipe we received for Jug Jug was written in Barbadian dialect and called for "guinea corn flour," which is nothing more than millet flour, available in many natural foods markets. If you can find only whole millet, grind it, in small amounts, to a cornmeal consistency in a blender. This is another recipe that is usually served as a side dish but is substantial enough to serve most mainlanders as a pasta-like main course. If you're a grains fan, you'll love millet's nutty, slightly sweet flavor. Why do they call it "jug jug"? It may be a bit of onomatopoeia: the mush goes "jug . . . jug" as it simmers in the pan, bubbling up like a highly edible lava.

1 cup (½ pound) dried pigeon peas (*gandules*), rinsed
    and picked over
½ pound corned beef, cut into 1-inch cubes
7 cups water
2 chicken thighs
2 medium onions, finely chopped
3 scallions, chopped
½ teaspoon dried thyme
1 tablespoon chopped fresh chives, or 1 teaspoon dried
1 cup millet flour (available at natural foods markets)
2 tablespoons unsalted butter
¼ teaspoon salt
⅛ teaspoon freshly ground black pepper

1. In a large saucepan, combine the pigeon peas with enough water to cover by 1 inch; bring to a boil over high heat. Boil for 1 minute. Remove the pan from the heat, cover tightly, and let stand for 1 hour.

JUG JUG
Meat-Seasoned Millet
Polenta
(BARBADOS)

"Christmas wouldn't be Christmas without Jug Jug," says Rita Springer, a Bajan author of several books on Caribbean cooking. "It is made mainly of crushed pigeon peas mixed with guinea corn flour [what Americans call millet], which binds it. Jug Jug has the pudding-like texture of couscous. It can be very rich, especially in the past when a lot of lard was used."

(Or soak the peas overnight in a large bowl with enough cold water to cover by 3 inches.) Drain well and set aside.

2. Meanwhile, bring the corned beef and 6 cups of the water to a boil in a large saucepan over high heat. Reduce the heat to medium-low and simmer, partially covered, for 1 hour. Add the chicken thighs and drained pigeon peas. Cover partially and cook until the beef and peas are tender, and the chicken shows no sign of pink at the bone when prodded with the tip of a sharp knife, about 45 minutes.

3. Drain the mixture into a colander set over a large bowl, reserving both the liquid and the solids. Allow the meats to cool; then remove and discard the bones and skin. Coarsely chop the meat together with the peas to form a rough paste, and set aside. (This is done most efficiently by pulsing the mixture in a food processor.)

4. In a large saucepan, combine 3½ cups of the reserved cooking liquid with the onions, scallions, thyme, and chives; bring to a boil over medium heat. In a medium bowl, Whisk the millet and the remaining 1 cup water together until smooth. Gradually whisk the millet mixture into the boiling liquid. Reduce the heat to low and cook, stirring often, for 10 minutes.

5. Stir in the chopped meat and peas mixture, and continue cooking, stirring often, until a spoon can stand straight up in the mixture for at least 10 seconds, 20 to 30 minutes. Stir in 1 tablespoon of the butter and the salt and pepper.

6. Transfer the Jug Jug to a warmed serving bowl, dot with the remaining 1 tablespoon butter, and serve immediately.

RED RICE

Cook's Notes: Red rice is a festive side dish, and is often embellished with a cup of cooked shrimp or ham, stirred in at the last minute to heat through.

Serves 4 to 6

2 tablespoons unsalted butter
1 medium onion, chopped
1½ cups long-grain or popcorn rice
1 (35-ounce) can peeled plum tomatoes chopped, with their juice
1⅔ cups water
1 (6-ounce) can tomato paste
½ teaspoon dried oregano
½ teaspoon salt
¼ teaspoon hot pepper sauce
1 cup (4 ounces) cooked baby shrimp
Chopped fresh parsley, for garnish

1. Heat the butter in a medium saucepan. Add the onion and cook over medium heat, stirring often, until softened, about 5 minutes. Add the rice and stir until opaque, about 1 minute.
2. Stir in the tomatoes with their juice, water, tomato paste, oregano, salt, and hot pepper sauce; bring to a boil. Reduce the heat to medium-low, and cook until the rice is tender and has absorbed all the liquid, about 20 minutes. Stir in the shrimp, if desired, and let stand, covered, for 2 minutes. Sprinkle the rice with the chopped parsley, and serve immediately.

RED RICE
(UNITED STATES)

"In the South during my grandmother's childhood, her family would go crabbing in the river nearby their house, and sometimes they'd do some shrimping in the bay," says Audie Odum-Stallato. "When my grandparents moved up North, my grandmother, mother, and aunt would buy whole shrimp and take lots of time cutting off the tails and cleaning them. It was funny because it took less time to cook the shrimp than to clean them. But we thought the effort was worth it. Sometimes we used precleaned shrimp for this dish, but they weren't as good. The shrimp was tougher when frozen than when fresh. We served red rice with long-grain Louisiana popcorn rice, which was excellent. It cooks nicely and doesn't get sticky. Louisiana long-grain is different from your usual white rice in that long-grain has an almost nutty flavor. It smells almost like popcorn when it's cooking." (See page 335 for mail-order sources.)

"Red rice can be either a main course or a side dish. We usually served it as main course, and had salad on the side," Audie says.

There are many guesses about how Hoppin' John, arguably the most famous and myth-shrouded of African-American meals, came by its name. Sheila Ferguson, in her book *Soul Food*, recounts three theories: that there was a man named John who would come a-hoppin' when his wife took this black-eyed pea and rice dish off the stove; that children would hop once around the table before the dish was served; and that the dish was named after an exceptionally animated waiter. According to John Thorne in *Beans and Rice*, etymologists believe Hoppin' John is a corruption of *pois à pigeon*, French for "pigeon pea," another food that was brought to this country from Africa and which is the basis of many dishes in the Caribbean.

Like many African-Americans, Catherine Bailey comes from a tradition of eating Hoppin' John on New Year's Day for good luck: "We always have Hoppin' John on the Kwanzaa menu because of my childhood in Virginia. We learned the myth that black-eyed peas must be eaten on New Year's Day for luck, and Imani is always on January first."

HOPPIN' JOHN

Cook's Notes: Black-eyed peas and rice cooked with sausage, known throughout the South as Hoppin' John, is one of those dishes that often requires a lifetime of kitchen experience. South of the Mason-Dixon line, the sign of a truly fine cook is whether he or she takes the hard way and cooks the rice directly *in* the beans or "cheats" and cooks the rice separately. It is mightily hard to judge exactly how much rice you should stir into the beans (as the exact amount of beans and their cooking liquid changes from batch to batch), a skill acquired by trial and error or, we suspect, after years of cooking for church socials. In order to avoid a sticky mess, we must recommend the simpler tactic. The saucy taste of the long-simmered black-eyes will be deliciously correct, and only the most hard-hearted traditionalist will admonish your rice-making.

1 pound dried black-eyed peas, rinsed and picked over
1 pound spicy bulk pork sausage
1 large onion, chopped
2 garlic cloves, minced
2 quarts water
2 tablespoons crushed hot red pepper flakes
1½ teaspoons freshly ground white pepper
1½ teaspoons salt
4 cups beef broth, homemade or canned
2 tablespoons unsalted butter
3 cups long-grain rice

1. In a large saucepan, bring the peas and water to a boil over high heat. Boil for 1 minute. Remove the pan from the heat, cover tightly,

and let stand for 1 hour. (Or in a large bowl, combine the peas with enough cold water to cover by 3 inches, and let stand overnight at room temperature.) Drain well.

2. In a 5-quart Dutch oven, cook the sausage, onion, and garlic over medium heat, stirring often to break up the sausage, until it loses its raw look, about 10 minutes. Pour off all excess fat.

3. Add the drained beans, water, and red and white peppers. Bring to a boil, reduce the heat to low, and simmer, covered, until the peas are tender, about 1¼ hours. Stir in ½ teaspoon of the salt.

4. Meanwhile, bring the beef broth, butter, and remaining 1 teaspoon salt to a boil in a medium saucepan over high heat. Add the rice, reduce the heat to medium-low, and simmer, covered, until the rice is tender and the liquid has been absorbed, about 20 minutes. Fluff the rice and transfer it to a deep serving bowl.

5. Pour the peas over the rice, mix well, and serve immediately.

CARRINGTON

189

GARLIC-CHEDDAR GRITS SOUFFLÉ
(UNITED STATES)

"Grits and I grew up together," recalls Mavis Young. "My family used to have grits for breakfast, as cereal. However, we never put sugar on it, only salt and butter. Sometimes, for a change, we would have grits and gravy in the morning. I started to fancy it up and call it a soufflé when my sister and I opened our catering business. I began experimenting by adding eggs, milk, and cheese to give it a different consistency. The milk especially seems to penetrate the grits and make them softer. I think when people say 'soufflé' they think they are getting something special. And it is. But in the end it's just dressed-up grits."

GARLIC-CHEDDAR GRITS SOUFFLÉ

Cook's Notes: Humble grits are fluffed up with beaten eggs, Cheddar cheese, and garlic, then baked to create a tempting side dish.

Serves 4 to 6

2 tablespoons unsalted butter
1 small onion, minced
2 garlic cloves, minced
2½ cups water
½ teaspoon salt
½ cup grits (not "instant")
1 cup evaporated milk
¼ teaspoon freshly ground black pepper
4 large eggs, at room temperature
1½ cups (6 ounces) shredded sharp Cheddar cheese

1. Position a rack in the center of the oven, and preheat to 325°. Lightly butter a 7- by 11-inch baking dish.
2. Heat the butter in a small saucepan. Add the onion and garlic. Cover, and cook over medium-low heat, stirring occasionally, until softened, about 6 minutes; set aside.
3. Meanwhile, bring the water and salt to a boil over high heat. Gradually whisk in the grits, and reduce the heat to low. Cover, and cook, stirring often to discourage scorching, for 20 minutes. Stir in ½ cup of the evaporated milk, cover, and cook, stirring often, until quite thick, about 15 minutes. Transfer the grits to a medium bowl.
4. Whisk in the remaining ½ cup evaporated milk and the pepper. Whisk in the eggs one at a time, beating well after each addition. Stir in 1 cup of the Cheddar cheese. Spread the mixture evenly in the prepared dish.

5. Bake until the casserole is set and the top is lightly browned, about 50 minutes. Sprinkle the top with the remaining ½ cup cheese, return the dish to the oven, and bake until the cheese has melted, about 5 minutes. Let stand 5 minutes before serving.

CONFETTI HOMINY

Cook's Notes: If you like corn, you'll love hominy. This plain-Jane staple of southern cooking gets the "company's coming" treatment with a little bacon, basil, sweet pepper, and onion.

Serves 4 to 6

3 slices bacon, cut into 1-inch pieces
1 small onion, chopped
1 small red bell pepper, seeded and chopped
2 (12-ounce) cans hominy, drained
¼ teaspoon dried basil
⅛ teaspoon salt
⅛ teaspoon freshly ground black pepper

1. Cook the bacon in a medium saucepan over medium heat, stirring often, until crisp and browned, about 5 minutes. Using a slotted spoon, transfer the bacon to paper towels to drain, leaving the fat in the pan.
2. Add the onion and bell pepper to the pan, and cook until softened, about 5 minutes. Stir in the reserved bacon, hominy, basil, salt, and pepper. Bring to a simmer, and cook to blend the flavors, about 5 minutes. Serve immediately.

CONFETTI HOMINY
(UNITED STATES)

"My mother used to make hominy," says Mavis Young. "Before she would cook it, she'd go through this very long process: She'd take the dry corn, put them in water with potash or a little lye, then boil them, which would loosen the husk. Then she'd wash them several times to get the lye out, and take the cobs off by hand, and then wash them some more. Today I just buy it in a can."

KAHLÚA-SOAKED
DRIED FRUIT COMPOTE
(UNITED STATES)

"This is a recipe I like to use for brunch," says Mavis Young. "It's attractive because of the assortment of fruits. And you can serve it hot, like a jam, with rolls or biscuits."

KAHLÚA-SOAKED
DRIED FRUIT COMPOTE

Cook's Notes: Any kind of dried fruit works well here, but we like the combination of apricots, apples, and prunes because they are each so different from one another. As Mavis says, it is a nice breakfast or brunch dish, served up with biscuits, especially with sautéed ham slices. For supper, it would go beautifully with Baked Ham with a Secret Glaze (page 101).

Serves 10 to 12

2 cups water
1 cup granulated sugar
½ cup Kahlúa or other coffee-flavored liqueur
8 tablespoons (1 stick) unsalted butter
Grated zest of 1 large lemon
¾ teaspoon ground cinnamon
1 tablespoon cornstarch
6 ounces dried apples
6 ounces dried apricots
6 ounces dried pitted prunes

1. In a large saucepan, combine the water, sugar, Kahlúa, butter, lemon zest, cinnamon, and cornstarch. Bring to a boil over medium-high heat, stirring often to dissolve the sugar. Add the dried apples, apricots, and prunes; return to the boil. Reduce the heat to low and simmer until the liquid is syrupy, about 10 minutes.
2. Transfer the compote to a medium bowl and allow to cool completely. Then cover, and refrigerate until chilled, at least 2 hours or overnight.

CURRIED BROWN RICE WITH VEGETABLES

Cook's Notes: Empress Akweke serves her Curried Brown Rice as a vegetarian main course, but it is also an outstanding side dish with meat ragouts, such as Kiddie Stew (see page 109).

Serves 4 to 6 as a main course, 8 as a side dish

3 tablespoons soy margarine (available at natural foods stores)
    or unsalted butter
1 medium onion, chopped
1 medium Granny Smith apple, cored and chopped
1 medium red bell pepper, seeded and chopped
1 medium carrot, chopped
2 garlic cloves, minced
1 tablespoon curry powder
1½ teaspoons Vege-Sal (available at natural foods stores)
4 cups Winter Garden Vegetarian Consommé (see page 49)
1 bay leaf
2 cups organic short-grain rice
1 cup chopped fresh spinach leaves
½ cup chopped scallions

1. Heat 2 tablespoons of the margarine or butter in a large skillet. Add the onion, apple, bell pepper, carrot, and garlic. Cook over medium heat, stirring often, until softened, about 6 minutes. Add the curry powder and Vege-Sal, and stir for 1 minute. Stir in the consommé and bay leaf, and bring to a boil.
2. Stir in the rice, and reduce the heat to medium-low. Cover tightly, and cook until the rice is tender and all the liquid has been absorbed,

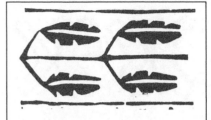

CURRIED BROWN RICE WITH VEGETABLES
(UNITED STATES)

"My former husband's father was from Sri Lanka, which is near India. He was a master of curry," says Empress Akweke. "I had made curry dishes before, but it was from tasting his curry that I learned how to use it, how to bring it out in the foods you are preparing. One of the things you must know is the different properties of different kinds of curries. For instance, Jamaica has its own curry, which they flavor with thyme and allspice in addition to the traditional East Indian spices. The Jamaican curry is also a Day-Glo yellow-orange, a clue to its richer flavor."

COU COU
Cornmeal and Okra Polenta
(BARBADOS)

Variations of cou cou (also spelled *coo coo*) are common throughout the Caribbean. In Trinidad, it is called *fungee*, and in Antigua, *fungi*. It can be made from plantain flour or breadfruit as well as cornmeal. According to Rita Springer, who contributed this recipe, the North Africans put a variety of vegetables into the semolina mix that closely resembles cou cou. "In Barbados we use okra," Springer says. "Its viscous texture helps bind the cornmeal. Cou cou is a basic local food. Other islands use cornmeal, but they don't use okra. On Barbados we especially like to eat cou cou with steamed flying fish."

about 50 minutes. Then stir in the spinach, scallions, and remaining 1 tablespoon margarine or butter. Remove from the heat, cover, and let stand 5 minutes. Serve immediately.

COU COU
Cornmeal and Okra Polenta

Cook's Notes: Creamy golden yellow with a soothing texture, this is the comfort dish *ne plus ultra* for okra-lovers. In fact, since the unpopular gluey texture of the vegetable is negated in cou cou, it could probably even be served to non-okra-lovers.

Serves 4 to 6

6 cups water
2 teaspoons salt
¼ pound okra, stems and tips trimmed, cut into ½-inch-thick
    rounds
2 cups yellow cornmeal, preferably stone-ground
2 tablespoons unsalted butter

1. In a medium saucepan, bring 3 cups of the water and 1 teaspoon of the salt to a boil over high heat. Add the okra and cook until barely tender, about 3 minutes. Drain the okra in a sieve set over a medium bowl, reserving both the okra and the cooking liquid. Return the cooking liquid to the saucepan and bring to a boil.
2. In a medium bowl, gradually whisk the cornmeal into the remaining 3 cups water and 1 teaspoon salt. Whisk the cornmeal mixture into the boiling liquid, reduce the heat to low, and stir until the mixture has thickened, about 2 minutes. Fold in the reserved okra.

3. Cover the pan tightly, and place it in a larger saucepan or skillet of simmering water. Steam until quite thick (a wooden spoon will stand up in the mixture for 10 seconds), about 10 minutes. Stir in 1 tablespoon of the butter.

4. Transfer the mixture to a buttered 2-quart round bowl, cover, and let stand for 10 minutes. Invert onto a serving plate and unmold. Dot the top with the remaining 1 tablespoon butter. Cut the cou cou into thin wedges, and serve hot, warm, or at room temperature.

ARROZ CON COCO
Cartagenan Coconut Rice

Cook's Notes: Coconut rice is categorically the best side dish to serve with most Caribbean and African stews, acting as an authentically flavored "canvas" for emphatically seasoned sauces. In American culture and cuisine, coconut is usually eaten in desserts, so it is difficult for many of us to picture coconut in savory dishes. Coconut rice has just the barest, elusive sweetness and a delicate brown cast, and is thoroughly pleasing.

Making fresh coconut milk may not be the most familiar kitchen task in American households. After cracking scores of the hard and hairy nuts in the course of researching this book, we are happy to share our surefire (and easy) method—see page 197.

ARROZ CON COCO
Cartagenan Coconut Rice
(COLOMBIA)

I never knew that Central American and South American countries (other than Brazil) had black populations. But after finding recipes from Honduras and this one from Colombia, I did some investigating and found that in addition to those two countries, there are black populations in El Salvador and Mexico (especially in the state of Veracruz). You learn something new every day.

Serves 6 to 8

6 cups fresh unsweetened coconut milk (from 2 coconuts; see Note
and page 197)
2 cups long-grain rice
1 tablespoon granulated sugar
½ teaspoon salt
½ cup shredded fresh coconut, from squeezing the coconut milk
(optional; see page 197)

1. In a large saucepan over medium-high heat, boil the coconut milk
until it has reduced to 3 cups, about 15 minutes.
2. Stir in the rice, sugar, and salt. Reduce the heat to medium-low,
and simmer until the liquid level reduces to just under the top of the
rice, about 10 minutes.
3. Cover, and cook until the liquid has been absorbed and the rice is
tender. Stir in the shredded coconut, if desired, and serve immediately.

NOTE: You may substitute 1½ cups canned unsweetened coconut milk
plus 1½ cups water for the reduced fresh coconut milk in Step 1.
Bring it to a boil in a large saucepan, and proceed with Step 2.

HOW TO MAKE FRIENDS WITH A COCONUT

Dealing with a coconut in an American kitchen can be quite a frustrating experience—especially in an apartment kitchen, where most of the old-fashioned instructions just don't work ("To crack the coconut, throw it repeatedly onto a hard surface, such as concrete"). Here is our method for establishing a better working relationship with your coconut:

When cracking the coconut, work over a medium bowl, so that when the coconut opens you can collect the coconut liquid (this clear liquid is *not* coconut milk). Cradle the coconut in the palm of one hand, and grasp a hammer with the other hand. Rotating the coconut in your hand as if it were a ball, knock firmly with the hammer around the coconut's equator. (We learned this method from a Brazilian lady who tapped the coconut in a jaunty conga rhythm, rolling it in her hand like a star baseball player.) Eventually, depending on the age of the coconut and your aggressiveness with the hammer, the coconut will crack, and its liquid will be caught in the bowl.

An alternative method, one that skeptics or the weak-hearted may prefer, is to first pierce the soft "eyes" of the coconut with an ice pick or a hammer and nail. Then place the coconut on a baking sheet in a preheated 350° oven and bake it for 20 to 30 minutes, which shrinks the flesh slightly from the shell, making it easier to crack. Working over the bowl, hold the coconut in one hand and knock it a few times with the hammer to crack it. But learning to open the coconut dexterously, without the trip to the oven, saves you plenty of time.

To peel the coconut, pry the coconut flesh out of the shell with a small sharp knife. Using a vegetable peeler, peel the dark skin from the flesh. The peeling is an optional step, as the skin will not affect the flavor, but it is normally done for visual effect.

To shred or grate the coconut, the quickest, most efficient tool is a heavy-duty food processor fitted with the finest shredding blade available. If you are making desserts or candies, where a delicate, fluffy texture is desired, it's best to finely shred the coconut on a hand grater's small holes (but not the tiny ones for grating nutmeg and the like). Coarsely grated coconut will not hold together well, and its rough texture is unpleasant.

To make about 3 cups of fresh unsweetened coconut milk, break or chop the coconut flesh into 1-inch pieces. In batches in a blender or food processor (the blender works best), process the coconut pieces with the reserved clear coconut liquid and 3 cups boiling water until smooth. Transfer the mixture to a medium bowl, and let it stand for 30 minutes. Then take a large piece of cheesecloth (about 16 inches square), rinse it, and squeeze it dry. Set a sieve over a medium bowl, and line it with the cheesecloth. Pour the coconut mixture into the lined sieve, gather up the ends of the cloth, and squeeze every last bit of the liquid into the bowl. This is the *coconut milk*. The remaining softened, squeezed-out coconut flesh can be stirred into dishes to add texture, but it won't have much flavor on its own. You may substitute canned unsweetened coconut milk in recipes using cooked coconut milk (the best brands are from Thailand or the Philippines), but the canned variety may be too strong-tasting for uncooked desserts.

As the coconut milk stands, a thick, creamy layer, called *coconut cream*, will separate onto the top. It is richer in flavor than coconut milk (like the cream that rises to the top of farmhouse dairy milk), so skim it off and use it in recipes that call for smaller amounts of coconut milk. Heavily sweetened commercial "cream of coconut" is good only for making piña coladas, and cannot be used for the recipes in this book.

VEGETABLES

SHEILA'S THREE MIXED GREENS
(UNITED STATES)

"My great-grandmother cooked three mixed greens," says Sheila Johnson. "My grandmother would talk about the three mixed greens and even cook them occasionally, but not often. When I started making three mixed greens, I used my great-grandmother's recipe. But I added the broth for extra flavor, which I learned at the hotel and restaurant management program at New York City Technical College in Brooklyn. I serve this with meat, potato salad, or cole slaw. I wouldn't complicate the menu too much because it is already a rich, deep-tasting kind of dish. Sometimes I just cook it with extra smoked turkey wings and do it as a one-pot dish, with a potato salad on the side."

SHEILA'S THREE MIXED GREENS

Cook's Notes: Sheila Johnson's addition of beef broth to the dish not only improves the greens but makes the best-flavored pot liquor you'll ever dunk a hunk of cornbread into. (Yankees take note: Pot liquor is the cooking liquid of cooked greens.) Use any combination of available fresh greens, interchanging dandelion, mustard, or beet greens for the ones listed below.

Serves 6

2 (1-pound) smoked turkey wings, chopped into large pieces
    (see Note)
2 cups water
1 pound collard greens
1 pound turnip greens
1 pound dark curly kale
3 cups beef broth, homemade or canned
1 tablespoon cider vinegar
1 teaspoon granulated sugar
⅛ teaspoon crushed hot red pepper flakes, or to taste

NOTE: Like many health-conscious cooks, Sheila prefers to use smoked turkey parts instead of the traditional ham hocks. Turkey wings are much lower in fat, sodium, and calories. If you prefer to use the classic ingredient, score the skin of 2 ham hocks with a sharp knife, then simmer the ham hocks in water to cover for 1 hour. Discard all but 2 cups of the cooking liquid, and continue with the recipe. You may want to cut off the cooked ham hock meat (there won't be much), and stir it into the greens in Step 4.

1. In a 5-quart Dutch oven or soup kettle, bring the turkey wings or ham hocks and water to a boil over high heat. Reduce the heat to medium-low and simmer, covered, for 1 hour.

2. In a large sink of lukewarm water, agitate the collard and turnip greens and kale well to remove any hidden grit. Carefully lift the mixed greens out of the water and transfer them to a colander, leaving the grit on the bottom of the sink. In a sink of fresh water, repeat the procedure. Discard the thick stems, and chop the greens coarsely.

3. Increase the heat under the turkey wings to medium-high, and add one third of the greens to the pot. Cover, and let the greens wilt, about 5 minutes; then stir the greens down. Repeat the procedure in two more batches, until all the greens fit into the pot.

4. Stir in the broth, vinegar, sugar, and red pepper flakes, and bring to a boil. Reduce the heat to medium-low and cover partially. Cook, stirring occasionally, until the greens are very tender, about 1 hour.

5. You can keep the turkey wing chunks in the greens as they are, or remove the turkey meat from the bones, chop it coarsely, and stir the meat back into the greens, discarding the bones.

6. Using a slotted spoon, transfer the greens and turkey to a serving bowl. Use the pot liquor as a dip for hot cornbread, such as Grandma's Creamed Cornbread (see page 236).

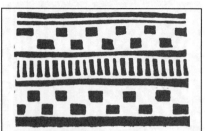

SUCCOTASH
(UNITED STATES)

"This is an old family favorite," says Audie Odum-Stallato of this succotash recipe. While it is generally agreed that the word comes from the Narraganset Indian language, there is a disagreement as to whether it literally means "something torn into bits" and has come to refer to this vegetable stew, or whether it always referred to some sort of similar vegetable dish. Audie, who grew up on a farm in southern New Jersey, remembers eating succotash in the summer, when she would pick the okra, tomatoes, and lima beans that go into the meal. "Grandmother, whom we called 'Mom,' would can some of the succotash for winter," Audie remembers. "So we had the dish summer and winter, usually over a bowl of rice."

SUCCOTASH

Cook's Notes: There's plain old succotash, and then there's this meaty version, which gets an extra boost by being cooked with a flavor-packed beef shin.

Serves 4 to 6

2 tablespoons vegetable oil
1 pound beef shin, cut into pieces about 1 inch thick
1 medium onion, chopped
3 cups water
1 teaspoon salt
¼ teaspoon freshly ground black pepper
1 bay leaf
8 medium plum tomatoes (about 1½ pounds), peeled, seeded and chopped, or 1 (28-ounce) can peeled plum tomatoes, drained and chopped
1 (10-ounce) package corn kernels, defrosted
1 (10-ounce) package baby lima beans, defrosted
½ pound fresh okra, stems and tips trimmed, cut into ½-inch-thick rounds

1. Heat the oil in a large saucepan. Add the beef shin pieces and cook over medium-high heat, turning often, until browned on all sides, about 5 minutes. Add the onion and cook, stirring often, until softened, about 5 minutes.
2. Add the water, salt, pepper, and bay leaf, and bring to a simmer, skimming off any foam that rises to the surface. Reduce the heat to medium-low and simmer, partially covered, for 1 hour.
3. Add the tomatoes and cook for 10 minutes, partially covered. Stir

in the corn, lima beans, and okra, and cook until the beef shins are tender, 10 to 15 minutes. Remove the beef shin pieces and discard any fat, gristle, and bones. Chop the remaining meat coarsely, stir it back into the succotash, and serve immediately.

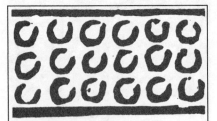

PUT-UP DILLED GREEN BEANS
(UNITED STATES)

"This recipe came from Mrs. Bauchum, who was like a second grandmother to me when I was growing up," remembers Hiram Bonner. "She was an elderly lady who lived alone in our neighborhood, and I spent nights at her house so that she would feel more secure. She gave me a lot of emotional support and guidance. I remember her once telling me that I should always do what makes me happy, as long as it doesn't hurt anyone. That's why I opted for the culinary field. We had her pickled green beans recipe on Thanksgivings, served at room temperature, with the roast turkey and the ham."

PUT-UP DILLED GREEN BEANS

Cook's Notes: What satisfaction you'll get from putting up these tangy, dilly green beans. They don't call for immersion in a boiling-water bath, so they're much simpler to make than many other preserving recipes. The crisp, piquant green beans are superlative when served with smoked ham.

Makes 2 quarts

2 (1-quart) canning jars with brand-new lids and rings (see "Notes on Canning and Preserving," opposite)
2 pounds fresh green beans, trimmed
4 large sprigs fresh dill
1 teaspoon celery seeds
4 garlic cloves, halved lengthwise
2 whole small dried chile peppers
¼ teaspoon peppercorns
4 cups cider vinegar
1 cup water
6 tablespoons pickling salt (see "Notes on Canning and Preserving")

1. Lay a hot sterilized canning jar on its side, and slip in half of the green beans. Stand the jar up, and add 2 dill sprigs, ½ teaspoon celery seeds, 2 garlic cloves, 1 dried chile pepper, and ⅛ teaspoon peppercorns. Repeat with the other jar.
2. Bring the vinegar, water, and pickling salt to a full rolling boil in a medium saucepan over high heat. Pour the hot liquid into the two jars, dividing it evenly. Wipe away any spills from the jars' lips.

Screw on the lids and rings, and let them cool completely at room temperature. Let the pickled green beans stand for at least 4 weeks before serving.

NOTES ON CANNING AND PRESERVING

• Always use brand-new lids and rings. If you are reusing the jars, make sure they are free of nicks and cracks. After filling a jar, wipe away any spilled canning liquid from the jar's lip with a clean, hot, moist kitchen towel before sealing.

• To sterilize the jars, rings, and lids, boil them in water to cover for at least 10 minutes, and remove from the water with kitchen tongs. Or wash in a dishwasher and use as soon as the drying cycle has ended. Always put up your pickles in hot jars.

• When filling up the jars with cooking liquid, leave a ¼-inch headspace between the level of the liquid and the top of the jar.

• Cool the pickles at room temperature; the long cooling period will seal the lids properly.

• None of the canning recipes in this book use the "hot water bath" method of preserving. These recipes include enough salt or sugar for preserving without the tedium and mess of the hot water bath. While the hot water method decreases the chance of bacterial growth, it also alters the color and texture of the fruits and vegetables being processed. However, to be on the safe side, it is recommended that you store these pickles in the refrigerator after they've cooled, not at room temperature.

PICKLED SPICED PEACHES
(UNITED STATES)

"I got this recipe from my father, who owned a bakery and made a lot of peach dishes," says Hiram Bonner. "He would pickle peaches on occasion. I like pickled peaches because of their unusual taste: sweet and tart."

PICKLED SPICED PEACHES

Cook's Notes: An easy-to-make pickle that cries out to be served with smoked ham. Make these in the summertime when peaches are inexpensive, and hoard them until the holiday season rolls around.

Makes 2 quarts

12 large firm but ripe freestone peaches (about 5½ pounds)
1 tablespoon whole cloves
2 cinnamon sticks
1 tablespoon pickling spices
5 cups granulated sugar
2 cups cider vinegar
2 (1-quart) canning jars with brand-new lids and rings (see "Notes on Canning and Preserving," page 205)

1. Blanch the peaches in a large saucepan of boiling water for 1 minute. Drain, rinse under cold water, and peel. Cut the peaches in half vertically, and remove the pits. Stud the peach halves with the cloves.
2. Tie up the cinnamon sticks and pickling spices in a squeezed-dry rinsed piece of cheesecloth. In a 5-quart nonreactive Dutch oven or soup kettle, bring the sugar, vinegar, and spices to a boil over medium-high heat, stirring just until the sugar has dissolved. Add the peaches, reduce the heat to low, and simmer gently just until the peaches are heated through, 3 to 5 minutes.
3. Using a slotted spoon, remove the peach halves from the syrup and pack them into the hot sterilized canning jars. Discard the spices and return the syrup to a full rolling boil. Pour the hot syrup into the jars, dividing it evenly. Wipe away any spills from the jars' lips, and screw on the lids and rings. Let cool completely at room temperature. Let stand for at least 1 week before serving.

HERB-STUFFED CHRISTOPHENES

Cook's Notes: Christophenes (also known as chayotes or mirlitons) are members of the squash family. They have a delicate flavor that makes them a perfect canvas for savory stuffings.

3 large chayotes (about 2½ pounds), halved horizontally
4 tablespoons (½ stick) unsalted butter
1 small onion, finely chopped
1 small celery rib with leaves, chopped
1 garlic clove, minced
1 medium plum tomato, peeled, seeded, and chopped
½ teaspoon dried thyme
½ teaspoon dried rosemary
½ teaspoon salt
¼ teaspoon freshly ground black pepper
1½ cups fresh bread crumbs

1. Place a steamer in the bottom of a large saucepan. Add enough boiling water to come within ½ inch of the steamer bottom. Steam the chayotes until barely tender when pierced with the tip of a sharp knife, 20 to 25 minutes. Allow them to cool slightly. Then, using a large spoon, scoop out the insides of the chayotes, leaving ½-inch-thick shells. Coarsely chop the chayotes pulp.
2. Position a rack in the top third of the oven, and preheat to 350°.
3. Heat 2 tablespoons of the butter in a large skillet. Add the chopped chayote, onion, celery, and garlic. Cook over medium heat, stirring often, until the onion has softened, about 5 minutes. Add the tomato, thyme, rosemary, salt, and pepper and cook, stirring often, just until the tomato is heated through, about 2 minutes. Stir in the bread crumbs.

HERB-STUFFED CHRISTOPHENES (UNITED STATES)

"This New Orleans dish is very good for the holidays, which, of course, now includes Kwanzaa," says Audie Odum-Stallato. "It's a different way to serve stuffing—inside an unusual vegetable rather than inside or on the side of a bird. When preparing the christophenes, make sure you don't scrape too much of the flesh away, because when you cook it, the stuffing will ooze out of the weak spots. Leave the outside rind kind of thick.

"I stumbled onto this recipe while exploring fruits and vegetables from other countries. I saw it in the fruit market and said, 'What is that!?' It looks like a dimpled pear, but it's not hard. The flesh has a very delicate flavor. You should not overpower this vegetable with seasoning. I've come across many, many recipes for christophenes, but I like this one, which I've adapted from a New Orleans chef's, the best."

4. Stuff each chayote shell with bread crumb mixture, molding the stuffing with your hands to form a dome. Place the stuffed chayotes in a lightly buttered baking dish, and dot the tops with the remaining 2 tablespoons butter.

5. Bake until the stuffing is lightly browned, about 20 minutes. Serve immediately.

STEWED SPINACH WITH PEANUT SAUCE

Cook's Notes: This is normally served as a main course, but it makes an admirable side dish too.

Serves 4 to 6

2 tablespoons vegetable oil

3 medium onions, thinly sliced

1 medium red bell pepper, seeded and chopped

1½ cups Winter Garden Vegetarian Consommé (see page 49)

½ cup unsalted sugar-free peanut butter (available at
    natural foods stores)

2 tablespoons cider vinegar

1 teaspoon salt, preferably sea salt

¼ teaspoon cayenne pepper, or to taste

2 pounds spinach, well washed, stems removed,
    and coarsely chopped

1. Heat the oil in a 5-quart Dutch oven or soup kettle. Add the onions and bell pepper, and cook over medium heat, stirring often, until the onions have softened, about 5 minutes. Add the consommé and bring to a boil.

2. Stir in the peanut butter, vinegar, salt, and cayenne. Add the spinach and cook, stirring often, just until the spinach has wilted, about 5 minutes. Serve immediately.

STEWED SPINACH WITH PEANUT SAUCE
(UNITED STATES)

When I was a child, my mother served a lot of greens—turnip greens, spinach, collard greens, kale. She would always admonish me to finish my greens. But had she served this dish, which comes from Gilbert Burnside, the chef at Yohimbe, a vegetarian soul food restaurant in Detroit, she might have had to admonish me not to lick my plate!

SUKUMA WIKI
Kenyan-Style Collard Greens in Lemon Sauce
(KENYA)

"There are many ways of making this very simple dish," says Maggie Marenga. "You can use just onions or just tomatoes. You can use heavy cream or half-and-half instead of the water in the lemon sauce. It's great with beef or chicken stew. Some people even put beef or chicken in their Sukuma Wiki. In Kenya, it is eaten on an almost daily basis."

SUKUMA WIKI
Kenyan-Style Collard Greens in Lemon Sauce

Cook's Notes: While these lightly cooked greens in their pungent sauce are a traditional side dish to Spicy Matoke (see page 94), you'll probably enjoy them so much that you'll want to serve them with more conventional all-American dishes too.

4 to 6 servings

2 pounds collard greens
1¾ cups water
2 tablespoons vegetable oil
1 medium onion, chopped
2 medium plum tomatoes, peeled, seeded, and chopped
1 fresh hot chile pepper, such as serrano, seeded and minced
2½ tablespoons fresh lemon juice
1 tablespoon all-purpose flour
½ teaspoon salt

1. In a large sink of lukewarm water, agitate the collard greens well to remove any hidden grit. Carefully lift the greens out of the water and transfer them to a colander, leaving the grit on the bottom of the sink. Repeat the procedure in a sink of fresh water. Remove and discard the woody stems. Stack the collard leaves a few at a time, and cut them crosswise into ½-inch-wide strips.
2. Bring 1 cup of the water to a boil in a large skillet. Add the collard greens, cover, and cook over medium heat, stirring often, until the greens are barely tender, about 10 minutes. Drain the greens well.
3. Heat the oil in a large skillet. Add the onion and chile pepper, and cook over medium heat, stirring often, until softened, about 5

minutes. Add the tomatoes and cook for 2 minutes. Stir in the drained greens.

4. In a medium bowl, whisk the remaining ¾ cup water with the lemon juice, flour, and salt until smooth. Stir this into the greens, reduce the heat to low, and simmer, stirring often, until the sauce has thickened and the flour flavor has cooked away, about 3 minutes. Serve immediately.

MUSTARD GREENS SOUFFLÉ
(UNITED STATES)

"I was thinking of foods that were familiar to me while I was growing up and ways of applying my French culinary training," Hiram Bonner remembers. "That's how I came up with this mustard greens soufflé. When I serve it, most of the time people will ask, 'What is it?' They are surprised to find out that it is only mustard greens, especially in the North, because many of them have never had it before."

MUSTARD GREENS SOUFFLÉ

Cook's Notes: The slight bitterness of mustard greens is cloaked in the smooth elegance of this superlative classic soufflé. Whether you choose to use it as a sophisticated first course or as an extravagant side dish, it will impress. Soufflés can be partially prepared ahead of time so you won't have any last-minute worries. Just be sure to serve it immediately after baking, before it loses its airy puff.

Serves 6 to 8

6 tablespoons (¾ stick) unsalted butter, at room temperature
2 tablespoons dried bread crumbs
6 ounces mustard greens (1 small bunch)
1 small onion, minced
1 garlic clove, minced
2 cups chicken broth, homemade or canned
2 tablespoons cider vinegar
¼ cup all-purpose flour
1¼ cups milk, heated
1 cup freshly grated Parmesan cheese
¼ teaspoon salt
¼ teaspoon cayenne pepper
⅛ teaspoon grated nutmeg
6 large eggs, separated, at room temperature
⅛ teaspoon cream of tartar

1. Position a rack in the center of the oven, and preheat to 400°. Lightly butter a 2½-quart soufflé dish with 1 tablespoon of the butter. Dust it with the bread crumbs, and tap out the excess crumbs.
2. In a large sink of lukewarm water, agitate the mustard greens well

to remove any hidden grit. Carefully lift the greens out of the water and transfer them to a colander, leaving the grit on the bottom of the sink. Repeat the procedure in a sink of fresh water. Remove and discard the woody stems. Tear the greens into 2- to 3-inch pieces.

3. Heat 1 tablespoon of the butter in a medium saucepan. Add the onion and garlic, and cook over medium heat, stirring often, until the onion has softened. Add the chicken broth and bring to a boil. Add the mustard greens and vinegar, reduce the heat to medium-low, and simmer, covered, until the greens are tender, about 30 minutes. Drain the greens and chop finely, either by hand or in a food processor. (The greens can be prepared up to 1 day ahead; allow to cool, then cover and refrigerate.)

4. In a heavy medium saucepan, heat the remaining 4 tablespoons butter over low heat. Whisk in the flour. Cook, stirring constantly, for 2 minutes, without allowing the mixture to brown. Whisk in the hot milk and bring to a boil. Reduce the heat to low and simmer, whisking often, for about 5 minutes, until thickened. Stir in the Parmesan cheese, salt, cayenne, and nutmeg. Transfer the soufflé base to a large bowl and allow it to cool until lukewarm, stirring often, about 5 minutes. (The soufflé base can be prepared up to 1 day ahead; allow to cool and then cover with plastic wrap pressed directly on the surface to prevent crusting, and refrigerate. Reheat in a saucepan over medium-low heat, stirring constantly, just until warm, before proceeding.)

5. Whisk the egg yolks, one at a time, into the soufflé base. Stir in the chopped cooked greens.

6. Using a hand-held electric mixer set at low speed, beat the egg whites in a grease-free medium bowl until foamy. Add the cream of tartar, increase the speed to high, and beat just until soft peaks form. Stir about one fourth of the beaten whites into the soufflé base to lighten the mixture, then gently fold in the remaining whites. Transfer the mixture to the prepared soufflé dish.

7. Place the dish in the oven and immediately reduce the heat to 375°. Bake until the soufflé is puffed and golden brown, and a long broom straw inserted into the puff comes out clean, 35 to 40 minutes. Serve immediately.

LONG-COOKED GREEN BEANS, TOMATOES, AND BACON
(UNITED STATES)

It's not written in stone that all vegetables must be cooked crisp-tender. They can be delicious any way you want to prepare them, and here's a recipe proving just that.

LONG-COOKED GREEN BEANS, TOMATOES, AND BACON

Cook's Notes: Long simmering allows a mingling of flavors that just can't be accomplished otherwise, and gives the vegetables a delicious melting texture. This is a classic example of the genre. Granted, the green beans' color is dulled somewhat, but the last-minute addition of chopped tomatoes brightens things up considerably. You can omit the bacon strips and use 2 tablespoons of olive oil to cook the chopped onion in Step 2, but the bacon is a time-honored indulgence.

Serves 6 to 8

6 strips bacon, cut into 1-inch pieces
1 large onion, chopped
1 pound green beans, trimmed, cut into 1½-inch lengths
½ cup chicken broth, homemade or canned
½ teaspoon salt
¼ teaspoon freshly ground black pepper
4 medium plum tomatoes, chopped into ½-inch pieces

1. In a large skillet, cook the bacon over medium heat, stirring often, until crisp, about 5 minutes. Using a slotted spoon, transfer the bacon to paper towels to drain, leaving the bacon fat in the pan.

2. Add the onions to the skillet and cook, stirring often, until lightly browned, about 6 minutes. Stir in the green beans, chicken broth, salt, and pepper; bring to a boil. Reduce the heat to medium-low and simmer, covered, until the green beans are very tender, about 40 minutes.

3. Add the chopped tomatoes, increase the heat to medium-high, and cook, stirring, just until the tomatoes are heated through, about 3 minutes. Transfer to a warmed serving dish, sprinkle with the reserved bacon, and serve immediately.

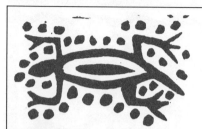

BROCCOLI AND CHERRY TOMATO SAUTÉ WITH CARAMELIZED ONIONS
(UNITED STATES)

Well, two of the colors of Kwanzaa—red and green—are celebrated in this colorful side dish. By expressing the principle of Creativity (Kuumba), maybe you can come up with the third.

BROCCOLI AND CHERRY TOMATO SAUTÉ WITH CARAMELIZED ONIONS

Cook's Notes: This side dish offers an enticing combination of textures and flavors—crisp green broccoli, tart red cherry tomatoes, and sweet tender onions.

Serves 6 to 8

5 tablespoons unsalted butter
2 large onions, thinly sliced
1 teaspoon granulated sugar
¾ teaspoon salt
2 teaspoons cider vinegar
1 bunch broccoli
1 pint cherry tomatoes, stemmed and halved
¼ teaspoon freshly ground black pepper

1. In a large skillet, melt 2 tablespoons of the butter over medium-high heat. Add the onions and cook, covered, stirring occasionally, until golden brown, 8 to 10 minutes. Stir in the sugar and ¼ teaspoon of the salt. Cook, uncovered, stirring often, until the onions are beginning to brown around the edges, about 3 minutes. Then stir in the vinegar, and set the skillet aside. (The onions can be prepared up to 1 day ahead; allow them to cool, then cover and refrigerate.)
2. Cut off the thick broccoli stems, pare them with a vegetable peeler, and cut them diagonally into ½-inch-thick pieces. Cut the remaining broccoli into florets. In a large saucepan of boiling salted water, cook the broccoli stems for 2 minutes. Add the florets, and cook until all the broccoli is just crisp-tender, about 2 more minutes. Drain, rinse

under cold water, and drain again. (The broccoli can be prepared up to 1 day ahead; wrap it in paper towels, close tightly in a plastic bag, and refrigerate.)

3. Heat the remaining 3 tablespoons butter in a large skillet. Add the broccoli and cook over medium-high heat, stirring often, until just heated through, about 5 minutes. Add the cherry tomatoes, remaining ½ teaspoon salt, and the pepper. Cook, gently stirring often, until the tomatoes are heated through, about 2 minutes. Transfer to a large warmed serving dish, and cover with aluminum foil to keep warm.

4. Return the caramelized onions to the skillet and cook, stirring constantly, until they are heated through, about 3 minutes. Spread the onions on top of the broccoli and tomatoes, and serve immediately.

ROOT CELLAR PURÉE

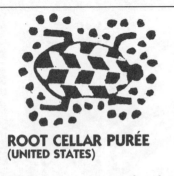

ROOT CELLAR PURÉE
(UNITED STATES)

While summertime produce has its own appeal, many folks look forward to the robust flavor of winter vegetables. Every farm down South had its own root cellar for storing long-keeping vegetables and tubers to sustain the family through nongrowing periods.

Cook's Notes: This combination of homey winter staples tastes extra-good doused with the gravy from Fresh Pork Roast Adobo (page 116). The recipe is easily doubled.

Serves 6 to 8

1 pound carrots, cut into 1-inch lengths
1 pound celeriac, cut into 2-inch chunks
2 large Russet potatoes, peeled and cut into 2-inch chunks
2 medium turnips, peeled and cut into 2-inch chunks
2 medium parsnips, peeled and cut into 2-inch lengths
1 cup milk, heated
4 tablespoons (½ stick) unsalted butter, at room temperature
¾ teaspoon salt
¼ teaspoon freshly ground black pepper
2 tablespoons minced fresh chives or scallions

1. In a pot of boiling salted water, cook the carrots, celeriac, potatoes, turnips, and parsnips until all the vegetables are tender, about 30 minutes. Drain well and return to the pot.
2. Press the vegetables through a ricer, or mash with a masher or hand-held electric mixer. Beat in the hot milk, butter, salt, and pepper.
3. Transfer to a warmed serving dish, sprinkle with the chives, and serve immediately.

SOUTH AFRICAN VEGETABLE CASSEROLE

Cook's Notes: This sumptuous casserole has chunks of yellow and green squash combined with a winning yogurt–peanut butter–curry sauce, and covered with a crunchy topping.

Serves 4 to 6

9 tablespoons (1 stick plus 1 tablespoon) unsalted butter
1 large onion, chopped
1 garlic clove, minced
3 medium zucchini (about 1 pound), cut into 2-inch chunks
3 medium yellow squash (about 1 pound), cut into 2-inch chunks
2 medium carrots, grated
1 teaspoon curry powder
¼ teaspoon salt
⅛ teaspoon cayenne pepper
1 cup plain yogurt
¾ cup unsalted, sugar-free peanut butter
1 cup crushed dry herbed stuffing

1. Position a rack in the top third of the oven, and preheat to 350°. Lightly butter a shallow 2-quart casserole.
2. In a large skillet, heat 8 tablespoons of the butter. Add the onion and garlic and cook, stirring often, until softened, about 5 minutes. Add the zucchini and yellow squash, and cook for 2 minutes. Add the carrots, curry powder, salt, and cayenne pepper, and stir for 1 minute. Set the skillet aside.
3. In a medium bowl, stir the peanut butter and yogurt together. Add the vegetables, and toss until combined. Transfer to the prepared

SOUTH AFRICAN VEGETABLE CASSEROLE
(SOUTH AFRICA)

This is a great make-ahead dish, and perfect for toting to potluck suppers.

casserole, top with the crushed stuffing, and dot with the remaining 1 tablespoon butter.

4. Bake until the casserole is bubbling and the top is golden brown, about 30 minutes. Let stand 5 minutes before serving.

EMPRESS'S ZULU GREENS
(UNITED STATES)

"Collard greens were such a staple in our family that my father used to eat them for breakfast," says Empress Akweke. "After eating them for the greater part of my life, I decided to cook them in different ways. I was talking to a friend of mine—his name is Shaka Zulu—and he asked me to make a special collard green for his birthday. And I'm thinking to myself, what can I do to make these collard greens really different. I'm thinking about Zulus, I'm thinking about Shaka Zulu, the warrior, and what I know about his history . . . and I'm thinking about the taste of the greens. Finally I was able to come up with this really immaculate taste—they're made with lots of hot pepper."

EMPRESS'S ZULU GREENS

Cook's Notes: While most greens recipes have some kind of smoked meat for flavoring, Empress Akweke, a committed vegetarian, enhances hers with loads of fresh vegetables, giving the dish a lovely light quality that makes it a perfect side dish.

Makes 6 to 8 servings

3 pounds collard greens
2 tablespoons vegetable oil
6 medium carrots, chopped
2 medium onions, chopped
1 medium Russet potato, scrubbed and chopped into 1-inch pieces
1 celery rib, chopped
1 tablespoon minced fresh ginger
2 fresh hot chile peppers, such as jalapeño, seeded and minced
1 garlic clove, minced
2 quarts water
1½ tablespoons Vege-Sal (available at natural foods groceries)
Cider vinegar, for sprinkling

1. In a large sink of lukewarm water, agitate the collard greens well to remove any hidden grit. Carefully lift the greens out of the water and transfer them to a colander, leaving the grit on the bottom of the sink. Repeat the procedure in a sink of fresh water. Cut off the woody stems, and chop them crosswise into ¼-inch-thick pieces. Coarsely chop the collard leaves.

2. Heat the oil in a 5-quart saucepan or soup kettle. Add the carrots, onions, potato celery, ginger, chile peppers, and garlic. Cook over medium heat, stirring often, until the vegetables have softened, about 6 minutes. Stir in the chopped stems and the water; bring to a boil. Add a batch of collard leaves, cover and let them wilt, about 5 minutes; stir the greens down. Continue to add the greens in batches until they all fit into the pot.

3. Reduce the heat to medium-low and cook, stirring often, until all the vegetables are just tender, about 1 hour. Stir in the Vege-Sal, cover tightly, and remove from the heat; let stand for 15 minutes. Serve with vinegar on the side, for each guest to season his or her own serving.

SWEET POTATO PUDDING
(UNITED STATES)

"This is my grandmother's recipe," says Sheila Johnson. "She was a great baker and a great chef. We used to have sweet potatoes all the time, but she only made this recipe for the holidays, so we didn't get it often. It is my favorite sweet potato recipe. It can be served as a dessert or as an excellent side dish. We used it for dessert most frequently, and then used the leftovers as a side dish the next day."

SWEET POTATO PUDDING

Cook's Notes: This marvelously creamy, spice-infused side dish is one of the best things you could ever serve to guests. (It is 100 percent guaranteed to move your usual holiday sweet potato recipe off the map.) Okay, some grouches could mumble that its sweetness level makes it most suitable for dessert, but they'll retract their doubts when it's served with glazed ham or roast turkey.

Serves 6 to 8

3 large sweet potatoes, "Louisiana yams," about 2 pounds, peeled and grated
4 tablespoons (½ stick) unsalted butter, melted
1½ cups granulated sugar
3 large eggs, at room temperature
1 (12-ounce) can evaporated milk
1 cup milk
½ teaspoon ground cinnamon
½ teaspoon ground allspice
½ teaspoon grated nutmeg
1 teaspoon vanilla extract
Grated zest of 1 lemon, or ½ teaspoon lemon extract

1. Position a rack in the center of the oven, and preheat to 375°. Lightly butter a 2-quart casserole.
2. Combine the sweet potatoes and butter in a large bowl. In a medium bowl, whisk together the sugar and eggs until light and lemon-colored. Add this to the sweet potatoes, and stir just until blended. Then gradually whisk in the evaporated and regular milks, cinnamon, allspice, nutmeg, vanilla extract, and lemon zest. Pour into the prepared casserole.

3. Bake, stirring well two or three times, until the sweet potatoes are tender and the top is lightly browned, about 1 hour. Remove from the oven and let stand 5 minutes before serving.

SPICED CANDIED SWEET POTATOES

Cook's Notes: Here's a carefree way to serve candied yams without resorting to the canned variety. Double or even triple the recipe for large groups.

Makes 6 to 8 servings

2 cups water
1 cup packed light brown sugar
8 tablespoons (1 stick) unsalted butter
Zest of 1 lemon, removed with a vegetable peeler
1 cinnamon stick, or ¼ teaspoon ground cinnamon
¼ teaspoon grated nutmeg
5 medium sweet potatoes, "Louisiana yams," about 2½ pounds,
    peeled and cut lengthwise into ½-inch-thick slices

1. In a large saucepan, combine the water, brown sugar, butter, lemon zest, cinnamon stick, and nutmeg. Bring to a boil over medium heat, and cook for 5 minutes.
2. Add the sweet potato slices and reduce the heat to medium-low. Cover, and cook until the sweet potatoes are just tender when pierced with the tip of a sharp knife, about 15 minutes.
3. Remove the lemon zest and cinnamon stick. Using a slotted spoon, transfer the sweet potatoes to a warmed serving dish. Pour some of the syrup over the top, and serve immediately.

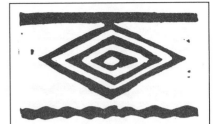

SPICED CANDIED SWEET POTATOES
(UNITED STATES)

The sweet potatoes we have at Thanksgiving (light brown skin, bright orange flesh) are not even a distant relative of the true yam. These two vegetables are members of different botanical families. The reason for the confusion, according to food historian John Mariani, is that in colonial times African-Americans called the sweet potato by one of a number of African or African-derived words: *njam* in Gullah, *nyami*, or *djambi* in Senegalese. They all mean "to eat." Sweet potatoes have become quite a staple in African-American meals. In his novel *The Invisible Man*, Ralph Ellison rhapsodizes about the different ways of preparing them—baked, fried, roasted, or, as in this recipe, candied. This dish was given to us by Hiram Bonner.

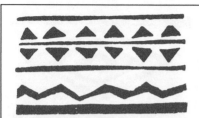

CAULIFLOWER AND MACARONI AU GRATIN
(UNITED STATES)

Take two favorite side dishes, cauliflower au gratin and macaroni and cheese, and mix them up to make one outstanding crowd-pleaser.

CAULIFLOWER AND MACARONI AU GRATIN

Cook's Notes: To turn this dish into a main meal, stir in 2 cups chopped cooked chicken, turkey, or ham before baking.

Serves 6 to 8

1 medium head cauliflower (about 1½ pounds), cut into florets
12 ounces elbow macaroni
4 tablespoons (½ stick) unsalted butter
3 tablespoons all-purpose flour
2 cups milk, heated
½ teaspoon salt
½ teaspoon hot pepper sauce
2½ cups (10 ounces) shredded sharp Cheddar cheese
½ cup fresh bread crumbs
½ cup grated imported Parmesan cheese

1. Position a rack in the top third of the oven, and preheat to 375°. Lightly butter a deep 3-quart casserole.
2. In a large saucepan of boiling salted water, cook the cauliflower over high heat until just tender, about 8 minutes. Using a slotted spoon, transfer the cauliflower to a colander. Rinse under cold running water, drain well, and pat dry with paper towels.
3. In the same boiling salted water, cook the elbow macaroni just until tender, about 8 minutes. Drain well.
4. Melt 3 tablespoons of the butter in a medium saucepan over medium-low heat. Whisk in the flour, and stir constantly without browning for 2 minutes. Whisk in the hot milk, salt, and hot pepper sauce; bring to a simmer. Simmer, whisking often, until thickened, about

2 minutes. Remove the sauce from the heat, and stir in the Cheddar cheese until smooth.

5. Toss the reserved cauliflower and macaroni with the cheese sauce in the prepared casserole until well combined. Sprinkle the top with the bread crumbs and Parmesan cheese, and dot with the remaining 1 tablespoon butter, cut into small pieces.

6. Bake until the mixture is bubbling and the top is golden brown, about 25 minutes.

SCALLOPED LEEKS AND POTATOES
(UNITED STATES)

Leeks, another treasure from the winter garden, make a guest appearance here in scalloped potatoes.

SCALLOPED LEEKS AND POTATOES

Cook's Notes: To clean leeks thoroughly of sand and grit, trim off the root ends. Make four lengthwise slits, each incision reaching through to the center of the leek, starting at the green part of the leek and going right down to the root end. Under cold running water, open up the leeks and rinse well. Cut off the green ends and proceed with the recipe.

Serves 4 to 6

2 tablespoons unsalted butter
4 medium leeks, white part only, cleaned and coarsely chopped
2 garlic cloves, minced
1 cup chicken broth, homemade or canned
⅔ cup milk
6 medium Russet potatoes (about 3 pounds), peeled and
  cut into ⅛-inch-thick slices
½ teaspoon salt
¼ teaspoon freshly ground black pepper
½ cup (2 ounces) grated Parmesan or sharp Cheddar cheese

1. Position a rack in the center of the oven, and preheat to 400°. Lightly butter a 9- by 13-inch baking dish.
2. Heat the butter in a medium skillet. Add the leeks and garlic, and cover. Cook over medium heat, stirring often, until softened, about 6 minutes.
3. Meanwhile, combine the broth and milk in a small saucepan, and bring to a simmer over medium heat.
4. Combine the potatoes, leeks and garlic, salt, and pepper in the prepared baking dish, and toss to combine. Spread the mixture out evenly, and pour in the hot broth and milk.

5. Bake until the potatoes are tender and the liquid has been absorbed, about 45 minutes. Then sprinkle the top with the cheese, and bake until the cheese has melted, another 5 minutes.

MEXICALI CASSEROLE

Cook's Notes: Almost a spoonbread, not quite a soufflé, this chunky yet creamy side dish will have everyone asking for more. When Mavis and Cyn make it for tenderfeet, they use sharp Cheddar cheese and substitute ground black pepper for the hot pepper sauce.

Serves 4 to 6

1 (16-ounce) can Mexican-style corn (with sweet peppers), drained
1 (16-ounce) can creamed corn
4 large eggs, at room temperature
½ cup all-purpose flour
1 tablespoon granulated sugar
1½ cups (6 ounces) shredded jalapeño Jack cheese (Monterey Jack with chile peppers)
½ cup heavy (whipping) cream
½ cup chopped scallions
1 garlic clove, minced
¼ teaspoon hot pepper sauce, or to taste

MEXICALI CASSEROLE
(UNITED STATES)

"This recipe came about because my family likes Mexican food and they also like spoonbread. So it was only natural to try them together," explains Mavis Young.

"When I used to work as a nurse full-time, I would pride myself on having dinner ready about an hour after I returned home from work," Mavis continues. "This dish, together with a salad and a roll, would be a complete dinner."

1. Position a rack in the center of the oven, and preheat to 375°. Lightly butter a 2-quart round casserole.

2. In a medium saucepan, bring both corns to a simmer over medium heat. Transfer to a medium mixing bowl.

3. Whisk the eggs, one at a time, into the corn, beating well after each addition. Whisk in the flour and sugar. Then whisk in 1 cup of the cheese, and the cream, scallions, garlic, and hot pepper sauce. Spread evenly in the prepared casserole.

4. Bake until the top is lightly browned and the casserole is set in the center (a toothpick will not necessarily come out clean), about 50 minutes. Sprinkle the top with the remaining ½ cup cheese, and bake until the cheese has melted, another 5 minutes. Remove from the oven and let stand 5 minutes before serving.

PLANTANOS FRITOS
Fried Plantains

Cook's Notes: It is important to select the correct ripeness and color of plantains to fit the recipe you are preparing. Green (unripe) plantains are hard and are used like potatoes, simmered to tenderness in stews or mashed to form a casserole topping. Yellow-ripe plantains will give when squeezed, and resemble a barely ripe banana in appearance and texture. Black-ripe plantains are very soft and sweet, and are found mainly in desserts.

Yellow-ripe plantains are normally fried or sautéed as a side dish. These are similar to our "home-fried" potatoes, and are served with *everything* in Latino coffee shops—and like home fries, they are darned good.

Serves 4

4 yellow-ripe plantains, peeled and quartered lengthwise
4 cups lukewarm water
1 tablespoon salt
¼ cup vegetable oil
Salt (optional)

1. Combine the plantains, lukewarm water, and salt in a medium bowl. Let it stand for 30 minutes to soften and mellow the plantains. Then drain the plantains well and pat dry with paper towels.
2. Heat the oil in a large skillet. Add the plantains and cook over medium-high heat, turning once, until golden brown on both sides, about 5 minutes. Using a slotted spatula, transfer the plantains to paper towels to drain briefly before serving. Season lightly with salt if desired, and serve immediately.

PLANTANOS FRITOS
Fried Plantains
(CARIBBEAN)

"In Puerto Rico, when we cook green *plantanos*, we eat them as a starch, almost like a potato," says Saalik Cuevas. "But when *plantanos* are ripe, we eat them in different ways. When I was growing up my grandmother would make them for us. They were a delicious treat. You can go to Harlem and find *cuchifritos* in little stores, where you can also buy all sorts of other Puerto Rican foods. You can find Plantanos Maduros as I've given them in this recipe, or buy them split in half lengthwise and filled with ground beef."

229

HOW TO PEEL PLANTAINS

Yellow-ripe and black-ripe plantains are relatively easy to peel—handle them just like bananas, being ready to pare away any stubborn peel with a small sharp knife if necessary. But green unripe plantains require a special technique:

Using a small sharp knife, trim away the stem and tip from the plantain. Cut the plantain in half crosswise. Make four shallow incisions down the entire length of each half, cutting just through the peel down to the flesh. Using the knife as an aid, pry, lift, and peel the tough skin away from the flesh.

BREADS

MOTHER'S CRACKLIN' BREAD
(UNITED STATES)

"There were cows and pigs on the farm where I grew up," says Mavis Young, "and every fall we'd slaughter some of the hogs. The fat part near the skin would be rendered out, called cracklin'. My mother would put it in cornbread batter, and we'd have it with our meal. You can use about a cup of chopped-up fried bacon if you don't feel like making cracklin'."

MOTHER'S CRACKLIN' BREAD

Cook's Notes: Warm from the oven, this robust bread is crunchy with cornmeal, tender with buttermilk, and richly seasoned with pork cracklings. People are not cooking with lard the way they used to, so while the cholesterol levels of many old-time dishes may be decreased, the flavors are altered as well. Cracklings, those crunchy bits of pork gathered from rendering pork fat, also aren't made at home much anymore. They can sometimes be found in the snack section of Latin American markets, labeled *chicarrones*. For those of you who occasionally want to use a dab of lard to bring back that old-fashioned taste, the recipe below gives instructions for both lard and cracklings.

LARD AND CRACKLINGS:
2 pounds fresh pork fatback
½ cup water

CORNBREAD:
2 cups yellow cornmeal, preferably stone-ground
1 cup all-purpose flour
2 tablespoons granulated sugar
1 teaspoon salt
½ teaspoon baking soda
1½ cups buttermilk
1 large egg, well beaten
4 tablespoons (½ stick) unsalted butter, melted
½ to 1 cup pork cracklings (optional; see Cook's Notes)

1. Make the lard and cracklings: Coarsely grind the pork fat in a food processor or meat grinder. In a medium saucepan, cook the ground fat and water over low heat until the fat has completely melted and

the solid bits in the saucepan are browned, 2 to 3 hours. Do not let the fat color beyond a light yellow. Strain the rendered fat (lard) into a jar reserving the browned bits (cracklings), and allow it to cool completely. Transfer the cracklings to paper towels to drain. The lard will keep, covered and refrigerated, for up to 6 months. The cracklings will keep at room temperature for up to 24 hours.

2. Make the cornbread: Position a rack in the center of the oven, and preheat to 350°. Lightly butter a 7- by 11-inch baking pan.

3. In a medium bowl, whisk together the cornmeal, flour, sugar, salt, and baking soda. Make a well in the center of this mixture, and pour the buttermilk, egg, and melted butter into the well. Stir together to form a slightly stiff batter. Stir in the cracklings. Spread the batter evenly in the prepared baking dish.

4. Bake until the top of the cornbread is golden brown and a toothpick inserted in the center comes out clean, 20 to 25 minutes. Remove the cornbread from the oven and let it stand for 5 minutes; then cut it into pieces and serve warm.

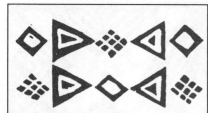

MARGARETTA'S HUSH PUPPIES
(UNITED STATES)

How did this fried cornmeal dumpling get its name? One story is that Kentucky hillbillies tossed them to their dogs to shut them up while dinner was cooking. In his book *Southern Cooking*, Craig Claiborne writes that Confederate soldiers cast them to dogs so that their barking would not give away the Confederates' position to the Yankee troops. One of the oddest stories is that the term comes from deep-frying the legs of a salamander—also called "dwarf water dog," "water dog," "water puppy," and "mudpuppy"—with cornmeal dough.

Mavis Young, who was given this recipe by a friend in South Carolina, remembers having this popular southern dish fairly frequently, usually, as with so many cornmeal dishes—cou cou, for instance, with fish."

MARGARETTA'S HUSH PUPPIES

Cook's Notes: This is what hush puppies are all about—moist, crunchy, full of flavor, and greaseless. Of course, your oil temperature must be just right (375°), but an electric skillet or an efficient deep-frying thermometer will handle that problem.

Makes about 3½ dozen

Vegetable oil, for deep-frying
2 cups yellow cornmeal, preferably stone-ground
1 cup all-purpose flour
1 tablespoon baking powder
½ teaspoon baking soda
1 teaspoon salt
¼ teaspoon cayenne pepper
1⅓ cups buttermilk
2 large eggs, well beaten
1 medium onion, minced
¼ cup minced red bell pepper

1. Preheat the oven to 200°.
2. In a large deep skillet, heat enough oil to reach halfway up the sides until very hot but not smoking. (An electric skillet set at 375° works perfectly for this.) Be sure the oil is at the right temperature before making the batter.
3. In a medium bowl, whisk together the cornmeal, flour, baking powder, baking soda, salt, and cayenne. Make a well in the center of this mixture, and pour the buttermilk and eggs into the well. Stir to make a stiff batter. Stir in the onion and bell pepper.
4. In batches without crowding, drop the batter by heaping tablespoons into the hot oil. Cook, turning once, until both sides are golden

brown, about 5 minutes. Using a slotted spoon, transfer the hush puppies to a paper towel–lined baking sheet to drain. Keep them warm in the oven while cooking the rest of the hush puppies. Serve immediately.

235

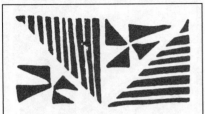

GRANDMA'S CREAMED CORNBREAD
(UNITED STATES)

"The ancestor to our cornbread was the humble corn pone: an Indian concoction of water, salt, and cornmeal that was mixed together, put on a makeshift griddle, and thrust over an open fire.

Cornbread was a ubiquitous fixture of the meals of my early childhood. My mother didn't like to cook, so I usually had the packaged mix variety. But there are those who can coax delicious and varied melodies from this unassuming dinner accompaniment."

Sheila Johnson's recipe comes from her great-grandmother, who usually served cornbread when they had fish for supper.

GRANDMA'S CREAMED CORNBREAD

Cook's Notes: You'd have to go a long mile to find a cakier, more finely textured cornbread than this one. The creamed corn has something to do with it, of course.

Makes one 9-inch round cornbread

4 tablespoons (½ stick) unsalted butter, melted
1 cup yellow cornmeal, preferably stone-ground
¾ cup all-purpose flour
2 tablespoons granulated sugar
1 tablespoon plus 1 teaspoon baking powder
½ teaspoon salt
1 (8-ounce) can creamed corn
1 cup milk
1 large egg, well beaten

1. Preheat the oven to 450°.
2. Pour 2 tablespoons of the melted butter into a 9-inch cake pan, and bake for 5 minutes, until the cake pan is very hot.
3. Meanwhile, in a medium bowl, whisk together the cornmeal, flour, sugar, baking powder, and salt. Make a well in the center of this mixture, and pour the creamed corn, milk, remaining 2 tablespoons butter, and egg into the well. Stir until smooth. Pour the batter into the hot cake pan.
4. Bake until the cornbread is golden brown and a toothpick inserted in the center comes out clean, 30 to 35 minutes. Remove the cornbread from the oven, and let it stand for 15 minutes before serving.

CARROT HONEY LOAF

Cook's Notes: Even though this carrot loaf is honeyed, it is not cloyingly sweet, so you can serve it at suppertime. It is also most welcome for brunch, spread with honey butter or your favorite low-sugar preserves.

Makes 1 loaf

¾ cup vegetable oil

¾ cup honey

2 large eggs, at room temperature

2 tablespoons blackstrap molasses

1½ teaspoons vanilla extract

½ teaspoon almond extract

1 cup all-purpose flour

1 cup whole-wheat flour

2 teaspoons baking powder

2 teaspoons ground cinnamon

1 teaspoon grated nutmeg

¼ teaspoon baking soda

2 cups grated carrots (about 5 medium carrots)

1. Position a rack in the center of the oven, and preheat to 350°. Lightly butter a 9- by 5-inch loaf pan.

2. In a large bowl, whisk together the oil, honey, eggs, molasses, and vanilla and almond extracts until smooth. Sift the two flours, baking powder, cinnamon, nutmeg, and baking soda into a medium bowl. Stir the flour mixture into the liquid mixture just until blended. Add the grated carrots, and stir well for 3 to 4 minutes. Transfer the dough to the prepared pan, and smooth out the top.

CARROT HONEY LOAF
(UNITED STATES)

This recipe is the product of a series of friendly baking contests between Dee Dee Dailey and a friend of hers. This carrot honey loaf was one of the many recipes Dailey developed from what amounted to a basic tea cake recipe. "Some people might consider this more of a loaf than a cake, because it isn't that sweet," says Dailey. "It's very simple. It tastes great with ice cream, and because it's not heavily sugared, you can use it as a breakfast cake."

3. Bake until a toothpick inserted in the center of the loaf comes out clean, about 45 minutes. Allow it to cool on a wire cake rack for 10 minutes. Then invert the pan onto the rack, unmold the loaf, and let it cool completely.

COCONUT AND RAISIN LOAVES
(UNITED STATES)

Here is another treasure from Dee Dee Dailey's baking contest.

COCONUT AND RAISIN LOAVES

Cook's Notes: Dee Dee's not-too-sweet tea loaf has admirable characteristics that you just can't get with sweetened coconut flakes. The rose water adds a charming "remembrance of times past" dimension. The recipe makes two loaves, so you may want to freeze one or to offer it as a Kwanzaa gift.

Makes 2 loaves

4 cups all-purpose flour
⅔ cup granulated sugar
1 tablespoon plus 1 teaspoon baking powder
1 teaspoon ground cinnamon
¼ teaspoon salt
¼ teaspoon grated nutmeg
2 cups grated unsweetened fresh coconut (from 1 coconut, see page 196)
¾ cup dark raisins
8 tablespoons (1 stick) unsalted butter, melted
½ cup milk, plus additional if necessary
2 large eggs, well beaten
2 teaspoons vanilla extract

1 teaspoon almond extract

1 teaspoon rose water (available at specialty markets and some
    pharmacies)

1. Position a rack in the center of the oven, and preheat to 350°.
Lightly butter two 8- by 4-inch loaf pans. Dust the pans with flour,
and knock out the excess.

2. In a large bowl, sift together the flour, sugar, baking powder,
cinnamon, salt, and nutmeg. Stir in the coconut and raisins. In a
medium bowl, whisk together the melted butter, milk, eggs, vanilla
and almond extracts, and rose water. Stir the liquid into the dry
ingredients to make a soft biscuit-like dough. (The exact amount of
milk depends on the moistness of the coconut. Stir in additional milk,
1 tablespoon at a time, if necessary.) Divide the dough evenly between
the two prepared loaf pans, smoothing the tops.

3. Bake until a toothpick inserted in the center of a loaf comes out
clean, 45 to 50 minutes. Cool the loaves for 10 minutes on a wire
cake rack. Then invert them onto the rack, unmold, and allow to cool
completely.

CARRINGTON

HIGH-RISE BISCUITS

**HIGH-RISE BISCUITS
(UNITED STATES)**

Next to cornbread, biscuits, in all their scrumptious variety, are the most ubiquitous bread accompaniment to African-American meals.

Cook's Notes: These flaky, buttery biscuits get their height from an old-fashioned leavening mixture of cream of tartar and baking soda. (That's what bakers used before the advent of double-acting baking powder.) Beautiful at breakfast, luscious at lunch, delightful at dinner—we'll eat these biscuits any way we can get them, but they're always best served piping hot.

Makes 1 dozen

1 cup cake flour (not self-rising)
1 cup all-purpose flour
2 teaspoons cream of tartar
1 teaspoon baking soda
½ teaspoon salt
8 tablespoons (1 stick) unsalted butter, chilled, cut into ¼-inch
    cubes
¾ cup half-and-half

1. Position a rack in the center of the oven, and preheat to 400°.
2. In a medium bowl, sift together the cake flour, all-purpose flour, cream of tartar, baking soda, and salt. Using a pastry blender or two knives, cut the butter into the flour until the mixture resembles small peas. Add the half-and-half, and stir gently just until a soft dough forms. Knead the dough in the bowl a few times, just until smooth. Do not overwork the dough.
3. On a floured work surface, roll out the dough to ¾-inch thickness. Using a 3-inch round cookie cutter, cut out biscuits. Gather up the scraps, reroll, and repeat the procedure until 12 biscuits are cut out. Transfer the biscuits to an ungreased baking sheet.
4. Bake until biscuits are golden brown, 12 to 15 minutes. Serve hot.

"MOCK" INJERA
American-Style Ethiopian Flatbread

Cook's Notes: See Doro Wat (page 130) for suggestions on how to enjoy this bread in the African manner.

Makes about 10 *injera*

1 cup buckwheat pancake mix
6 tablespoons all-purpose flour
2⅔ cups buttermilk
2 large eggs, beaten
Vegetable cooking spray

1. In a medium bowl, whisk together the pancake mix and flour. Make a well in the center, pour the buttermilk and egg into the well, and whisk just until smooth.
2. Spray a 9-inch nonstick skillet with vegetable cooking spray. Place the skillet over medium-low heat, and heat. Using about ⅓ cup batter for each *injera*, pour the batter into the center of the pan, swirling the pan by the handle in order to coat the bottom of the pan completely. Cook until the top is set and full of tiny holes, about 3 minutes. Transfer the *injera* to a plate, and continue with the remaining batter. Separate the cooked *injera* with pieces of waxed paper so they don't stick. The *injera* can be made up to 4 hours ahead of serving; store at room temperature, loosely covered with a clean kitchen towel.

"MOCK" INJERA
American-Style Ethiopian Flatbread
(ETHIOPIA)

"This comes from an Ethiopian friend of mine," says Roscoe Betsill. "This bread is generally made with millet flour, but I tried making it with buckwheat flour, and she agreed that it had a pretty authentic taste and texture. Quite frankly, it was the spongy, moist texture I was most concerned about. Ethiopian food is so spicy that it overwhelms the flavor of the bread anyway. But the bread is used as a utensil in Ethiopia. They use the bread to eat their food." Don't overcook the *injera*. They should be soft enough to wrap around your food like a thick tortilla.

TUSKEGEE INSTITUTE SWEET POTATO BREAD WITH RAISINS AND WALNUTS
(UNITED STATES)

George Washington Carver was known for, among other things, being able to make hundreds of products—many of them foods, such as peanut milk, chocolate bars, and instant coffee—from the lowly peanut. Given that track record, it shouldn't be surprising to find that Tuskegee —over which Carver exerted a strong influence from his arrival in 1896 almost until his death in 1943—published a series of bulletins on how to exploit other kinds of foods. For instance, the institute's Bulletin #13 contains recipes for cooking "cow peas," or black-eyed peas. Another bulletin is called "How to Grow the Tomato and 115 Ways to Prepare It." This recipe, along with the following biscuit and muffin recipes, is from Bulletin #38, which contains thirty-two ways to prepare sweet potato dishes. We have gussied these recipes up to give them a little more zest and variety.

TUSKEGEE INSTITUTE SWEET POTATO BREAD WITH RAISINS AND WALNUTS

Cook's Notes: The nutty-sweet flavor of sweet potatoes is enhanced by the raisins and walnuts in this yeast bread. It can be topped as a breakfast treat, toasted and buttered, then drizzled with a bit of honey.

Makes 1 loaf

1 medium (9-ounce) sweet potato, "Louisiana yam," unpeeled
1 package dry active yeast
2 tablespoons plus 1 teaspoon granulated sugar
¼ cup warm water (105°)
3 cups unbleached all-purpose flour
1 teaspoon salt
½ cup dark raisins
½ cup chopped walnuts
1 tablespoon milk

1. In a medium saucepan, cook the whole sweet potato in boiling (unsalted) water until tender when pierced with the tip of a sharp knife, about 20 minutes. Remove the sweet potato, reserving 1¾ cups of the cooking water. Let the sweet potato cool, then pare it and mash until smooth. You should have about 1 cup mashed sweet potato. Let the cooking water cool to warm (105° or less).
2. Sprinkle the yeast and 1 teaspoon sugar over the ¼ cup plain warm water in a small bowl, and let stand 5 minutes, until frothy; then stir until the yeast has dissolved. In a medium bowl, combine the mashed sweet potato, the yeast mixture, ⅓ cup of the flour, and 1¼ cups of

the reserved cooking water; stir until smooth. Cover with plastic wrap, and let stand in a warm place until the sponge has risen, about 1 hour.

3. Position a rack in the center of the oven, and preheat to 375°. Lightly oil a 9- by 5-inch loaf pan.

4. In a large bowl, combine the sponge, the remaining 2⅔ cups flour, the remaining 2 tablespoons sugar, the salt, and the remaining ½ cup reserved cooking water; stir until a smooth dough forms. On a lightly floured work surface, knead the dough until it is smooth and elastic, about 10 minutes. Then knead in the raisins and walnuts.

5. Press the dough out to form a thick 9-inch square, and roll it up into a cylinder. Pinch the seams closed, and fit it into the prepared loaf pan. Slash the top twice with a razor blade or very sharp knife, and brush it lightly with the milk.

6. Bake until the loaf is golden brown, about 45 minutes. (When removed from the pan, the bottom of the loaf will sound hollow when lightly tapped with your knuckles.) Cool the loaf in the pan on a wire cake rack for 10 minutes. Then unmold it onto the rack and allow it to cool completely.

SWEET POTATO BISCUITS
(UNITED STATES)

A delightful and surprising twist
on an old saw.

SWEET POTATO BISCUITS

Cook's Notes: One of the most successful appetizers we ever served
was a tray of these melt-in-your-mouth biscuits, spread with honey
mustard and stuffed with ham slices.

Makes 1 dozen

1 medium (9-ounce) sweet potato, "Louisiana yam," unpeeled
6 tablespoons (¾ stick) unsalted butter, melted
½ cup milk
2 tablespoons granulated sugar
1 large egg, beaten
1¼ cups cake flour
1¼ cups all-purpose flour
1 tablespoon plus 1 teaspoon baking powder
1 teaspoon salt

1. In a medium saucepan, cook the whole sweet potato in boiling
(unsalted) water until tender when pierced with the tip of a sharp
knife, about 20 minutes. Let the sweet potato cool, then pare it and
mash until smooth. You should have about 1 cup mashed sweet potato.
Let the cooking water cool to warm (105° or less).
2. Position a rack in the center of the oven, and preheat to 425°.
3. In a medium saucepan, stir the mashed sweet potato with the melted
butter until smooth. Transfer the mixture to a medium bowl. Stir in
the milk, sugar, and egg. Sift the cake and all-purpose flours, baking
powder, and salt into a medium bowl, and then stir into the liquids
to combine. Knead briefly in the bowl to form a soft dough.
4. On a floured work surface, roll out the dough to ¾-inch thickness.
Using a 2½-inch round cookie cutter, cut out biscuits. Gather up the

scraps, reroll, and repeat the procedure until 12 biscuits are cut out. Transfer the biscuits to an ungreased baking sheet.

5. Bake the biscuits until golden brown, 15 to 20 minutes. Serve hot, warm, or at room temperature.

MASHING SWEET POTATOES

When cooking sweet potatoes (also called Louisiana yams) to mash and use in baked goods, boil them whole and unpeeled. While it takes more time, the potatoes won't become waterlogged. Mashed sweet potatoes that are too wet can throw off the flour measurement in your dough, ruining the bread. For each cup of mashed sweet potatoes, allow 1 medium raw sweet potato, weighing about 9 ounces. For the smoothest mashed sweet potatoes, rub pared cooked sweet potatoes through a fine-mesh sieve or put them through a ricer. If you like little chunks of mashed taters in your breads (and they do add a certain character), use a masher or even an electric mixer. But do *not* put them in a food processor, which will turn them into a gluey mess.

SWEET POTATO MUFFINS WITH WALNUT STREUSEL
(UNITED STATES)

Put these treasures out on the table with other breads, and they will disappear first by a country mile.

SWEET POTATO MUFFINS WITH WALNUT STREUSEL

Cook's Notes: While these not-so-sweet muffins are welcome at breakfast time, they are also a fine supper accompaniment. Crunchy nut streusel and warm spices are nice additions to a classic recipe.

Makes 1 dozen

MUFFINS:

1 medium (9-ounce) sweet potato, "Louisiana yam"
1 cup milk
2 large eggs, well beaten
4 tablespoons (½ stick) unsalted butter, melted
2 cups all-purpose flour
½ cup granulated sugar
2 teaspoons baking powder
1 teaspoon grated nutmeg
1 teaspoon ground cardamom
¾ teaspoon salt

WALNUT STREUSEL:

2 tablespoons coarsely chopped walnuts
2 tablespoons light brown sugar
1 tablespoon unsalted butter, softened
1 tablespoon all-purpose flour
¼ teaspoon ground cinnamon

1. Make the muffins: Position a rack in the center of the oven, and preheat to 400°. Butter twelve 2½-inch diameter muffin cups.
2. In a medium saucepan of boiling salted water, cook the sweet potato

just until tender when pierced with the tip of a sharp knife, about 20 minutes. Allow it to cool, then pare and mash until smooth. You should have about 1 cup mashed sweet potato.

3. In a medium bowl, whisk the mashed sweet potato and milk until smooth. Whisk in the eggs, one at a time, and then the melted butter. In another medium bowl, sift together the flour, sugar, baking powder, nutmeg, cardamom, and salt. Stir the dry ingredients into the potato mixture just until blended. Do not overmix.

4. Make the streusel: In a small bowl, stir together the walnuts, brown sugar, butter, flour, and cinnamon until well combined.

5. Dividing the batter evenly among the muffin cups, fill each about two-thirds full. Sprinkle the streusel evenly over the muffin tops, patting it lightly so it adheres.

6. Bake the muffins until the streusel is lightly browned, 20 to 25 minutes.

7. Let the muffins stand in the pan for 5 minutes. Then run a sharp knife around the muffins to loosen them. Invert the muffin tin over a double thickness of kitchen towels, and unmold.

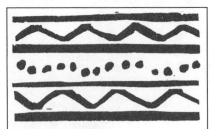

CHILE-SPIKED SPOONBREAD
(UNITED STATES)

"I'm the oldest of four children, and I started cooking when I was eight," says Mavis Young. "Mom said, 'Since you're the oldest, you'll have to help.' She started teaching me different things to cook, but most of the recipes I still use I got from simply observing her.

"We used to eat spoonbread with fish, similar to what you do with hush puppies. We'd also have spoonbread with greens."

CHILE-SPIKED SPOONBREAD

Cook's Notes: There are few dishes in the world more heartwarming than spoonbread, a steaming spoonable cornbread served right from its baking dish. Minced fresh chiles are stirred in here to add some spunk, but they can be omitted if your family prefers.

Serves 6

2 cups water
1 teaspoon salt
1 cup yellow cornmeal, preferably stone-ground
4 tablespoons (½ stick) unsalted butter
2 cups milk
3 large eggs, well beaten, at room temperature
1 fresh hot chile pepper, such as jalapeño, seeded and minced
2 teaspoons baking powder

1. Position a rack in the center of the oven, and preheat to 400°. Lightly butter a 1½-quart round casserole.
2. In a medium saucepan, bring the water and salt to a boil over high heat. Gradually whisk in the cornmeal. Reduce the heat to low, and cook, stirring constantly, until the cornmeal is quite thick, about 3 minutes.
3. Remove the pan from the heat, and stir in the butter until melted. Then whisk in the milk. Add the beaten eggs and whisk well. Whisk in the chile pepper and baking powder. Spread the batter evenly in the prepared casserole.
4. Bake until puffed and golden brown, about 45 minutes. Let stand 5 minutes before serving.

Nguzo Saba

Umoja (Unity)
Kujichagulia (Self-determination)
Ujima (Collective Work and Responsibility)
Ujamaa (Cooperative Economics)
Nia (Purpose)
Kuumba (Creativity)
Imani (Faith)

F rederick Douglass was one of America's greatest human rights leaders. Born enslaved in Maryland in 1818, he educated himself under great adversity (this excerpt doesn't give the half of it) and eventually escaped slavery. Douglass became a celebrated abolitionist, brilliant on the public lecture circuit and on paper. He wrote three autobiographies.

Everybody should read the works of Frederick Douglass—the story of his life is as inspiring as the style in which he told it. This selection is from his first autobiography, *Narrative of the Life of Frederick Douglass, an American Slave*. We are coming in just after Douglass has been transferred from a Maryland plantation to Baltimore, where he was to work as a house servant to Hugh Auld and his family. What attracted me to this passage is his Self-determination (Kujichagulia). Douglass would let no one except himself tell him what he could be or what he could do. Douglass was also single-minded—purposeful —and creative in his quest for literacy and freedom.

My new mistress proved to be all she appeared when I first met her at the door,—a woman of the kindest heart and finest feelings. She had never had a slave under her control previously to myself. I was utterly astonished at her goodness.

But, alas! this kind heart had but a short time to remain such.

Very soon after I went to live with Mr. and Mrs. Auld, she very kindly commenced to teach me the A, B, C. After I had learned this, she assisted me in learning to spell words of three or four letters. Just at this point of my progress, Mr. Auld found out what was going on, and at once forbade Mrs. Auld to instruct me further, telling her, among other things, that it was unlawful to teach a slave to read. To use his own words, further, "If you teach that [negro] how to read, it would forever unfit him to be a slave." These words sank deep into my heart. I now understood what had been to me a most perplexing difficulty—to wit, the white man's power to enslave the black man. From that moment, I understood the pathway from slavery to freedom. It was just what I wanted, and I got it at a time when I the least expected it. Whilst I was saddened by the thought of losing the aid of my kind mistress, I was gladdened by the invaluable instruction which, by merest accident, I had gained from my master. Though conscious of the difficulty of learning without a teacher, I set out with high hope, and a fixed purpose, at whatever cost of trouble to learn how to read.

I lived in Master Hugh's family about seven years. During this time, I succeeded in learning to read and write. In accomplishing this, I was compelled to resort to various stratagems. I had no regular teacher. My mistress, who had kindly commenced to instruct me, had, in compliance with the advice and direction of her husband, not only ceased to instruct, but had set her face against my being instructed by any one else.

She was not satisfied with simply doing as well as he had commanded; she seemed anxious to do better. Nothing seemed to make her more angry than to see me with a newspaper. I have had her rush at me with a face made all up of fury, and snatch from me a newspaper, in a manner that fully revealed her apprehension.

From this time I was most narrowly watched. If I was in a separate room any considerable length of time, I was sure to be suspected of having a book, and was at once called to give an account of myself.

All this, however, was too late. The first step had been taken. Mistress, in teaching me the alphabet, had given me the *inch*, and no precaution could prevent me from taking the *ell*.

The plan which I adopted, and the one by which I was most successful, was that of making friends of all the little white boys whom I met in the street. As many of these as I could, I converted into teachers. With their kindly aid, obtained at different times and in different places, I finally succeeded in learning to read. When I was sent on errands, I always took my book with me, and by going one part of my errand quickly, I found time to get a lesson before my return. I used also to carry bread with me, enough of which was always in the house, and to which I was always welcome; for I was much better off in this regard than many of the poor white children in our neighborhood. This bread I used to bestow upon the hungry little urchins, who, in return, would give me that more valuable bread of knowledge.

By trying often, the monkey learns to jump from the tree.

Proverb, Cameroon

The Cameroon proverb represents Purpose (Nia). In reading the biographies of successful men and women, one of the common components I've noticed is Purpose, an unflagging persistence which, while it doesn't always yield the success one is looking for, always, absolutely always, gets one further than quitting. And sometimes it yields a success beyond one's dreams.

Purpose is just one of the Kwanzaa principles illustrated in this excerpt about Berry Gordy. But this is not the Berry Gordy with whom you are most familiar. Because before there was Motown Records, a cultural phenomenon and one of America's foremost business success stories, before there was the Berry Gordy who founded Motown in 1960, before there was Berry Gordy's father, there was Berry Gordy's grandfather, also named Berry. The eldest Gordy, born in Georgia around 1854, set the philosophical and material foundation that would provide for the success of future generations.

In this selection from *Where Did Your Love Go: The Rise and Fall of the Motown Sound* by Nelson George, there are a number of principles at work. As I mentioned there is Purpose (Nia), in that while he was breaking his back working for someone else, he held to his goal—acquiring land and keeping it for future generations of Gordys; Self-determination (Kujichagulia), in that the eldest Gordy didn't allow other people to determine who he was or what he could do; and Cooperative Economics (Ujamaa) and Collective Work and Responsibility (Ujima), in that the eldest Gordy got his family, especially his son and namesake, involved with the business of the farm. This was essential in holding on to the farm.

By his mid-twenties Berry was recognized by his neighbors, both white and black, as a local leader, a "big dog." A shrewd, thoughtful, self-reliant businessman, Berry was respected by blacks and many whites in the community for being self-reliant. He worked for a decade on a local plantation, bending and bowing to make another man's fortune. But by the time most of his offspring were walking, Berry had so carefully budgeted his earnings that in the 1890s, when he was in his forties, he was able to purchase 168 acres in Oconee County and go into business for himself. Cotton was his chief cash crop, though he supplemented his income by growing corn, potatoes, peanuts, okra, cabbage, collard greens, sugar cane, and various fruits.

Most of his black neighbors were deep in debt to the white landowners on whose land they resided and toiled, and to the shopkeepers from whom they purchased their supplies. Ill educated by the local government, blacks would have their books kept and their busi-

nesses managed by the white men with whom they did business. For a hundred years after the Civil War, well into the 1960s, this system of economic neo-slavery effectively kept many blacks in constant debt. No matter how prosperous a black family was one season, it could never overcome the debts that prevented it economic freedom.

Berry would have none of this. He and he wife, Lucy, kept every bill, every loan statement, every scrap of paper pertaining to the business. To their neighbors the Gordys appeared almost fanatical in their desire to account for every dime, as if the accumulation of money and the keeping of records—and not the Good Book—held the key to salvation.

As Berry preached his dedication to business to his children every day, his most attentive student was his namesake, who mirrored his father in many ways. Berry II was short (tagged a runt even by friends), feisty, and always seemed to follow his daddy's lead as closely as possible. While the other Gordy children would play in the fields, little Berry lingered around the adults, supposedly playing by himself but actually listening closely to what they said. As his parents discussed bills and crop prices, he'd be underfoot, quietly itching to join their world.

His interest didn't go unnoticed. When he was ten his father started taking him to Sandersville on Saturdays to sell farm produce, where little Berry's job was to calculate the value per pound of the family's cotton. An awareness of the worth of things and the necessity of keeping one's own counsel about them became part of the young boy's makeup.

His father bought him a law book and encouraged him to study it. The education continued as his father's business expanded. After his initial 168-acre purchase, the elder Gordy bought another 100-acre tract, one complete with a large white house, a general store, and a well-stocked barn. Later he opened a blacksmith shop in town, employing another worker and, on occasions, one of his sons.

The Gordy family's unity and the depth of the lessons the elder Gordy taught his family were put to the ultimate test in the days following May 31, 1913. At noon, before lunch, the two Berry Gordys surveyed the family property, father showing son idiosyncrasies of the plantation that young Berry had never noticed. The elder Gordy had proved himself as a farmer and a businessman, and on this dark, cloudy morning he savored his considerable achievement, sharing that pleasure with his closest son. By the time they reached their back porch the sky had turned black and was filled with lightning. Rain began falling on the Gordys' piece of sweet Georgia soil.

A day later Sandersville's blacks and whites stood by the grave of Berry Gordy as his namesake fell to his knees, tears streaming down his cheeks. After he'd left him on the porch, a bolt of lightning had struck his father down, killing him instantly. Berry II quickly assumed the role of family leader, organizing his father's funeral.

A few days later, with the family still in mourning, some of the elder Berry's business acquaintances, most of them white, began visiting the house. Since Reconstruction, it had become customary for white businessmen, playing upon the still strong paternal ties between blacks and whites, to offer themselves as supervisors of the black family's land any time a black father died. They would serve as "administrators," making all of the business decisions relating to the family's land, property, and finances. Berry and his mother, still shocked by the elder Gordy's sudden death, planned to follow tradition and name a white merchant administrator. But luck was with them. On the way to town they stopped at the home of a white woman the family had befriended. After they told her of their plans, she put the situation to them bluntly: any white man you get as administrator will steal your land.

Lucy and Berry II went to the county clerk's office and named themselves administrators, an unusual move that seemed to confirm local speculation that the Gordys' "big dog" days were over. Berry,

not quite twenty-five when his father died, was considered an untried "boy" by local merchants. In the months that followed, local businessmen constantly approached him, always seeking his signature on contracts to purchase cars and other items that required monthly payments. Looking into the law book his father had given him, Berry saw that if an administrator failed to meet any of his obligations, his land could be seized as payment. Once he fully understood all the implications of his newfound power, Berry realized why his signature was suddenly so popular. As the bills came in, his father's insistence on careful record-keeping stood him in good stead. Whenever the local white merchants challenged the Gordys over a bill—and they seemed to take every opportunity to do so—Berry and his mother would refer to their records. The Gordys even won a court case based on the evidence their records presented.

This folktale, from *Bantu Tales* by Patti Price, was introduced to me by the storyteller Eshu Bumpus—and Bumpus first heard Danny Kaye tell it on an album he recorded in 1960. So you never know where you'll find something for your Kwanzaa celebration! I find that my four-year-old son really enjoys it, which is one of the reasons it appeals to Bumpus. "Kids like the repetition," Bumpus says, "but I like it because it's one of the few stories written with children in mind that has substance."

The lesson I draw from this tale is Purpose (Nia). It is through his unwavering intent that one of the animals succeeds in his goal.

Let me give one word of warning to potential storytellers: Be sure to practice saying "Oowungalema" (which to my knowledge is just a nonsense word). You might even want to warm up the way singers do before going on stage. Telling this tale unprepared can be embarrassing.

* * *

Once there was a terrible drought in the land of the animals. A kindly king came from over the mountain and planted a special tree. He told them that this tree would bear fruit all year round in any kind of weather. All they had to do to get the fruit was to speak its name. The name of the tree was Oowungalema.

The animals thanked the kind old king, and he returned to his own land far over the mountain. The animals then sounded the Great Drum to call everyone for miles around. When all were gathered at the tree, the lion asked Anansi to speak the name of the tree.

"I thought you were going to remember the name!" said Anansi.

"I don't remember the name!" said the lion. "Someone must know it!"

They asked everyone who had been there when the old king planted the tree, but not one of them could remember the name of the tree. They decided to send someone to ask the king for the name. They were all very hungry, so they decided to send someone fast. They sent the hare.

The hare ran as fast as he could through villages, across the river, through the bush, over the mountain, and straight to the court of the kindly old king. The king told him, "The name of the tree is Oowungalema."

The hare ran back, repeating the name to himself as he went along. On the way home, he stopped at the river to rest and take a drink. The water was nice and cool. It felt good after all that running. The hare splashed around for a while to cool himself off, then he got out of the water and started back to the tree. When he got back, the animals all cheered. "Now we can have the fruit!" they shouted.

The hare went up to the tree to speak the name, "Oomagamoomoo . . . No, Oobapadoopa . . . Noomooogamooga . . ."

Try as he might, the hare just couldn't remember the name.

"We have to send someone else," the lion said at last.

257

So the springbok, a beautiful African antelope, was sent. She ran all the way to the king over the mountain and tried to keep the name in her head all the way home, but coming through the forest, she tripped over a root and bumped her head. The name was lost again.

Next they sent leopard, but on the way back he started chasing a monkey who was teasing him. He forgot the name as well.

Many others tried and failed until, finally, the tortoise asked if she might go. Most of the animals laughed because the tortoise is so slow.

"Give her a chance!" Anansi said. "She may succeed where the rest of us have failed."

The tortoise went to her mother and asked, "What do you do if you must remember something very important?"

Her mother told her to keep repeating it no matter what happens. So the tortoise set out on her journey. When she reached the king over the mountain, he said, "The name of the tree is Oowungalema."

The tortoise kept repeating it over and over to herself all the way home. When the monkeys teased her in the forest, she only said, "Oowungalema."

When she passed by the river and the sound of the water made her thirsty, she looked at the water and said, "Oowungalema."

And when she got near her house and her family came running to her, she only said, "Oowungalema."

Finally the tortoise came to the tree. All the other animals were anxiously waiting. The lion spoke: "Tortoise, please speak the name of the tree."

Tortoise said, "Oowungalema."

And at last the animals were able to eat the fruit.

BEVERAGES

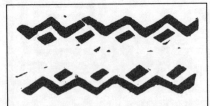

MINTED ICED TEA
(UNITED STATES)

Catherine Bailey serves mint tea (regular tea prepared with dried mint leaves) as the guests arrive for her Kwanzaa celebrations. Mavis Young remembers as a child picking mint from the family flower garden and putting the leaves in either hot water or regular tea, then serving it with tea cookies. The peoples of the northwest region of Africa take regular hot mint tea breaks, pouring the sugary brew from small brass pots into three-inch-high glasses.

MINTED ICED TEA

Cook's Notes: This recipe gives you iced tea in a jiffy. In the Deep South iced tea is always heavily sweetened, but you can leave the sugar out if you prefer.

Makes about 3 quarts, 12 servings

3 quarts water
1 cup granulated sugar
1 cup chopped fresh mint leaves
12 orange pekoe tea bags, or ¼ cup loose tea
Ice cubes

1. In a medium saucepan, bring 1 quart of the water and the sugar to a boil over high heat, stirring to dissolve the sugar. Remove the pan from the heat, and stir in the mint leaves and tea. Cover, and let stand for 10 minutes. Strain the tea into a large pitcher.
2. Stir in the remaining 2 quarts water. Add the ice cubes and let stand until well chilled before serving.

FRUIT SLUSH PUNCH

Cook's Notes: A fruity punch is a must at holiday gatherings with a lot of kids, or one with grown-ups who prefer to avoid liquor. Here, a mélange of fruits are blended and frozen to form a decorative block that serves two purposes. First, it keeps the punch cold, and second, as it melts into a slush, it flavors the drink too. Nonteetotalers will find that this punch is sensational when spiked with rum or vodka.

Makes about 30 servings

½ cup granulated sugar

¼ cup water

2 ripe bananas, peeled and sliced

½ cup fresh or frozen sliced strawberries

5 cups orange juice

2 cups pineapple juice

4 quarts ginger ale

1. In a small saucepan, bring the sugar and water to a boil, stirring just until the sugar has dissolved. Remove the syrup from the heat.
2. In a food processor or blender, purée the bananas, strawberries, and sugar syrup. Combine the purée, orange juice, and pineapple juice in a large bowl. Pour the fruit mixture into a 9-cup fluted tube mold. Cover it with foil, and freeze until very solid, at least 24 hours or up to 3 days.
3. Run hot water around the outside of the mold. Remove the foil and unmold it into a large punch bowl. Pour 2 quarts of the ginger ale around the fruit block. As the punch is served add additional ginger ale as necessary.

FRUIT SLUSH PUNCH
(UNITED STATES)

"A friend of mine, an old colleague from my nursing career, gave me this recipe about seven years ago," remembers Mavis Young. "She and I and a lot of people on the unit where we worked used to have potlucks. One day she brought this punch and I begged her for the recipe. She made me swear not to give it away, but of course I just have."

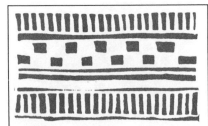

WEST AFRICAN GINGER BEER
(WEST AFRICA AND CARIBBEAN)

Ginger beer is a favorite drink in West Africa and the Caribbean, where it floats from island to island in slightly different forms. Audie Odum-Stallato created her version from one she had in West Africa. "I love the way the pepperiness of the ginger in this drink plays on your tongue," she says.

WEST AFRICAN GINGER BEER

Cook's Notes: Honey gives this version an elusive sweetness, tempering the spicy sharpness of the fresh ginger. There's no reason to peel the fresh ginger (in this or any other recipe) unless the esthetics of the skin bother you. If you insist on peeling, a vegetable peeler does a quick and efficient job. Yes, it is very fine with a little rum sneaked into the glass, but it's not *de rigueur*.

Makes about 2½ quarts, 10 servings

2 quarts water
½ pound fresh ginger, thinly sliced
½ cup fresh lemon juice
1 cup honey
Ice cubes

1. In a medium saucepan, combine 2 cups of the water with the ginger, and simmer over medium heat for 20 minutes. Stir in the lemon juice and honey, and let cool completely.
2. Strain the ginger mixture into a large pitcher, and add the remaining 1½ quarts water. Add the ice cubes, and let stand until well chilled before serving.

SORREL
Spiced Hibiscus Blossom Iced Tea

Cook's Notes: The purple-red color and citrusy flavor of these dried hibiscus blossoms are more familiar than you'd imagine—they appear in a number of popular commercial herb teas. The Jamaicans call the blossoms *sorrel*. You are most likely to find them in Latin American markets, where they are called *flor de Jamaica* ("Jamaican flowers").

Makes about 3 quarts, 12 servings

3 quarts water
1 cup turbinado or raw sugar
2 cups (2 ounces) dried sorrel (*flor de Jamaica*)
¼ cup grated fresh ginger
1 zest of orange, removed with a vegetable peeler
1 zest of lemon, removed with a vegetable peeler
1 cinnamon stick
¼ teaspoon whole cloves
15 grains of rice (optional)
Ice cubes

1. In a large saucepan, bring the water and sugar to a boil over high heat, stirring to dissolve the sugar. Add the sorrel, ginger, orange and lemon zests, cinnamon, and cloves. Let stand at room temperature for 24 hours. Then strain the beverage into a large bowl and discard the solids.
2. If desired, add the rice grains and let the beverage stand for another 24 hours to allow for slight fermentation.
3. Pour into a large pitcher, add the ice cubes, and let stand until well chilled.

SORREL
Spiced Hibiscus Blossom Iced Tea
(JAMAICA)

"Sorrel is a cold drink that we have mostly from around Christmastime into New Years," says Georgia Dunn. "The hibiscus flower, from which it is made, blooms in December, which is when it is harvested. The hibiscus flower grows in the rural areas of Jamaica on shrublike trees. There may be a lot of them on one stalk. It looks like a small rose, four or five petals with a seed in the middle. The seed can be itchy to the touch, like poison ivy. My parents and grandparents would take it home in bunches, and we children would sit around and pick the floral part of the sorrel off the stalk. It was one of the chores that you did at that time of the year, and you'd develop the art of picking these things off so that you avoided getting the seed on you."

REAL LEMONADE
(UNITED STATES)

Empress Akweke's classic version
of this basic beverage.

REAL LEMONADE

Cook's Notes: The trick in this recipe is to blend the lemon seeds into the juice, so they can release their intensely scented oils into the lemonade.

Makes about 1½ quarts, 6 servings

7 large lemons
¾ cup granulated sugar
4 cups water
Fresh mint sprigs
Ice cubes

1. Roll six of the lemons on a work surface, pressing hard to bruise them slightly so they release more juice. Cut the remaining lemon into thin slices and reserve.
2. Cut the six lemons in half and squeeze them, reserving the juice and seeds. You should get about 1 cup juice.
3. In a blender, blend the lemon juice and seeds with the sugar until the sugar has dissolved and the seeds are pulverized. Strain into a large pitcher, add the water, and stir to combine. Add the mint sprigs, ice cubes, and reserved lemon slices. Let stand until well chilled before serving.

HOT SPICED HOLIDAY DRINK

Cook's Notes: This heavenly scented beverage is worth making just to have the spicy fragrance wafting through the kitchen. It's easy to fix in a large coffee maker (which also keeps the drink hot), but if you don't have one, then simply simmer it in a large pot and keep it warm on a hot plate. Be sure to tie up the spices so they don't clog up your percolator's spout.

Makes about 2½ quarts, 10 servings

4 cinnamon sticks
2 teaspoons whole allspice
1 teaspoon whole cloves
2 cups water
2 cups granulated sugar
2 quarts orange juice
2 quarts pineapple juice
Dark rum or brandy, to taste

1. Tie the cinnamon, allspice, and cloves together in a piece of rinsed, squeezed-dry cheesecloth. In a small saucepan, bring the water, sugar, and spices to a boil, stirring to dissolve the sugar.
2. In a 12-cup or larger electric percolator, combine the sugar syrup, spice bag, and orange and pineapple juices. Perk until the machine indicates that the drink is hot. Remove the spice bag.
3. Serve with a bottle of dark rum or brandy next to the coffee maker, so each guest can add liquor to taste. The right amount seems to be about 2 tablespoons per serving.

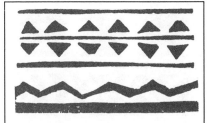

HOT SPICED HOLIDAY DRINK
(UNITED STATES)

"This recipe came from a friend of mine a long time ago," says Mavis Young. "She was one of the first people I met when I married my husband, who was in the Air Force. She was a military wife also. So, as I said, the recipe is hers, but it was my idea to make it in the percolator. I like the way the percolator sends the festive aroma of the punch throughout the house."

EGGNOG WITH VANILLA ICE CREAM FLOAT
(UNITED STATES)

While this version of the typical holiday drink does not contain the ale that its name would imply —"nog" is an old English word for ale—this recipe does call for brandy, rum, and bourbon. So watch out!

EGGNOG WITH VANILLA ICE CREAM FLOAT

Cook's Notes: When serving from a punch bowl, it's always a headache to keep the beverage cold but undiluted. This world-class eggnog solves the problem by floating vanilla ice cream in the bowl. When it melts into the eggnog, it's a plus, not a minus.

Makes about 2 quarts, 12 servings

6 large eggs, separated, at room temperature
1¼ cups granulated sugar
1½ quarts half-and-half
1 cup golden rum
1 cup brandy
¼ cup bourbon
2 pints high-quality vanilla ice cream

1. In a large bowl, whisk the egg yolks and sugar together until thick and pale yellow, about 1 minute. Whisk in the half-and-half, rum, brandy, and bourbon.
2. In a medium grease-free bowl, using an electric mixer set at low speed, beat the egg whites until foamy. Increase the speed to high, and beat just until the whites form soft peaks. Fold the beaten whites into the egg yolk mixture. Cover, and refrigerate until well chilled, at least 2 hours.
3. Pour the eggnog into a large punch bowl. Cut down the sides of one of the ice cream containers with a sharp knife, and then peel away the container to remove the ice cream in one piece. Float the ice cream in the eggnog. When necessary, unmold the remaining ice cream and add it to the punch bowl.

MAVIS'S PINEAPPLE-PAPAYA PUNCH

Cook's Notes: Wait until you try fresh pineapple juice! As if that's not enough, it's blended with chopped papaya and fresh citrus juices, then served over ice with a float of dark rum on top. Of course, it's equally excellent as a rum-free libation.

Makes about 2 quarts, 8 servings

1 large ripe pineapple
3 cups water
½ cup granulated sugar
Grated zest of 1 lime
⅔ cup fresh grapefruit juice
⅓ cup fresh orange juice
3 tablespoons fresh lime juice
1 ripe papaya, peeled, seeded, and finely chopped
Ice cubes
1 cup dark rum

1. Using a sharp knife, cut away the crown of leaves and the pineapple rind. Quarter the pineapple, then remove the tough core from each quarter. Cut the pineapple into 1-inch chunks.
2. In batches, in a food processor or blender, purée the pineapple with the water and sugar. Transfer the purée to a fine sieve placed over a large bowl, and strain it, pressing down hard on the solids with a wooden spoon to extract as much juice as possible. Pour the strained pineapple juice into a large pitcher, discarding the solids.
3. Stir in the lime zest and the grapefruit, orange, and lime juices. Add the chopped papaya and ice cubes, and let stand until well chilled.
4. Pour the punch into individual glasses, and spoon 2 tablespoons dark rum on top of each serving. Serve immediately.

MAVIS'S PINEAPPLE-PAPAYA PUNCH
(UNITED STATES)

"I just hate store-bought punch," says Mavis Young, "because you never get a true flavor. It always tastes flat and artificial. And I'm not alone in holding that opinion. When we cater an affair, people say, 'We don't like that red punch stuff.' My punch is made with real fruit juices. I figure people can't complain about fruit juices. And in the five years I've served it, nobody has."

CAIPIRINHA
High-Octane Brazilian Cocktail
(BRAZIL)

"*Caipirinha* literally means the 'little hillbilly.' The people who drink cachaça, the liquor in the drink, are considered hillbillies: rough uncultured people," says Isabella Bravim. "Cachaça is very strong. Like tequila, it burns you on the way down. Caipirinha, with its sugar and crushed ice, is a softer, but still potent, drink."

CAIPIRINHA
High-Octane Brazilian Cocktail

Cook's Notes: Margarita fans will line up at the blender for seconds of these lime-infused libations. But bartender beware—they are as potent as they are tasty. The main ingredient is *cachaça,* a type of Brazilian rum that can be found in Portuguese/Brazilian neighborhoods in urban areas like Miami and Newark. Cachaça comes in two varieties, silver and gold (which are interchangeable in this concoction), and tastes like a cross between rum and *eau-de-vie.*

Serves 8

8 limes
2 cups cachaça, light rum, or vodka
1 cup superfine sugar
Crushed ice

1. Roll the limes on a work surface, pressing hard to bruise them slightly so they release more juice. Halve and squeeze 6 of the limes; you should have about ¾ cup juice. Halve the remaining 2 limes.
2. In a blender, combine the lime halves, lime juice, cachaça, and sugar. Blend until the lime halves are puréed, about 1 minute.
3. Pour the mixture into glasses filled with crushed ice, and serve immediately.

Nguzo Saba

Umoja (Unity)
Kujichagulia (Self-determination)
Ujima (Collective Work and Responsibility)
Ujamaa (Cooperative Economics)
Nia (Purpose)
Kuumba (Creativity)
Imani (Faith)

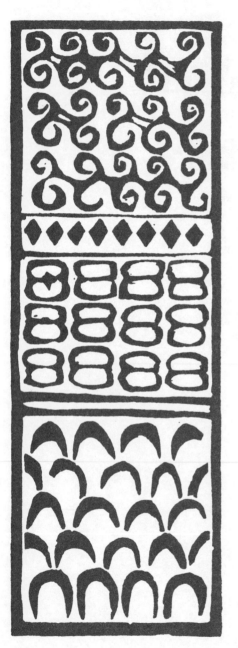

The moon moves slowly, but it crosses the town.

Ashanti proverb

Faith (Imani) and Purpose (Nia): that's what the Ashanti adage symbolizes to me. For almost four centuries black men and women, famous and obscure, have stood up to prejudice. They have sought constructive ways to fight it and to advance our position in American society. They have exhibited faith in their actions, despite apparent setbacks. They have continued to fight as if their success were as inevitable as the course of the moon.

Ida B. Wells is a vivid example of one of those who toiled for justice for black Americans. During her long career in journalism, she wrote about lynching, and kept track and published the numbers, hoping to draw public attention to the issue. Wells was born in Holly Springs, Mississippi, in 1869. Although she was only fourteen years old when her parents died of yellow fever, she raised her four younger siblings and still continued her education. She had to leave the South when she was twenty-three, after writing that the reason three black grocers from Memphis had been lynched was because they were successfully competing with white grocers.

This extract from Wells's autobiography, *Crusade for Justice*, is about her efforts to get a fair trial for twelve black men. The "riot" Wells refers to occurred when whites poured through the streets of an Arkansas town after black farmers refused to sell their cotton for less than market value. Yes, at times in her account Wells is self-congratulatory. But she also illustrates the Nguzo Saba in her life in general, and in this chapter in particular, where she demonstrates Unity (Umoja), Collective Work and Responsibility (Ujima), and Purpose (Nia) in her resolve to free the falsely jailed young men; Creativity (Kuumba) in the way she went about bringing attention to their case; Self-determination (Kujichagulia) in ignoring people who said what she was doing was impossible; and Faith (Imani) in her belief that her efforts were not in vain.

I arrived late at the September meeting, and inquired if any action had been taken about the Elaine, Arkansas, riot, which had taken place the week before.

Mr. Taylor [President of the Equal Rights League in Chicago] said they had considered it. "But," I said, "Mr. President, what have you *done* about it?" He replied, "There is nothing we can do." I said, "We can at least protest against it and let the world know that there is one organization of Negroes which refuses to be silent under such an outrage. I move, Mr. President, that we appoint a committee to send resolutions of protest to the President of the United States, Senator McCormick, Congressman Madden, and Governor Brough of Arkansas."

This was done and I was made chairman of the committee which sent letters to each of the officials named.

When Congressman Madden received his letter, he wired to Mr. DePriest [one of the letter signers] asking the names of the men lynched and other details, showing that he had not known of the riot. Mr. DePriest sent the telegram to me with the request that I answer it. This I did, and I took the reply to his office so that he might sign it,

271

which he did. Mr. DePriest then invited me to the following Sunday meeting of the People's Movement to tell them about it and bring a good strong resolution for them to act upon. I was very pleased to accept this first invitation, especially as he said he wanted me to come at once to the platform and he would stop the program to enable me to present it.

A letter of mine had already appeared in the Chicago *Defender* calling attention to the fact that the riot had been precipitated by the refusal of colored men to sell their cotton below market price because they had an organization which advised them so to do. I appealed to the colored people of the country to use their influence and money for those twelve men, who had been found guilty of murder in the first degree and then sentenced to be electrocuted.

This letter published in the *Defender* had a widespread response. Many people all over the country sent in contributions to assist in securing legal talent. One of the letters received came from one of the twelve men who said that they were so glad to see "the piece that the people in Chicago had spoke for them in the *Defender*." They thanked us for what had been said and done, and said it was the first word or offer of help they had from their own people. The letter ended by saying that if I had anything that I wanted them to know to send the reply to a certain address in Little Rock. For after scores of helpless Negroes were killed, scores more of them were herded into prison in Helena, Arkansas, where the mob tried to lynch them and where they were shocked by electricity, beaten, and tortured to make them confess they had a conspiracy to kill white folks. After the mockery of a trial, twelve of them were sentenced to be electrocuted.

The resolution I offered at the People's Movement that Sunday afternoon said that thousands of Negroes had left Arkansas because of dreadful treatment and were now living in Chicago; and that we pledged ourselves that if those twelve men were electrocuted we would use our influence to bring a thousand persons in that meeting that afternoon, and the resolution was unanimously adopted.

It was sent to Governor Brough, and it was the only one of the resolutions of protest he received to which he paid any heed. When he got our resolution he said he was going to let his own people there in Arkansas decide the matter. Our pledge in it was one that he could not very well ignore.

Accordingly, he [Governor Brough] called a conference of white and colored people. The spokesmen for the colored people were Bishop J. C. Connor of the A.M.E. church, Rev. Morris, president of the National Baptist Convention, and Dr. J. C. Booker; they were invited to express their opinion as to whether those twelve men had received a fair trial. Each one was duty bound to say they had not. Governor Brough then announced that he would see that the prisoners had a new trial. As a result of this promise, they were not electrocuted on the date originally planned, but were removed to the penitentiary at Little Rock while awaiting a new trial.

I took the train for Little Rock in January 1922, arrived there Sunday morning, and went directly to the address that had been given me in the letter sent me by one of the twelve men. I found the wives and mothers preparing to go up to the penitentiary on a visit to their sons and husbands. I made myself look as inconspicuous as possible, joined them, and thus had no trouble whatsoever in gaining entrance to the prison. It was my first return to the South since I had been banished thirty years before.

When we came into the building in which these twelve men were incarcerated, we were readily admitted. Mrs. Moore, the leading spirit among the wives, who was well known because of her frequent visits, said, "Boys, come and shake hands with my cousin who has come from Saint Louis to see me." The iron bars were wide enough apart to enable us to shake hands.

When we got up close to the bars, Mrs. Moore whispered, "This is Mrs. Barnett from Chicago." An expression of joy spread over their faces, but I put my finger to my lips and cautioned them not to let on, and immediately a mask seemed to drop over the features of each

273

one. I talked to them about their experiences, asked them to write down everything they could recollect about the rioting, and what befell each one of them.

I asked them also to tell me the number of acres of land they had tilled during the year, how much cotton and corn they had raised, and how many heads of cattle and hogs they owned, and be sure to say what had become of it all. They told me that since they had been moved to Little Rock they had been treated with a good deal of fairness and consideration; but that while they were in jail in Helena they were in constant torment. First a mob tried to get into the jail to lynch them. Then they were beaten, given electric shocks, and in every possible way terrorized in an effort to force them to confess that their organization was a conspiracy for the purpose of murdering white people and confiscating their property.

Then Mrs. Moore said, "Boys, don't you want to sing for my cousin?" Whereupon they sang a song of their own composition and many others. I listened to those men sing and pray and give testimony from their overburdened hearts, and sometimes the women would take up the refrain. They shed tears, and the burden of their talk and their prayers was of the hereafter.

Finally I got up and walked close to the bars and said to them in a low tone, "I have been listening to you for nearly two hours. You have talked and sung and prayed about dying, and forgiving your enemies, and of feeling sure that you are going to be received in the New Jerusalem because your God knows that you are innocent of the offense for which you expect to be electrocuted. But why don't you pray to live and ask to be freed? The God you serve is the God of Paul and Silas who opened their prison gates, and if you have all the faith you say you have, you ought to believe that He will open your prison doors too.

"If you do believe that, let all of your songs and prayers hereafter be songs of faith and hope that God will set you free; that the judges who have to pass on your cases will be given the wisdom and courage to decide in your behalf. Quit talking about dying; if you believe your God is all-powerful, believe He is powerful enough to open these prison doors, and say so. Dying is the last thing you ought to even think about, much less talk about. Pray to live and believe you are going to get out."

I went away and spent nearly all night writing down the experiences of the women who were also put in prison in Helena, and within two days I had written statements of each one of those twelve men of the facts I had requested. It is a terrible indictment of white civilization and Christianity. It shows that the white people did just what they accused the Negroes of doing: murdered them and stole their crops, their stock, and their household goods. And even then they were invoking the law to put the seal of approval on their deeds by executing those twelve men who were found guilty after six minutes' deliberation!

In the meantime the lawyers who had been engaged by the colored people themselves had included Mr. Scipio Jones, a colored lawyer there. Mr. Jones, hearing I was in town, sent for me to come to his office. When I got there, he said, "Well, Mrs. Barnett, when the matter was first broached, I didn't believe we had a ghost of a chance. Since then a new trial has been granted, colored people of the state themselves are organized, and they are raising money all over the United States to help in this case." I visited the committee which had been organized to receive funds and complimented them that they had at last gotten a move on themselves in the effort to defend and protect innocent men of the race.

The following winter I came home one Sunday evening and knocked on the door for admittance. A strange young man opened it. He said, "Good evening, Mrs. Barnett. Do you know who I am?"

"I do not," I said.

He said, "I am one of the twelve men that you came down to Arkansas about last year."

He was well dressed and had been living in Chicago for three

CARRINGTON

months; he said he had been looking for me all that time. He wanted to tell me how much he felt indebted for my efforts.

When my family came in to be introduced, he said, "Mrs. Barnett told us to quit talking about dying, that if we really had faith in the God we worshiped we ought to pray to him to open our prison doors, like he did for Paul and Silas. After that," he said, "we never talked about dying any more, but did as she told us, and now every last one of us is out and enjoying his freedom."

Brer Rabbit strikes again, in another of Julius Lester's adaptations of the Uncle Remus stories. This yarn is from Lester's *More Tales of Uncle Remus: Further Adventures of Brer Rabbit, His Friends, Enemies and Others*. The story is wonderful for Kwanzaa because it illustrates Brer Rabbit's Creativity (Kuumba). It also illustrates, by its absence in Brer Bear, the need for Unity (Umoja), Collective Work and Responsibility (Ujima), and Cooperative Economics (Ujamaa). In short, in a time of famine (and you can take that literally or figuratively), the honey of life needs to be spread around. Ask trumpeter Wynton Marsalis, who unselfishly makes time to visit high schools to conduct jazz workshops and whose ensemble has helped launch a new generation of jazz musicians, how important this is.

One year famine came to the community. The animals put their seed in the ground to make a crop, but the sky turned to iron and not a drop of rain fell. The leaves on the trees looked like they were going to turn to powder, and the ground was like it had been cooked. Old Man Hungriness had taken off his clothes and was parading around everywhere.

All the animals—horn, claw, and wing—lived there in the community together, and they all shared the same fate. When times were good, they all prospered. And when times were bad, they all suffered.

When the famine came, it was one of the suffering times. Wasn't no food to be had, no money, and no jobs. It was all the animals could do to scuffle along and make the buckle and tongue meet. Most of them went to bed hungry every night.

All of them, that is, except Brer Bear. The skinnier they got, the fatter he got. He was just wallowing in fat. Shoots! Brer Bear was so fat, he couldn't keep the flies off himself.

Everyday the animals talked among themselves about how come Brer Bear was so fat and they were so skinny. Brer Rabbit was tired of talking and decided to keep an eye on Brer Bear.

Before long he noticed that Brer Bear was acting mighty strange. Instead of staying up at night talking politics and watching television, he was going to bed same time as the chickens and was up and gone by first light. It wasn't natural to go to bed with the sun and get up with it. If God had meant for folks to live like that, he wouldn't have invented electricity.

One night Brer Rabbit went over to Brer Bear's house. He scraped his foot on the porch and cleared his throat. Miz Brune . . . came to the door, and when she saw it was Brer Rabbit, she invited him in out of the evening chill.

Miz Brune pulled him a chair up close to the fireplace, and Brer Rabbit crossed his legs and allowed as to how he hadn't seen Brer Bear in a coon's age.

"Times is so hard," Miz Brune said, "that my ol' man been working soon and late just to make both ends meet." She got up and said she had to fix a bag of ashes for Brer Bear to take to work with him in the morning.

"What in the world Brer Bear do with a bag of ashes, Miz Brune?"

She laughed and said she didn't know. "But I got to get a bag together every night and leave it for him in the corner by the chimney."

"Where is Brer Bear?"

"You sit here long enough, you won't have to ask where he at 'cause you be hearing him." She laughed. "I ain't never heard nobody snore like he do."

They chatted on for a while longer, and then Brer Rabbit said it was time for him to be getting on down the road. But he didn't go no farther than it took to find a place where he could hide and watch the house. He spent the night there, chasing lightning bugs and getting the frogs all confused by making frog sounds.

Long about the time the chickens started crowing up the sun, Brer Bear came out of the house, the bag of ashes over his shoulder, and made for the woods. Brer Rabbit was scared to follow too close. First thing he knew, Brer Bear was out of sight, and for the life of him Brer Rabbit couldn't figure out which way he'd gone.

Brer Rabbit went home, worrying about what Brer Bear could be doing with a bag of ashes.

That night he went back to Brer Bear's house. After he was sure Miz Brune was good and asleep, he sneaked in and found the bag of ashes next to the chimney. He picked it up. It was sho' 'nuf heavy. He set the bag down and tore a tiny hole in one corner. Some of the ashes got up his nose, and he was about to sneeze. He held his breath and ran out of the house, and when that sneeze came out—goodness gracious!—the chickens started cackling and Sister Moon swayed for a minute like she wasn't sure she was going to be able to hang on to her perch. Brer Rabbit decided to get on out of there.

When morning came, he went back along the way Brer Bear had gone the day before until he saw a little trail of ashes. That was the reason he'd put the hole in the sack. Everytime Brer Bear took a step, he jolted the ashes out. Brer Rabbit followed the ashes, uphill and downhill, through bushes and through briars, until he came on Brer Bear.

Now, what you think Brer Bear was doing? If you said he was in a tree eating honey off a honeycomb, you would be right. He was eating the good stuff, the natural, stark-naked bee juice.

When Brer Rabbit saw him, though, he liked to have fainted, because Brer Bear had poured the sack of ashes over himself, and he was a horrible-looking sight. I reckon he'd covered himself with ashes so the bees wouldn't sting him. Brer Bear was way up in the tree, eating honey by the handful, with the bees zooming all around him. Brer Rabbit looked around, and everywhere were hollow poplar trees, and every one was so full of honeycombs that the honey was dripping down the sides.

Brer Rabbit watched Brer Bear eat honey until his stomach started saying *Want some! Want some!*

Brer Rabbit shouted up, "Please, Brer Bear! I'm awful hungry! I sho' would be pleased if you'd hand me down a handful of honey."

"You better get away from here, you trifling, good-for-nothing cottontail nuisance."

"Please, Brer Bear! Just a handful."

"Get on away from here before I come down and make you into a pair of gloves for one of my children."

The next day Brer Rabbit got all the animals together—horn, claw, and wing—and told 'em how come Brer Bear was rolling in fat.

"Don't understand how he could do that to us," Brer Possum said.

"He could've at least let us smell some of that honey even if we couldn't taste it," said Brer Rat.

"Speak for yourself. I want me some of that honey!" said Brer Fox.

"And we gon' feast on honey before the sun start running from the moon," said Brer Rabbit.

"How?" all the animals asked at once.

"We gon' start a hurricane!"

If the animals hadn't known Brer Rabbit so well, they would've thought he'd lost his mind. But if Brer Rabbit said he was going to start a hurricane, a hurricane was coming.

Brer Rabbit led them quietly out to the honey orchard. He put

all the big animals behind big trees and the little animals behind little trees.

"Now, when I holler, y'all rub and shake these trees."

He told all the ones with wings who could fly to get up in the trees. "When I holler, you beat your wings as hard as you can."

All the ones with wings who could run but not fly high he put in the weeds. "When I holler, run through the grass as hard as you can."

When everybody was in place, Brer Rabbit took a long rope, and he went way back in the woods. Then he ran toward the honey orchard, dragging the rope and yelling and hollering.

Brer Bear looked down from the top of the tree. "What's wrong, Brer Rabbit?"

"Hurricane coming! Hurricane coming! I got to go somewhere and tie myself to a tree before I get blown all the way to Jamoca Junction. Can't you hear it, Brer Bear?" Brer Rabbit hollered real loud.

The animals behind the trees started shaking them, and the birds in the weeds started running back and forth, and the birds in the trees started fluttering, and it sounded like the world was coming to an end.

Brer Bear scrambled out of that tree and hit the ground—*kerbiff!* "Brer Rabbit! Tie me to the tree with you! Tie me, too!"

The animals were into it now, and they were shaking the trees and fluttering and running back and forth and creating such a commotion that even Brer Rabbit started to get a little scared. He hurried and tied Brer Bear real tight to the tree, and when he tied the last knot, he called to the animals, "Come and look at Brer Bear!"

All the animals came and laughed at Brer Bear, and then they went to work on that honey orchard. They ate their fill and then took a lot of honey home for their wives and children. I expect that somebody came along eventually and untied Brer Bear.

John Jones was yet another African-American who put his comfort, indeed his very life, on the line to help other African-Americans, and to help this country realize its promise. I found Jones's story in William Loren Katz's eye-opening book *The Black West*. Jones shows Purpose (Nia) in his drive to set up a secure financial base, and Unity (Umoja), Collective Work and Responsibility (Ujima), and Cooperative Economics (Ujamaa) in using a portion of his money (not to mention his time) to better the lot of all black people. He also shows Creativity (Kuumba) in the nimbleness with which he lobbies to abolish slavery and end the "black laws." Black Americans today realize the need for Jones's flexibility.

In 1845, as antislavery agitation mounted in the nation, a young black man from North Carolina arrived in Chicago with only $3.50 in his pocket. He was destined to become a wealthy man and to play a vital part in the long battle against both slavery and discrimination. While his fellow residents admired his prosperity and forthright opposition to slavery and prejudice, few knew that their black neighbor was deeply involved in the illegal underground railroad and the activities of John Brown. John Jones's well-bred manner and business acumen cloaked his fine hand for conspiracy.

Born in North Carolina in 1816 to a German father and a free black mother, John Jones was apprenticed to a trader who pledged to protect him from possible enslavement. After working in Memphis and Alton, Jones returned to North Carolina when he was twenty-two and secured his "free papers." In 1841 he married Mary Richardson, daughter of a blacksmith. The couple left for Chicago in 1845, and starting with that $3.50, eventually set up both a home and a tailoring establishment. Here Jones taught himself to read and write.

Although he devoted enough time to business to amass a fortune of $100,000, his real interest lay in aiding his oppressed fellow black men. He became active in the underground railroad; his home became one of its many "stations." As a man who had much to lose if discovered, he was able to convince many less fortunate black people to lend their homes to the cause. When in 1853 the state of Illinois passed a law halting black immigration, Jones took a leading part in battling this latest of "black laws." He lectured, donated money, and in 1864 published his pamphlet *The Black Laws of Illinois and a Few Reasons Why They Should Be Repealed.* He pointed out that rich white men who employed black wagon drivers (as most did) stood to lose enormous amounts of money if these wagons were robbed. Since the black laws prohibited testimony from blacks, their drivers would never be allowed to provide evidence to convict thieves. He also pointed out that he was paying taxes on $30,000 in assets and yet was denied the vote. Jones escalated his civil rights activities during the Civil War, organizing black and white people in every part of the state to demand repeal of black laws and effectively lobbying for repeal in the state capital. In January 1865, Illinois revoked its black laws, and a few months later it became the first state to adopt the Thirteenth Amendment, abolishing slavery.

By this time the need for illegal action had passed and John Jones, seeing the value of political involvement, sought election to the Cook County Board of Commissioners. He was elected and then re-elected. From this public rostrum he battled to integrate the Chicago public schools, and in 1874, his last year in office, he achieved success.

By the time of his death in 1879, John Jones was a wealthy and prominent Chicagoan. He was buried at the Graceland Cemetery near the grave of Allan Pinkerton, head of the Union Army's secret service and a fellow supporter of the underground railroad and John Brown.

DESSERTS

BLACKBERRY SLUMP
(UNITED STATES)

"This recipe is from Miss Emma, a friend of the family's when I was growing up, and an excellent cook," says Audie Odum-Stallato. "Every now and then if I had picked too many blackberries for preserves or the pie my mother was making, I would bring the extras to Miss Emma's house and she would make blackberries with dumplings. She'd start cooking it and before you knew it she would be done, and of course we'd *have* to stay for dinner. And then dessert!"

BLACKBERRY SLUMP

Cook's Notes: A slump is a cousin of the baked cobbler, only simmered on top of the stove. It must be served hot from the skillet, preferably with a big scoop of the best vanilla ice cream you can find (read "homemade").

Serves 6

BLACKBERRY STEW:
5 cups fresh blackberries
⅔ cup granulated sugar
⅔ cup water
1 teaspoon vanilla extract

SWEET DUMPLINGS:
1¾ cups all-purpose flour
2 tablespoons granulated sugar
2½ teaspoons baking powder
¾ teaspoon salt
⅓ cup unsalted butter, chilled, cut into ½-inch pieces
½ cup plus 3 tablespoons milk

1 pint vanilla ice cream, preferably homemade

1. Make the blackberry stew: In a 10-inch skillet, bring the blackberries, sugar, and water to a boil over medium heat, stirring occasionally to help dissolve the sugar. Reduce the heat to low and simmer until slightly thickened, about 5 minutes. Stir in the vanilla.
2. Meanwhile, make the sweet dumplings: Sift the flour, sugar, baking powder, and salt into a medium bowl. Using a pastry blender or two

knives, cut the butter into the flour mixture until it resembles coarse meal. Stir in the milk just until a soft dough forms.

3. Drop the dough by heaping tablespoons into the simmering stew, making 12 dumplings. Simmer, uncovered, for 10 minutes. Then cover, and simmer until the dumplings are cooked through, 10 to 12 minutes.

4. Divide the slump evenly among six dessert bowls. Top each with a scoop of vanilla ice cream, and serve immediately.

SNOWBALL CAKE

SNOWBALL CAKE
(UNITED STATES)

"Every summer my family and I would go to the South—Georgia, Florida, and North and South Carolina—to see all our relatives," remembers Audie Odum-Stallato. "We'd bounce around from one relative's house to the next. My cousin Hady Mae (everyone in the South seemed to be named "Mae"), in Appleton, South Carolina, made wonderful cakes of all kinds. The snowball, or coconut, cake seemed to be a kind of hallmark of the South. Almost everyone had a recipe for it. You'd have it on birthdays, holidays, get-togethers . . . just about anytime you sat down for dessert, it seemed.

My grandmother would toast the coconut before putting it on the cake. It gives the cake a nice color, makes it more 'coconutty,' and adds a bit of crunch. But some people like the coconut to remain white so that the cake really looks like a snowball."

Serves 8

COCONUT CAKE:
2 cups all-purpose flour
1 tablespoon baking powder
1 teaspoon salt
¾ cup milk
¼ cup canned unsweetened coconut milk (not "cream of coconut")
1 teaspoon vanilla extract
8 tablespoons (1 stick) unsalted butter, at cool room temperature
1½ cups granulated sugar
3 large eggs, at room temperature

COCONUT FROSTING:
3 cups confectioners' sugar, sifted
⅓ cup unsalted butter, at cool room temperature
2 tablespoons milk
1 teaspoon vanilla extract
¼ teaspoon coconut extract
1½ cups sweetened coconut flakes

1. Make the cake: Position a rack in the top third of the oven, and preheat to 350°. Lightly butter two 8-inch round, 1½-inch-deep, cake pans. Line the bottom of each pan with a circle of waxed paper. Dust the sides of the pans with flour, and tap out the excess.
2. In a medium bowl, sift together the flour, baking powder, and salt. In a 2-cup measuring cup, combine the milk, coconut milk, and vanilla.

3. Using a hand-held electric mixer set at high speed, cream the butter and granulated sugar together in a large bowl until light in color and texture, about 2 minutes. Add the eggs, one at a time, beating well after each addition. In thirds, alternately add the flour and milk mixtures, beating just until mixed after each addition, scraping the sides of the bowl well with a rubber spatula as necessary. Divide the batter evenly between the prepared cake pans, smoothing the tops.

4. Bake until the cakes are golden brown and a toothpick inserted in the center comes out clean, 25 to 30 minutes. Cool the cakes in the pans on wire racks for 10 minutes. Then run a knife around the inside of the pans to release the cakes, and invert them onto the wire racks. Remove the cake pans and the waxed paper, and allow to cool completely.

5. Make the frosting: In a large bowl, using a hand-held electric mixer set at low speed, mix the confectioners' sugar and butter until crumbly. Add the milk, vanilla, and coconut extract, and mix until smooth.

6. Brush away any loose crumbs from the cooled cake layers. Place one layer, rounded side down, onto a serving platter. Spread about ½ cup of the frosting over the layer. Top with the second layer, rounded side up. Frost the top and sides of the cake with the remaining frosting. Using your cupped hand, press the coconut onto the top and sides of the cake. Let it stand at room temperature until ready to serve.

CARRINGTON

GINGER CUSTARD ICE CREAM
(UNITED STATES)

"My proudest cooking achievement has been ginger custard ice cream, which I have finally more or less perfected," says Catherine Bailey. "My guests, I believe, would not come if I left it off the menu! I use the food processor to prepare the fresh gingerroot, because chopping ginger by hand would be much too tiring, especially with all the other time-consuming steps involved—making the candied ginger, the custard, and freezing and storing all that."

GINGER CUSTARD ICE CREAM

Makes about 2 quarts, about 8 servings

½ pound fresh ginger, peeled and sliced paper-thin
2 cups water
2¼ cups granulated sugar
1 envelope plain unflavored gelatin
2 cups milk, chilled
⅛ teaspoon salt
2 large eggs, separated, at room temperature
1 cup half-and-half
1 cup heavy (whipping) cream

1. In a small saucepan, bring the ginger and water to a simmer over low heat. Cook, partially covered, until the ginger is quite soft, about 1 hour. Process the ginger and the cooking liquid in a blender until smooth.
2. Return the ginger purée to the saucepan, and cook over medium heat, stirring often, until it is reduced to ¾ cup, about 10 minutes. Then stir in ¾ cup of the sugar and cook, stirring often, until the sugar has dissolved and the mixture is quite thick, about 5 minutes. Set the ginger jam aside.
3. In a small bowl, sprinkle the gelatin over ¼ cup of the cold milk; let it stand for 5 minutes.
4. In a heavy medium saucepan, combine the remaining 1¾ cups milk, 1½ cups sugar, and salt, and bring just to a low simmer over medium heat.
5. In a grease-free medium bowl, using a hand-held electric mixer set at low speed, beat the egg whites until foamy. Increase the speed to high, and beat just until stiff peaks form.

6. In a medium bowl, whisk the egg yolks until thickened and pale yellow. Gradually whisk the hot milk mixture into the yolks. Return the yolk-milk mixture to the saucepan, and whisk in the beaten egg whites. Cook, stirring constantly with a wooden spatula, until a thermometer inserted in the mixture reads 170°. (The mixture will barely coat the wooden spatula.) Remove the pan from the heat, and add the gelatin mixture; whisk until the gelatin has dissolved. Whisk in the reserved ginger jam. Using a wooden spoon, rub the mixture through a fine-mesh sieve set over a large bowl, discarding the ginger fibers left in the sieve. Stir the half-and-half into the ginger custard.

7. In a chilled medium bowl, whip the heavy cream until soft peaks form. Whisk the whipped cream into the ginger custard. Cover with plastic wrap and refrigerate until well chilled, at least 4 hours or overnight.

8. Pour the ginger custard into the freezing container of an ice cream mixer, and freeze according to the manufacturer's directions. Transfer the ice cream to an airtight container, and freeze in the freezer compartment of the refrigerator for at least 4 hours before serving.

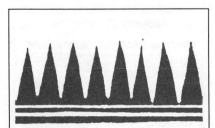

CONKIES
Individual Cornmeal and Raisin Puddings in Banana Leaves
(BARBADOS)

This Bajan favorite is probably descended from the Ghanaian dish *kenky*. Conkies can be made with meat, plantain, or, as it is in this recipe from Rita Springer, cornmeal. It is a traditional holiday snack. "We used to make conkies on Guy Fawkes Day," notes Springer, referring to the British holiday celebrating the discovery of a plot to blow up their parliament. "Conkies were convenient because you did a lot of walking around. Since Barbados became independent in 1966, we don't celebrate British holidays such as Guy Fawkes Day. Now we observe our independence on November 30, and conkies are eaten during that celebration."

CONKIES
Individual Cornmeal and Raisin Puddings in Banana Leaves

Cook's Notes: Please don't be put off by conkies' unusual combination of ingredients. They result in soul-soothing warm mini-puddings, similar to the New Englander's Indian pudding. If you can't find banana leaves, you can use aluminum foil and waxed paper wrappings, as described below, but the banana leaves add moisture and a subtle flavor that you won't get from substitutes. If you're not up to making forty conkies, the recipe can easily be halved. Simply freeze the remaining grated coconut for another time.

Makes 40 conkies

1 pound banana leaves, defrosted if frozen (available at Filipino and Latin American markets)
1⅓ cups packed light brown sugar
1 cup milk
2 large eggs
1 teaspoon ground cinnamon
1 teaspoon grated nutmeg
1 teaspoon almond extract
12 tablespoons (1½ sticks) unsalted butter, melted
2 cups yellow cornmeal, preferably stone-ground
½ cup all-purpose flour
1 teaspoon salt
1 coconut, finely shredded (see page 197)
¾ pound *calabaza* squash or sugar pumpkin, seeded, pared, and shredded

290

1 medium (8-ounce) *boniato* (*batata*) or sweet potato "Louisiana yam," peeled and shredded

½ cup dark raisins

1 cup heavy (whipping) cream

2 tablespoons confectioners' sugar

1 teaspoon vanilla extract

1. Using scissors, cut some of the banana leaves into forty 9- by 9-inch squares. Following the veins in the remaining leaves, tear off forty ¼-inch-wide strips about 12 inches long. In a large saucepan of boiling water, blanch the squares and strips until pliable, 1 to 2 minutes. Drain, rinse under cold water, and drain well. (Or cut out forty each aluminum foil and waxed paper squares.)

2. In a large bowl, whisk the brown sugar, milk, eggs, cinnamon, nutmeg, and almond extract until smooth. Whisk in the melted butter. Add the cornmeal, flour, and salt, and whisk well. Stir in the shredded coconut, *calabaza, boniato,* and raisins.

3. Place about 2 tablespoons of the cornmeal mixture in the center of a leaf square. Fold over the top and bottom of the square to completely enclose the filling, then fold in the sides to form a plump parcel. Lightly flatten the filling to an even thickness of about 1 inch. Using a leaf strip, tie up the parcel to keep the side flaps from unfolding. (Or place the filling on a waxed paper–lined foil square, then proceed.) Continue with the remaining ingredients.

4. Place a steamer in the bottom of a large saucepan. Add enough boiling water to come within ½ inch of the steamer bottom. Arrange the packets, standing up in concentric circles, in the steamer. Cover tightly and steam over medium-low heat until the packets are firm, about 1 hour, adding more boiling water if necessary.

5. In a chilled medium bowl, whip the heavy cream just until it forms soft peaks. Beat in the confectioners' sugar and vanilla.

6. To serve, place the packets on dessert plates. Let guests unwrap their own packets, and serve the whipped cream on the side.

PEACHES AND VANILLA BEAN ICE CREAM
(UNITED STATES)

"We had pear and peach trees on our farm, but peach trees were very special because we didn't have many of them," remembers Mavis Young of her Texas childhood. "My mom would can the peaches we didn't eat, and we'd have them during the months they were not in season. One of the special things we made with the peaches was peach ice cream. Turning the crank of the ice cream freezer was the children's job. We'd want to be the first or last to turn it. The first one had the easiest time of turning the crank since nothing was frozen yet; the last one got to open it and pull out the dasher, and eat the peaches that clung to it. That was a big treat!"

PEACHES AND VANILLA BEAN ICE CREAM

Cook's Notes: Fresh wintertime peaches (from New Zealand or Chile) can be found at many groceries and specialty markets in December. You can also use 2 (8-ounce) cans of drained canned peaches if you prefer and skip Step 1. Reserve ⅓ cup of the peach syrup to use in place of the fresh peaches' macerated juices. In either case, your guests will savor the extraordinary taste of this homemade peach ice cream.

Makes 3 quarts, about 12 servings

4 ripe medium peaches, pitted and chopped into ¼-inch dice
1½ cups granulated sugar
4 cups milk
1 tablespoon all-purpose flour
2 cups heavy (whipping) cream
3 large eggs
1 vanilla bean, split

1. Toss the peaches with ¼ cup of the sugar in a medium bowl. Cover tightly with plastic wrap, and refrigerate until the peaches give off their juice, at least 4 hours or overnight.
2. In a small bowl, whisk ½ cup of the milk with the flour.
3. Combine the remaining 3½ cups milk with the heavy cream and the vanilla bean in a medium saucepan, and cook over medium-high heat until small bubbles appear around the edges of the liquid, about 3 minutes.
4. Whisk the eggs and remaining 1¼ cups sugar in a heavy medium saucepan until well blended. Gradually whisk in the flour-milk mixture, then the scalded milk-cream mixture. Cook over low heat, stirring constantly with a wooden spoon, until an instant-reading thermometer

reads 170°. (The mixture will lightly coat the spoon.) Don't let the mixture come near a boil, or the eggs will scramble. Immediately strain the custard through a sieve placed over a medium bowl. Using the tip of a small knife, scrape the tiny seeds out of the vanilla bean into the custard, and discard the bean. Place the bowl of custard in a larger bowl of iced water.

5. In a food processor or blender, purée about half of the chopped peaches with their juice. Stir the purée into the custard. Let it stand, stirring often, until chilled, about 30 minutes. Stir in the remaining chopped peaches and juice.

6. Pour the mixture into the container of an ice cream maker, and freeze according to the manufacturer's directions. (If your ice cream machine has less than a 6-quart capacity, freeze the mixture in batches, using fresh ice and salt as necessary for each batch.)

7. Transfer the ice cream to a large bowl, cover tightly with plastic wrap, and freeze for at least 4 hours before serving, or overnight. (Homemade ice cream is best if enjoyed within 24 hours.)

SWEET POTATO TARTS IN PEANUT BUTTER CRUSTS
(UNITED STATES)

"To accompany the ice cream that we often serve, we may have cookies or some kind of cake," explains Catherine Bailey. "An unusual choice that has become a favorite is sweet potato tarts in peanut butter crusts."

SWEET POTATO TARTS IN PEANUT BUTTER CRUSTS

Makes 18 tarts

PEANUT BUTTER PASTRY:

2½ cups all-purpose flour

1 teaspoon baking powder

¼ teaspoon salt

8 tablespoons (1 stick) margarine, chilled, cut into ¼-inch cubes

½ cup smooth peanut butter, at room temperature

⅓ cup ice water

SWEET POTATO FILLING:

2 medium sweet potatoes, "Louisiana yams," about 1 pound

8 tablespoons (1 stick) unsalted butter, softened

1½ cups granulated sugar

1 teaspoon vanilla extract

1 teaspoon ground cinnamon

1 teaspoon grated nutmeg

½ teaspoon salt

⅛ teaspoon ground allspice

1 cup evaporated milk

2 large eggs, well beaten

¾ cup heavy (whipping) cream, chilled

2 tablespoons confectioners' sugar

⅓ cup finely chopped unsalted peanuts, for garnish (optional)

1. Make the pastry dough: In a large bowl, whisk together the flour, baking powder, and salt. Using a pastry blender or two knives, cut

in the margarine and peanut butter until the mixture resembles coarse meal. Tossing the flour mixture with a fork, sprinkle in the ice water, mixing just until the dough is moist enough to hold together when pinched between your thumb and forefinger. (You may have to add more ice water.) Gather the dough up into a thick flat disk, and wrap it in waxed paper. Refrigerate for at least 1 hour or overnight.

2. Meanwhile, in a large saucepan of boiling water, cook the (unpeeled) sweet potatoes until tender when pierced with the tip of a knife, about 25 minutes. Drain, rinse under cold running water, and drain again. Allow the sweet potatoes to cool slightly, then pare and mash them. You should have 1½ cups mashed sweet potatoes.

3. In a large bowl, combine the warm mashed sweet potatoes with the butter, and stir until the butter has melted. Stir in the sugar, vanilla, cinnamon, nutmeg, salt, and allspice. Beat in the milk, then the eggs. Refrigerate filling, covered until ready to use, up to 8 hours.

4. On a lightly floured work surface, roll out half the dough to form a circle about 12 inches in diameter and ⅛ inch thick. Using a 4½-inch round cookie cutter or drinking glass, cut out pastry rounds. Gather up and reserve the scraps. Repeat with the remaining dough. Lightly knead the scraps together and roll them out, repeating the procedure until you have eighteen pastry rounds.

5. Preheat the oven to 350°. Lightly butter eighteen 3-inch muffin cups.

6. Fit the pastry rounds into the muffin cups, pressing the pastry against the sides to remove any air bubbles. Using a fork, prick the bottom and sides of the pastry shells well. Fill each pastry shell with about ¼ cup of filling.

7. Bake until a knife inserted in the center of the filling comes out clean, 35 to 40 minutes. Cool the tarts in the tins for 10 minutes. Then carefully run a dinner knife around the inside of each cup to release the pastry. Tilting the tin to help them slide out easily, use the knife as an aid to lift out the tarts. Cool the tarts to room temperature.

COCONUT MOUSSE WITH RUM-SOAKED CHERRIES
(BARBADOS)

"Coconut mousse is only one way of using coconut in a dessert form, and only one of the many recipes my mother made with it," says Rita Springer. "It's a very popular fruit."

8. In a chilled medium bowl, whip the cream and confectioners' sugar just until soft peaks form. Top each tart with a dollop of whipped cream, and sprinkle with chopped peanuts if desired. (The tarts are also delicious warm, with the whipped cream and peanuts served on the side, or chilled.)

COCONUT MOUSSE WITH RUM-SOAKED CHERRIES

Serves 6 to 8

3 cups fresh coconut milk (from 1 coconut; see page 197)
1 (12-ounce) can evaporated milk
½ cup plus 2 tablespoons superfine sugar
½ cup shredded fresh coconut (reserved after making coconut milk)
¼ teaspoon almond extract
3 envelopes plain unflavored gelatin
½ cup cold water
2 large egg whites, at room temperature
1½ pounds fresh cherries, pitted and coarsely chopped
3 tablespoons dark rum or kirsch

1. In a large bowl, combine the coconut milk, evaporated milk, ¼ cup plus 2 tablespoons of the sugar, shredded coconut, and almond extract. Mix thoroughly.
2. Sprinkle the gelatin over the cold water in a small bowl, and let it stand for 5 minutes. Then place the bowl in a small saucepan of simmering water. Stir the gelatin mixture often until the gelatin has

dissolved, about 3 minutes. Stir about 1 cup of the coconut mixture into the gelatin. Then whisk the gelatin mixture into the remaining coconut mixture.

3. Place the bowl of coconut mixture in a larger bowl filled with iced water. Let it stand, stirring often, until partially set, about 5 minutes. Remove the bowl from the iced water.

4. In a small grease-free bowl, using a hand-held electric mixer set at low speed, beat the egg whites until foamy. Increase the speed to high, and beat just until soft peaks form. Fold the whites into the coconut mixture.

5. Lightly oil a 1-quart fluted mold. Pour in the coconut mousse, smoothing the top with a rubber spatula, and cover tightly with plastic wrap. Refrigerate for at least 6 hours or overnight.

6. In a medium bowl, combine the chopped cherries, remaining ¼ cup sugar, and rum. Cover and refrigerate for at least 4 hours or overnight.

7. To unmold the mousse, wet a clean kitchen towel with hot water and wring it out. Invert the mold onto a serving platter, and wrap the hot moist towel around the mold; let it stand for 30 seconds, and remove the towel. Hold the mold and the platter together, and shake firmly once or twice to unmold the mousse onto the platter. Remove the mold.

8. Cut the mousse into wedges, and transfer them to dessert plates. Spoon marinated cherries and their juice over each serving.

CARRINGTON

PASSION FRUIT MOUSSE WITH TROPICAL FRUITS
(BRAZIL)

"Passion Fruit Mousse is something I created when someone wanted me to do the food for a reception," says Isabella Bravim. "I wanted to do something new, something no one would have had before.

"Passion fruit is used a lot, especially in the Brazilian state of Espírito Santo, which has a lot of African and Italian influence in the culture. Throughout Brazil you'll find all kinds of things made with the fruit: passion fruit tea, ice cream, you name it."

PASSION FRUIT MOUSSE WITH TROPICAL FRUITS

Serves 8

20 ripe passion fruits (see Note)
6 large eggs, separated, at room temperature
1¾ cups granulated sugar
2 tablespoons cornstarch
Grated zest of 1 large lemon
2 packages plain unflavored gelatin
6 tablespoons cold water
1 ripe papaya, peeled, seeded, and cut into ½-inch-thick slices
1 ripe mango, pitted, peeled, and cut into ½-inch-thick slices
2 ripe kiwis, peeled and cut crosswise into ¼-inch-thick rounds
1 medium banana, peeled and cut into ¼-inch-thick rounds
Grated zest and juice of 1 medium lime

1. Using a serrated knife, cut the passion fruits in half crosswise. Using a dessert spoon, scoop the yellow pulp and seeds out of the shells and place them in a fine sieve set over a medium bowl.
2. Using a wooden spoon, rub the pulp in the sieve to extract the juices; discard the seeds in the sieve. You should have ¾ cup plus 2 tablespoons juice.
3. In the top part of a double boiler, whisk the egg yolks with 1½ cups of the sugar until thick and pale yellow, about 2 minutes. Whisk in the passion fruit juice and cornstarch.
4. Cook the juice mixture over simmering water, stirring constantly with a wooden spoon, until a thermometer inserted in the mixture reads 175° and it lightly coats the spoon, 8 to 10 minutes. Stir in the

lemon zest. Remove the top of the double boiler from the heat.

5. In a small bowl, sprinkle the gelatin over the cold water; let it stand for 5 minutes. Then place the bowl in a small saucepan of simmering water, and stir constantly until the gelatin has dissolved, about 2 minutes. Whisk the gelatin into the passion fruit mixture. Refrigerate, whisking occasionally, until the mixture is cool and beginning to set, about 15 minutes.

6. In a large grease-free bowl, using a hand-held electric mixer set at low speed, beat the egg whites until foamy. Increase the speed to high and beat just until the whites form soft peaks. Gradually beat in the remaining ¼ cup sugar, beating just until the whites form stiff, shiny peaks. Stir about one fourth of the beaten whites into the passion fruit mixture. Then gently fold in the remaining whites.

7. Lightly grease a 2-quart fluted mold. Pour in the passion fruit mousse and smooth the top. Cover tightly with aluminum foil, and refrigerate until firm, at least 6 hours or overnight.

8. In a large bowl, combine the papaya, mango, kiwis, banana, lime zest, and lime juice. Cover tightly with plastic wrap and refrigerate until ready to serve, up to 1 day.

9. To unmold the mousse, wet a clean kitchen towel with hot water and wring it out. Invert the mold onto a serving platter, and wrap the hot, moist towel around the mold; let it stand for 30 seconds, and then remove the towel. Hold the mold and the platter together and shake firmly once or twice to unmold the mousse. Remove the mold.

10. Surround the mousse with the tropical fruits. Cut the mousse into wedges, and garnish each serving with a spoonful of the fruit.

NOTE: You may substitute ¾ cup bottled passion fruit juice (available at health food stores) plus 2 tablespoons passion fruit liqueur (such as La Grande Passion) for the ripe passion fruit juice. Use only 1 cup sugar in Step 3.

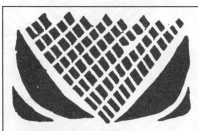

PEAR AND CUSTARD TART FRANÇAISE
(UNITED STATES)

On French-speaking islands such as Haiti, Guadeloupe, and Martinique, the haute cuisine influence is strongly felt. This is another Caribbean-inspired favorite contributed by Dee Dee Dailey.

PEAR AND CUSTARD TART FRANÇAISE

Cook's Notes: This classic tart features pears, one of winter's best fruit values. Bosc pears are your best choice, as they hold their shape well after baking and won't give off a lot of juice, which could dilute the custard and throw off the baking times.

Serves 8 to 10

BUTTERY TART DOUGH:

1¼ cups all-purpose flour

1 tablespoon packed light brown sugar

½ teaspoon salt

8 tablespoons (1 stick) unsalted butter, cut into ¼-inch cubes

3 tablespoons ice water

1 egg yolk, lightly beaten

POACHED PEARS:

3 quarts water

2 tablespoons fresh lemon juice

4 firm baking pears, such as Bosc (about 2 pounds), peeled, halved, and cored

2 tablespoons packed light brown sugar

½ teaspoon ground cinnamon

¼ teaspoon grated nutmeg

CUSTARD:

1 cup half-and-half

2 large eggs

¼ cup granulated sugar

1 teaspoon vanilla extract

1. Make the dough: In a medium bowl, stir together the flour, brown sugar, and salt. Using a pastry blender or two knives, cut in the butter until the mixture resembles coarse meal. In a small bowl, mix together the ice water and egg yolk. Tossing with a fork, gradually sprinkle this into the flour mixture, tossing just until the mixture holds together when pressed between your thumb and forefinger. Gather up the dough to form a thick flat disk, and wrap it in waxed paper. Refrigerate for at least 1 hour or overnight.

2. Prepare the poached pears: In a large saucepan, bring the water and lemon juice to a simmer over medium-high heat. Add the pear halves, reduce the heat to low, and simmer just until the pears are tender when pierced with the tip of a sharp knife. Using a slotted spoon, carefully transfer the pears to a plate to cool slightly.

3. Position a rack in the bottom third of the oven, and preheat to 350°.

4. On a lightly floured work surface, roll out the dough to form a 14-inch circle about ⅛ inch thick. Transfer it to a 10½-inch fluted tart pan with removable bottom. Gently press the dough into the tart pan, leaving no air bubbles. Fold any excess dough inside the tart pan, pressing it against the sides of the pan so it rises ¼ inch above the rim.

5. Using a small sharp knife, cut three or four lengthwise slices through the pears, keeping the slices connected about ½ inch from the top of the pears. Arrange the pears in a spoke pattern on the pastry, stem ends pointing at the center. Spread out the slices in each pear slightly to form a fan design. Combine the brown sugar, cinnamon, and nutmeg in a small bowl; sprinkle this over the pears. Place the tart pan on a large baking sheet.

6. Prepare the custard: In a medium bowl, whisk together the half-and-half, eggs, sugar, and vanilla. Pour the custard into the center of the tart, allowing it to surround, but not cover, the pears. Carefully transfer the tart to the oven.

7. Bake until the custard is set and the tart crust is golden brown, 30 to 40 minutes. Cool the tart completely on a wire cake rack. Then lift the tart (still on the pan bottom) from the pan sides, and serve.

PEACHY BREAD PUDDING

Cook's Notes: Fresh peaches or nectarines could be used at Kwanzaa time if your market flies them in from Chile or New Zealand. This is a superlative dessert, even with the less pricey canned fruit.

Serves 4 to 6

2¼ cups milk
½ cup granulated sugar
2 large eggs
1 teaspoon vanilla extract
½ teaspoon grated nutmeg
6 slices day-old white bread, cut into 1-inch squares (about 2½ cups)
1 (8-ounce) can sliced peaches in heavy syrup, drained
½ cup dark or golden raisins

1. Preheat the oven to 350°. Lightly butter an 11- by 7-inch baking dish.
2. In a large bowl, whisk the milk, sugar, eggs, vanilla, and nutmeg until well mixed. Add the bread, peaches, and raisins; let stand 5 minutes. Transfer to the prepared baking dish.
3. Bake until the custard is set in the center (a knife inserted into it will not necessarily come out clean), about 50 minutes. Remove the pudding from the oven and let it stand for 10 minutes; serve warm. Or let it cool completely, cover, and refrigerate until chilled.

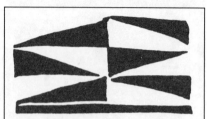

PEACHY BREAD PUDDING
(UNITED STATES)

"This recipe originated with my grandmother, who passed it on to my aunt," says Hiram Bonner of this bread pudding. "It was a staple dessert in our household. It gives me the feeling of the stability of home."

SOUR CREAM POUND CAKE

Cook's Notes: With the first buttery bite of this tender-crumbed, crunchy-topped cake, our minds raced at the myriad opportunities to use it—and *often!* It has since served as an excellent shortcake, a first-class trifle, a resting place for a scoop of ice cream drizzled with hot fudge sauce, and (perhaps most importantly) as the ultimate after-school treat with a cold glass of milk for dunking. While a vanilla flavor is most popular, some cooks add one of the following along with the vanilla for a variation: grated zest of 1 lemon or orange, 1 teaspoon orange blossom or rose water, ½ teaspoon rum or brandy extract.

Serves 8 to 10

3 cups cake flour
½ teaspoon salt
¼ teaspoon baking soda
½ pound (2 sticks) unsalted butter, at room temperature
3 cups granulated sugar
6 large eggs, separated, at room temperature
2 teaspoons vanilla extract
1¼ cups sour cream, at room temperature

1. Position a rack in the center of the oven, and preheat to 350°. Lightly butter a 10-inch tube pan. Dust the pan with flour, and tap out the excess.
2. Sift together the flour, ¼ teaspoon of the salt, and the baking soda. In a large bowl, using a hand-held electric mixer set at high speed, beat the butter until creamy, about 1 minute. Add the sugar and beat until light in color and texture, about 2 minutes. Beat in the egg yolks, one at a time, beating well after each addition. Then add the

SOUR CREAM POUND CAKE (UNITED STATES)

"Mom, who gave me this recipe, was an RN and spent a lot of her spare time investing in real estate," says Hiram Bonner. "And between private nursing duty and being on the nursing staff of a hospital and taking care of her investments, she had little free time. But when she had an opportunity, she would cook for her four children. I especially remember this recipe because it tastes so good."

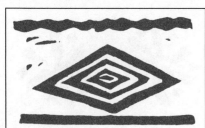

OLD-FASHIONED RICE PUDDING
(GUYANA)

This is a traditional dessert from Guyana, a country with many ethnic groups, located in the northeastern corner of South America. Those of African descent have been there longer than any other of the nation's nonindigenous population.

vanilla. Reduce the speed to low, and in thirds, alternately beat in the flour mixture and sour cream.

3. In a large greaseproof bowl, using a hand-held electric mixer (with clean beaters) set at low speed, beat the egg whites until foamy. Add the remaining ¼ teaspoon salt, increase the speed to high, and beat until the whites just form stiff peaks. Stir about one fourth of the beaten whites into the batter; then fold in the remaining whites. Transfer the batter to the prepared cake pan, smoothing the top.

4. Bake until the cake is golden brown and a long broom straw or bamboo skewer inserted into it comes out clean, 1¼ to 1½ hours. Cool the cake completely on a wire rack. Run a long thin knife around the edges to release the cake from the pan, then unmold.

OLD-FASHIONED RICE PUDDING

Cook's Notes: Unadorned vanilla-scented rice pudding is delicious simplicity personified. However, sometimes it's nice to stir in ½ cup of raisins or chopped crystallized pineapple after the custard has been made.

½ cup long-grain rice
2 cups milk
4 large eggs, separated, at room temperature
¾ cup granulated sugar
½ teaspoon vanilla extract
¼ teaspoon salt

1. Position a rack in the top third of the oven, and preheat to 400°. Lightly butter a 7- by 11-inch baking dish.

2. In a medium saucepan of boiling salted water, cook the rice until just tender, about 10 minutes. Drain well, rinse under cold water, then drain again.

3. Combine the rice and milk in a small saucepan over medium heat, and cook just until tiny bubbles appear around the edges of the milk. Remove the pan from the heat.

4. In a heavy medium saucepan, whisk the egg yolks and ½ cup of the sugar well. Gradually whisk in the scalded rice and milk mixture. Return the pan to low heat and stirring constantly with a wooden spoon, until an instant-reading thermometer reads 170° (the mixture will lightly coat the spoon). Stir in the vanilla and the salt. Transfer the rice pudding to the prepared baking dish.

5. In a medium grease-free bowl, using a hand-held electric mixer set at low speed, beat the egg whites until foamy. Increase the speed to high, and continue beating just until the whites form soft peaks. Gradually beat in the remaining ¼ cup sugar just until the whites form stiff peaks. Swirl the meringue on top of the pudding, making sure that the meringue touches all four sides of the dish.

6. Bake until the meringue is lightly browned, 4 to 6 minutes. Serve hot, warm, or chilled.

LEMONY TEA COOKIES
(UNITED STATES)

"My mom used to make these at the bat of an eye," says Mavis Young. "You could run into the house, grab one, and keep moving . . . keep playing. They are real simple. You can make them in any shape and sometimes you might sprinkle a little sugar on top because they are not very sweet. One thing you don't want is to overcook them—they get too crunchy. As a child, I usually had them with a glass of cold buttermilk. As I got older, I'd have them with tea or coffee."

LEMONY TEA COOKIES

Cook's Notes: Perfect for when you want a little nibble to perk up a dull afternoon, these sugar cookies are easy to make and bake. Lemon zest and spices give them an extra "lift," and they are just the thing for dipping in your favorite tea.

Makes about 4 dozen

2 cups all-purpose flour
1 teaspoon baking soda
½ teaspoon salt
½ teaspoon ground cinnamon
¼ teaspoon grated nutmeg
8 tablespoons (1 stick) unsalted butter, at room temperature
1 cup granulated sugar
Grated zest of 1 lemon
1 large egg, at room temperature
1 teaspoon vanilla extract
Granulated sugar, for sprinkling

1. Sift together the flour, baking soda, salt, cinnamon, and nutmeg. In a large bowl, using a hand-held electric mixer set at high speed, beat the butter until creamy, about 1 minute. Add the sugar and continue beating until the mixture is light in color and texture, about 2 minutes. Beat in the lemon zest, egg, and vanilla. Reduce the speed to low and beat in the flour mixture just until blended. Gather up the dough to form a thick flat disk, wrap it in waxed paper, and refrigerate until firm, at least 1 hour or overnight.
2. Position racks in the top third and the center of the oven, and preheat to 375°.

3. On a lightly floured work surface, in batches, roll the dough out ¼ inch thick. Using a 3-inch round cookie cutter, cut out rounds. Place the rounds on ungreased cookie sheets. Sprinkle each cookie with about ⅛ teaspoon granulated sugar, and press it lightly so it adheres. Gather up the scraps, reroll, and repeat the procedure with the remaining dough.

4. Bake the cookies for 3 minutes; then switch the positions of the cookie sheets from top to bottom, and continue baking until the cookies are barely browned, about 6 minutes total. Let them cool for 5 minutes on the sheets; then transfer the cookies to wire cake racks to cool completely.

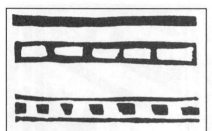

APPLE AND SPICE COBBLER
(UNITED STATES)

A spicy variation on an American standard.

APPLE AND SPICE COBBLER

Cook's Notes: The right variety of apple will make the difference between a successful apple cobbler and, well, one that isn't so successful. Choose an apple that will hold its shape after baking, such as Ida Red, Northern Spy, Jonathan, Granny Smith, or Macoun. (Red Delicious and Macintosh are best eaten out of hand or as applesauce, as they disintegrate easily upon cooking.) The sour cream pastry has a hint of tanginess that beautifully complements the apples.

SOUR CREAM PASTRY:

2 cups all-purpose flour

2 tablespoons granulated sugar

½ teaspoon salt

8 tablespoons (1 stick) unsalted butter, chilled, cut into ¼-inch cubes

1 cup sour cream, chilled

APPLE SPICE FILLING:

4 pounds baking apples, peeled, cored, and cut into ½-inch-thick slices

1⅓ cups packed light brown sugar

2 tablespoons all-purpose flour

Grated zest of 1 lemon

1 teaspoon ground cinnamon

¼ teaspoon ground allspice

¼ teaspoon grated nutmeg

⅛ teaspoon ground cloves

4 tablespoons (½ stick) unsalted butter, cut up

2 tablespoons heavy (whipping) cream

2 tablespoons granulated sugar

1. Make the pastry dough: In a medium bowl, stir together the flour, sugar, and salt. Using a pastry blender or two knives, cut in the butter until the mixture resembles coarse meal. Then stir in the sour cream just until the mixture is moistened (do not overwork the dough). Press the dough together to form a flat disk, wrap it in waxed paper, and refrigerate for at least 1 hour or overnight.

2. Position a rack in the top third of the oven, and preheat to 400°. Lightly butter a 9- by 13-inch baking pan.

3. Make the filling: In a large bowl, combine the apples, brown sugar, flour, lemon zest, cinnamon, allspice, nutmeg, and cloves. Toss until well combined. Transfer the apple mixture to the prepared baking pan, and dot it with the butter.

4. On a lightly floured work surface, roll out the dough to form a 10- by 14-inch rectangle about ⅛ inch thick. Arrange the dough over the top of the baking dish, letting the excess hang over the sides. Fold 1 inch of the overhanging dough under, and press this thick border of dough directly onto the rim of the baking dish so it adheres. With a sharp knife, cut four slashes in the dough to allow steam to escape. Brush the dough lightly with the heavy cream, and sprinkle with the granulated sugar. Place the baking dish on a baking sheet.

5. Bake for 10 minutes. Reduce the heat to 350° and continue baking until the crust is deep golden brown and the juices are bubbling and thickened, 35 to 45 minutes. (If the pastry begins to overbrown, cover with aluminum foil.) Serve the cobbler hot, warm, or at room temperature.

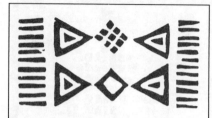

COCADA PUXA PUXA
Coconut Candy
(BRAZIL)

"Puxa puxa literally means to pull from one side to the other," explains Isabella Bravim.

COCADA PUXA PUXA
Coconut Candy

Cook's Notes: Traditionally Cocada Puxa Puxa is served with Queijo de Minas, a Brazilian fresh white cheese similiar to mozzarella. It is certainly welcome on its own, particularly cut up, wrapped in colorful plastic, and presented as a holiday gift. The confection's texture is unusual, with the chewiness of coconut balanced by a creamy yet crumbly candy.

Makes about 1 pound

2½ cups (about 1¼ pounds) turbinado or raw sugar
½ cup water
Pinch of ground cloves
1 coconut, finely shredded (see page 197)

1. In a heavy medium saucepan, bring the sugar, water, and cloves to a boil over medium-high heat, swirling the pan to dissolve the sugar (do not stir the sugar or it will crystallize). Cook until the syrup caramelizes and turns a light golden brown, 5 to 7 minutes.
2. Stir in the shredded coconut. Reduce the heat to low and continue cooking, stirring occasionally, until the syrup has been almost completely absorbed by the coconut, 6 to 8 minutes.
3. Meanwhile, lightly butter a large piece of aluminum foil.
4. Turn the candy out onto the prepared foil, spreading it out to form a 10-inch circle. Let the candy cool completely at room temperature. Then, using a large sharp knife, cut it into pieces to serve. Store the candy at room temperature in an airtight container.

PECAN PRALINES

Cook's Notes: Proper Crescent City pralines have a creamy, almost fudgelike consistency, and are not brittle-crisp like the French version. And these are as authentically delicious as you can get! Cool the praline mixture only to the point where it has thickened slightly—if it's too hot, it will spread out thinly on the waxed paper; if it's too cold, it will congeal and be impossible to spoon out. As with all syrup-based candies, avoid making pralines in humid or rainy weather, as they will take an inordinate amount of time to set up properly.

Makes about 32

3 cups granulated sugar
1 cup evaporated milk
4 tablespoons (½ stick) unsalted butter
2½ cups (about 10 ounces) coarsely broken pecans

1. Line a work surface (about 2 feet square) with lightly buttered sheets of waxed paper.
2. In a large skillet at least 2 inches deep, cook 1 cup of the sugar over medium heat, shaking and swirling (not stirring) the pan occasionally, until the sugar has melted and caramelized to a light golden brown, 5 to 7 minutes. (Stirring the sugar will cause crystallization.)
3. Meanwhile, in a deep medium saucepan, combine the remaining 2 cups sugar with the evaporated milk. Bring to a full boil over medium-high heat, stirring occasionally to dissolve the sugar.
4. Gradually stir the milk mixture into the caramelized sugar, and cook, stirring and scraping the bottom of the skillet constantly, until a candy thermometer reaches 238° (soft-ball stage), about 4 minutes. Remove the skillet from the heat, add the butter, and stir until the

PECAN PRALINES
(UNITED STATES)

Curtis Moore, who owns the Praline Connection, a New Orleans soul food restaurant, says this recipe comes from his grandfather. "This recipe has been handed down three generations," Moore says. "My grandfather started selling them in front of the church on Sundays." As for cooking hints, Moore says, "This is not something you can just walk away from while you're cooking it, or it will burn at the bottom of the pot. You have to stay with the candy."

butter has melted. Add the pecans, and stir just until the mixture has cooled and thickened slightly.

5. Drop tablespoons of the praline mixture about 2 inches apart on the prepared paper. Cool at room temperature until the pralines are set, at least 2 hours. (They will dull in color upon cooling, which is the way they should be.) Store the pralines at room temperature in an airtight container.

CREOLE PEAR AND RUM PUDDING

Cook's Notes: As French culture permeates New Orleans social traditions, French cuisine influences Creole cooking. This pear pudding resembles the French *clafouti*, also a warm cakelike pudding.

Serves 6 to 8

6 medium Bosc pears (about 3 pounds) cored and cut into ¼-inch-thick slices

2 tablespoons dark rum

½ teaspoon ground cinnamon

¼ teaspoon grated nutmeg

1 cup all-purpose flour

1 cup granulated sugar

3 large eggs, at room temperature

8 tablespoons (1 stick) unsalted butter, melted

½ cup milk

½ cup water

1 teaspoon vanilla extract

¼ teaspoon salt

1. Position a rack in the top third of the oven, and preheat to 400°.
2. Arrange the pear slices in a lightly buttered 9- by 13-inch baking pan, and sprinkle them with the rum, cinnamon, and nutmeg.
3. In a blender, combine the flour, sugar, eggs, butter, milk, water, vanilla, and salt. Process, scraping down the sides of the container, until smooth. Pour the batter over the pears.
4. Bake until the top is puffed and golden brown, 25 to 30 minutes. Cool slightly before serving.

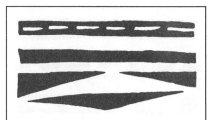

CREOLE PEAR AND RUM PUDDING
(UNITED STATES)

For a touch of the Big Easy around Kwanzaa time, try this delicious dessert. It's sure to inspire recollections of the great jazz trumpeter Louis Armstrong, the rollicking New Orleans blues pianist Professor Longhair, rock and roll's greatest shouter, Little Richard, and other legends of the Crescent City.

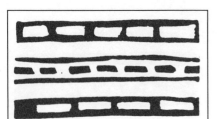

SWEET POTATO AND PRALINE PIE
(UNITED STATES)

Karen Grigsby Bates credits Paul Prudhomme's sweet potato–pecan pie as the inspiration for her recipe. "But rather than the rich, gooey pecan-pie top in his recipe, this version is slightly less sinful," she says. "I've used a crunchy praline topping to complement the texture of the traditional sweet potato pie beneath. Because the top contains brown sugar, the body of the pie is less sweet than usual. Use your favorite pie crust recipe, or the one here."

SWEET POTATO AND PRALINE PIE

Serves 6 to 8

PIE CRUST:
1⅓ cups all-purpose flour
1 teaspoon granulated sugar
¼ teaspoon salt
7 tablespoons unsalted butter, chilled, cut into ¼-inch cubes
¼ cup ice water

SWEET POTATO FILLING:
2 medium sweet potatoes, "Louisiana yams," about 1¼ pounds
½ cup granulated sugar
2 large eggs, well beaten
1 teaspoon ground cinnamon
½ teaspoon vanilla extract
¼ teaspoon grated nutmeg
⅛ teaspoon ground cloves
⅛ teaspoon salt
2 tablespoons milk
2 tablespoons all-purpose flour

PRALINE TOPPING:
1 cup (¼ pound) coarsely chopped pecans or walnuts
½ cup packed light brown sugar
2 tablespoons unsalted butter, melted

2 pints vanilla ice cream

1. Make the pie crust dough: In a large bowl, whisk together the flour, sugar, and salt. Using a pastry blender or two knives, cut in

the butter until the mixture resembles coarse meal. Tossing the flour mixture with a fork, sprinkle in the ice water, mixing just until the dough is moist enough to hold together when pinched between your thumb and forefinger. (You may have to add more ice water.) Gather the dough up to form a thick flat disk, and wrap it in waxed paper. Refrigerate for at least 1 hour or overnight.

2. Meanwhile, make the filling: In a large saucepan of boiling water, cook the (unpeeled) sweet potatoes until tender when pierced with the tip of a knife, about 25 minutes. Drain, rinse under cold running water, and drain again. Allow the sweet potatoes to cool slightly, then pare and mash them. You should have about 2 cups mashed sweet potatoes.

3. Mix the mashed sweet potatoes with the sugar in a large bowl. Add the eggs and beat well. Beat in the cinnamon, vanilla, nutmeg, cloves, and salt. Add the milk and beat well. Beat in the flour. Cover with plastic wrap, and refrigerate until ready to use, up to 8 hours.

4. Make the praline topping: In a medium bowl, combine the pecans and brown sugar. Drizzle with the melted butter, and combine with your fingertips until moistened and crumbly. Set aside at room temperature.

5. On a lightly floured surface, roll out the dough to form a 14-inch circle about ⅛ inch thick. Transfer it to a 10-inch round pie plate. Fold over 1 inch of the excess dough, and flute the edges decoratively. Pour in the filling and spread it out evenly. Crumble the praline topping over the filling.

6. Bake until the filling is set, about 35 to 40 minutes. Cool on a wire cake rack until warm, about 10 minutes. Serve warm, with scoops of vanilla ice cream.

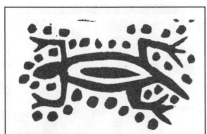

SUE'S LEMON PUDDINGCAKEPIE
(UNITED STATES)

"This is not your typical lemon meringue pie," warns Mavis Young, who got the recipe from a friend. "You mix the meringue in the pie filling and then cook it. The result is flatter and smoother than a meringue. And this is tarter, too—more lemony."

SUE'S LEMON PUDDINGCAKEPIE

Cook's Notes: You know those lemon sponge puddings, the kind that develop a delicious cake layer on top after baking? Mavis uses the pudding as a zesty filling for her famous pie, and what a match made in dessert heaven!

Serves 8

PIE DOUGH:
1½ cups all-purpose flour
¼ teaspoon salt
½ cup vegetable shortening, chilled, cut into small pieces
About ⅓ cup ice water

FILLING:
6 tablespoons (¾ stick) unsalted butter, at room temperature
1½ cups granulated sugar
4 large eggs, separated, at room temperature
⅓ cup fresh lemon juice
Grated zest of 2 large lemons
4½ tablespoons all-purpose flour
¼ teaspoon salt
1½ cups milk

1. Make the dough: In a large bowl, whisk together the flour and salt. Using a pastry blender or two knives, cut in the shortening until the mixture resembles coarse meal. Tossing the flour mixture with a fork, sprinkle in the ice water, mixing just until the dough is moist enough to hold together when pinched between your thumb and forefinger. (You may have to add more ice water.) Gather the dough up

to form a thick flat disk, and wrap it in waxed paper. Refrigerate for at least 1 hour or overnight.

2. Position a rack in the lower third of the oven, and preheat to 425°.

3. Make the filling: In a medium bowl, using a hand-held electric mixer set at high speed, beat the butter until creamy, about 1 minute. Add the sugar and continue beating until the mixture is crumbly and pale yellow, about 2 minutes. Beat in the egg yolks, lemon juice and zest, flour, and salt. On low speed, beat in the milk.

4. In a grease-free medium bowl, using a hand-held electric mixer (with clean beaters) set at low speed, beat the egg whites until foamy. Increase the speed to high, and beat just until the whites form stiff peaks. Stir about one fourth of the beaten whites into the lemon mixture, then fold in the remaining whites.

5. On a lightly floured surface, roll out the dough to form a 14-inch circle about ⅛ inch thick. Transfer it to a 10-inch round pie plate. Fold over 1 inch of the excess dough, and flute the edges decoratively. Pour in the filling, and place the pie plate on a baking sheet.

6. Bake for 10 minutes. Then reduce the oven temperature to 350° and continue baking until the top of the pie is deep golden brown and springs back when pressed in the center, 35 to 45 minutes. Cool the puddingcakepie completely on a wire cake rack before serving.

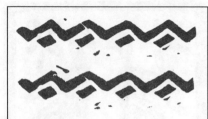

'NANA 'N' COOKIE PUDDING
(UNITED STATES)

"My mother made this all the time," Mavis Young recalls. "I guess because it is fairly quick and simple. And cheap. Sometimes I vary it. Instead of putting meringue on top of it, I spread it with whipped cream and make it real light."

'NANA 'N' COOKIE PUDDING

Cook's Notes: Ripe banana slices and vanilla wafers in a creamy pudding is one of the glories of down-home cooking. Now that you have this recipe, you should never *ever* be tempted to make it with instant vanilla pudding. Some cooks blatantly top 'Nana 'n' Cookie Pudding with a hearty dollop of sweetened whipped cream, but others are shocked at this gilding of the lily. Before deciding which tactic to take, step onto your bathroom scale.

Serves 6

1⅓ cups plus ½ cup granulated sugar
¼ cup all-purpose flour
3 large eggs, separated, at room temperature
3 cups milk, heated
1 teaspoon vanilla extract
1 (12-ounce) box vanilla wafers
6 ripe bananas, cut into ¼-inch-thick rounds
⅛ teaspoon cream of tartar

1. Position a rack in the top third of the oven, and preheat to 350°.
2. In the top part of a double boiler, whisk together 1⅓ cups of the sugar, the flour, and the egg yolks. Gradually whisk in the hot milk. Cook over simmering water, stirring constantly with a wooden spatula, until an instant-reading thermometer reads 180°. Do not bring near the boil or the eggs will scramble. (The mixture will barely coat the wooden spatula—this is a thin custard.) Remove the top part of the double boiler from the bottom, and stir in the vanilla.
3. In a 7- by 11-inch baking dish, spread about one third of the vanilla wafers in a single layer. (You can also use a 9- by 13-inch baking dish,

but the final result will be less plump.) Pour half of the vanilla pudding over the wafers. Arrange half of the bananas over the pudding. Top them with half of the remaining wafers. Pour the remaining pudding over the wafers, and top with the remaining bananas. Finish with the remaining wafers. Place the baking dish on a baking sheet.

4. In a grease-free medium bowl, using a hand-held electric mixer set at low speed, beat the egg whites until foamy. Add the cream of tartar, increase the speed to high, and beat just until the whites form soft peaks. Still beating, gradually add the remaining ½ cup sugar and beat until the whites form stiff, shiny peaks. Swirl the meringue over the top of the pudding, making sure that the meringue touches all four sides of the dish. (This will keep the meringue from shrinking after baking.)

5. Bake until the meringue is lightly browned, 5 to 10 minutes. Cool completely on a wire rack. Refrigerate until the pudding is thickened and chilled, at least 2 hours.

Nguzo Saba

Umoja (Unity)
Kujichagulia (Self-determination)
Ujima (Collective Work and Responsibility)
Ujamaa (Cooperative Economics)
Nia (Purpose)
Kuumba (Creativity)
Imani (Faith)

At age fifteen Lorene Cary seemed to be just another adolescent girl from West Philly. But she was soon to be attending a 125-year-old New Hampshire boarding school named St. Paul's, which Cary called with a touch of sarcasm "boot camp . . . for America's leaders." It was a rare opportunity for a teenager of any color. School was brutal. Not only did Cary have to deal with the usual difficult course load, not only did she have to deal with the usual adolescent emotional turmoils, but as a black and as a woman in 1971, she had to deal with her rush of feelings about being there—about being part of some "liberal-minded experiment." Yet she stayed. She suffered a bout of nervous exhaustion. She persevered. She graduated an academic success, and several years later returned to teach and to act as a trustee before continuing her career as a journalist and fiction writer.

What Lorene Cary is celebrating in this passage from her book *Black Ice* is her discovery, in Vernon Jordan, of a symbol of Unity (Umoja) and Collective Work and Responsibility (Ujima). Lorene Cary herself, through her candor in this wonderful book, stands as a symbol of both of these principles too.

I received a note to meet a visitor [to St. Paul's]: Mr. Vernon Jordan, president of the National Urban League. During his talk to students, Mr. Jordan referred to incidents in the history and current affairs of black and white racial relations that I had never heard. I felt the relief of a child after she has walked a very long way trying to be brave. Afterward I could not think of one intelligent question to ask him. It felt good simply to ride awhile. The next morning a fellow student, Alma, and I met him at Scudder, the guest house. Mr. Jordan was finishing breakfast when we arrived. He asked us about ourselves and the school. Alma described my involvement in Student Council and teased me about my reluctance to talk. "She's usually a big talker," she said.

I told him about Alma's athletic achievements, her varsity letters in basketball and lacrosse. We mentioned our Third World Coalition, and admitted our squabbles, our struggles, how at times we felt constricted but could not figure out what to do.

He understood us. He caught up our words and showed us what we meant. "This is a new phase of civil rights," he said. "Just a few years ago, it was a lot clearer. You could point to outrageously racist laws. Now it's more subtle. You kids here are feeling the effects. I mean you're here—" he motioned his hand in the air to take in the graceful room. We could hear Mrs. Burrows washing dishes in the kitchen. "And it's hard not to become a part of all this. It's hard not to forget where we came from."

How could I tell him: forgetting wasn't the problem, it was finding a new way to fight. If we couldn't fight, we'd implode. I tried to say that. I tried to ask him what we should do now, in this new phase. It was time for him to go, but he hadn't told us how to go on. I wanted to beg, to demand that he show us the way. "The most important thing," he said, "is to get everything you can here. You kids are getting a view of white America that we never even got close to." He shook his head. "We couldn't even dream of it."

I thought of the scene in *Native Son*—I'd have to teach it soon to the Fourth Formers—where the two boys stand on the sidewalk looking at an airplane. Only white boys could fly, they said.

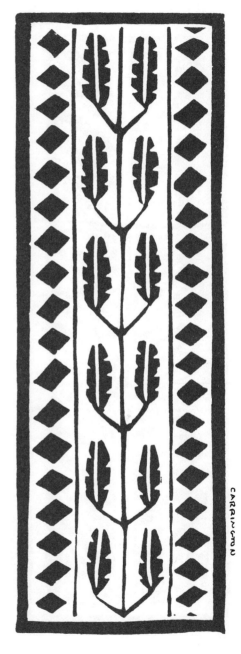

"You've got to get as much as you can here, be the best that you can, so that when you come out, you'll be ready. But you cannot forget where you've come from."

When I had been eleven years old, the year before Martin Luther King was shot, I had written to the Southern Christian Leadership Conference headquarters in Atlanta asking them what I could do to help the struggle. They had said the same thing. Stay in school. Prepare yourself. Then what?

"The fact is," he said, "there's no blueprint for what we're doing now. It's all uncharted water. We're going to need you. We're going to need every one of you."

This is another Ashanti story, the title tale from Harold Courlander's book, *The King's Drum and Other African Stories*. When I tell this story to my son, I change the line "It is for the king we labor" to "Because we work for our people." I make this change because Kwanzaa is a time for celebrating the indomitable spirit of the black community. Year in and year out, the fruits of any black person's labor contribute to the community. Every success, no matter how small or obscure, is a stepping stone for a subsequent success. I read this every year to my son, to emphasize the principle of Collective Work and Responsibility (Ujima). And because it is one of his favorites.

The king of the forest once called a meeting of all his subjects. His messengers went out to distant villages, and when the animals heard the king's command, they put on their best clothes and began their trip. But many weeks passed before they arrived.

When they had all gathered before his house, the king said to them: "When a meeting is called, many days pass before we are gathered. This is not good. What if we are in danger? What if the enemy is coming? We must find a way to gather quickly."

Anansi the spider was the king's councillor. He said, "What is needed is a drum. When the royal drum is beaten, it will be heard everywhere. Everyone will come quickly."

The animals applauded Anansi's suggestion. It was agreed that there should be a drum. The king ordered that a drum should be made. The animals were organized into work squads. Each squad was to take its turn at the making of the drum. First, one squad went out and cut a tree. Another squad went out to trim the tree. Another squad took adzes and cut the tree into the shape of a drum. The drum was hollowed. After that, carvers were set to work to decorate the drum. Only the monkey did not do any work. While the others labored, the monkey found a shady place and slept, or he went off looking for berries. When they came back to the village, the animals sang:

> *Life is labor,*
> *We are tired,*
> *We are hot,*
> *It is for the king we labor.*

The monkey also sang:

> *Life is labor,*
> *I am tired,*
> *I am hot,*
> *It is for the king I labor.*

But Anansi saw that the monkey shirked and rested while the others labored. He said nothing.

A time came when the drum was finished. The king announced: "Let the drum be brought in. There will be a ceremony. The drum will be initiated. After that, the assembly will be ended. When the people are wanted again, the royal drum will be sounded."

Anansi said: "Yes, the drum shall be brought in. There is only one problem remaining. Who shall carry the drum?"

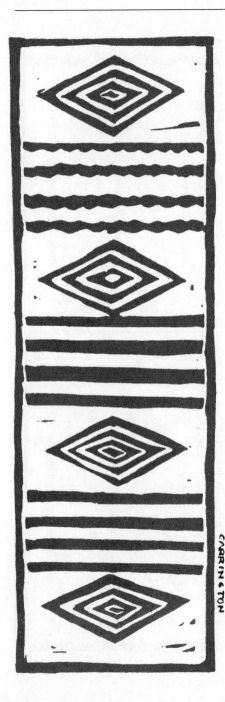

The drum was very large. It was heavy. The distance was great. No one wanted to carry it.

The leopard said, "Let the lion receive the honor."

The lion said, "No, it is the antelope who should carry it."

The antelope declared, "No, it is more fitting for the elephant to do it."

Each animal suggested that another should have the honor.

Anansi said: "It appears that each person wants someone else to do the carrying. Therefore, I suggest that the person to carry the drum is he who is most lazy."

The king said, "Yes, that is the way to do it."

The animals considered the question. They looked at each other. They tried to think who was the laziest. First, one looked at the monkey, then another looked at the monkey. The monkey looked here, looked there. Everywhere he looked, he saw people looking at him.

He went to the middle of the crowd and said: "I wish to make a statement. I refuse to carry the drum. Never, never will I carry the drum. That is all I have to say."

All the animals laughed. The antelope said: "Why are you here? No one mentioned your name."

The porcupine said: "Why do you speak? No one asked you to carry the drum."

The crowd called out, "Yes, no one said even a word to him."

Once more the monkey said: "I want it to be made clear. I will not carry the drum. These are my words."

Again the animals laughed.

Anansi said to the king: "No one mentioned the monkey's name. People were thinking to themselves, 'Who is the laziest?' They could not make up their minds. But the monkey was sure. He came forward. He said, 'I want it made clear that I will never carry the drum.' Thus he confessed that he is the laziest. With his own mouth he has said it."

The animals answered, "It is true, the monkey is the laziest of all!"

And so when at last the great drum was brought from the forest to the king's house, it was the monkey who carried it.

As historian Lerone Bennett, Jr., paints it, there once was a time where it appeared that, at least as far as race relations were concerned, the United States was on the cusp of a Golden Age. There was an African-American senator, a governor, lieutenant governors, judges, lawyers, state treasurers, generals of state militias, and mayors. As Bennett put it in his book *Before the Mayflower*: "Negroes and whites were going to school together, riding on streetcars together and co-habiting. . . . An interracial board was running the University of South Carolina, where a Negro professor was teaching white and black youth metaphysics and logic." Lower on the economic ladder, "Never before . . . had there been so much hope. A black mother knew that her boy could become governor. Had not Blanche Kelso Bruce been suggested as a possible vice-presidential candidate? Black mothers could hope. Black boys could dream." The period Bennett described was between 1865 and 1877. Robert Smalls, a Civil War hero, was among the African-American politicians then. This is my version of Smalls's life based on many different accounts.

Robert Smalls was born into slavery on April 5, 1839, in Beaufort, South Carolina. As a youngster, Smalls heard about Frederick Douglass, who was also born into slavery but escaped to work for emancipation through articles in the newspaper he founded and owned, the *North Star*, and through speeches he made overseas. The story of Frederick Douglass captured Smalls's imagination and served to ignite his own ambition.

Smalls was sent to Charleston, South Carolina, where he worked as a hotel waiter, a hack driver, and a rigger. He was impressed into the Confederate navy and was a deckhand on the *Planter*, a gunboat. Soon he was promoted to pilot, but he never forgot his early dreams of freedom. Along with the other twelve slaves who manned the ship, he devised a daring plan of escape. When the Confederate officers were on shore, Smalls and the others smuggled their wives and children on board and sailed away. They found a cache of pistols, rifles, and other weapons, and a Confederate uniform, which one of them would wear to help get them past Rebel checkpoints. When they finally got past the southern defenses, they were spotted by a Union vessel, which almost blew them out of the water. Smalls and his crew were still flying the Confederate flag. It was only the thundering of the Union drums that warned Smalls that they were about to strike. But before the Union ships could fire, Smalls's crew hoisted the white surrender flag, and then they turned the gunboat over to the Union navy.

This episode brought Smalls a lot of fame throughout the North. In Washington, where he lived for a very brief time after the incident, he worked to help African-Americans who had escaped slavery, and lectured against the institution. Soon Smalls returned to the *Planter*, this time as a pilot under the Union flag. One day, while returning from one of their missions, Smalls's gunboat was attacked. The captain wanted to surrender, but Smalls, risking a charge of mutiny, took command of the ship and refused to surrender. The boat was hit and Smalls was wounded. But he still managed to guide the boat to safety and to keep it out of Confederate hands. As a result of his actions, Smalls was promoted and became captain of the *Planter*.

During Reconstruction, that period after the Civil War, Smalls was chosen as one of the delegates to write a new constitution for South Carolina. One of the areas he was especially active in was lobbying to end the Black Codes. (Although all African-Americans were declared free with the Emancipation Proclamation, many southern states created these special laws, which were designed to prevent African-Americans from voting and exercising other rights, such as traveling where they pleased or obtaining certain jobs.) Smalls also lobbied for free public education in South Carolina, a first for that state.

Smalls continued his career in government, first as a state representative, then a state senator, and then a congressman. This was quite an accomplishment, considering that blacks were frequently intimidated and threatened by violence at the polls. The Ku Klux Klan in the South in general, and a group that called themselves "red shirts" in South Carolina in particular, seemed to work around the clock to deprive blacks of their still-nascent power.

Shortly after becoming a congressman, Smalls was convicted, without any evidence, of accepting a $5,000 bribe while in the Senate, and was sentenced to three years in prison. (He was pardoned by the governor of South Carolina while free on bail.) Despite the arrest, Smalls was elected to the Congress of the United States, where he continued to push for rights for African-Americans. He was elected and re-elected for four terms, or eight years. It is even suspected that his eventual loss in 1887 was not because of his constituents' disloyalty or dissatisfaction, but because of voting irregularities and the continuing violent intimidation of blacks by whites at the polls. In 1895 he delivered a moving speech before the South Carolina constitutional convention, addressing the virtual disenfranchisement of blacks. He spent the rest of his life talking to children about the importance of education and civic involvement, before dying in 1915.

The Congo proverb illustrates Faith (Imani): that no matter what happens, in the end we of African descent will flourish, as individuals and as a people.

No matter how long the night, the day is sure to come.

Proverb, Congo

EPILOGUE

Kwanzaa means different things to different people. A child might remember the dance and music, having the family all together, sweets to eat, and the celebration table, laden with all the symbols of Kwanzaa.

For a grandparent or elder, it's a time when proper and special attention is paid, a time when the gift given and gladly received is the gift of history, something carried off in the heads and hearts of a family, not something carted off in the back of a station wagon.

A busy parent finds in Kwanzaa a time of rejuvenation, a time to stop and reflect, a time to raise sights and set goals, for self and family. The reflection of the candles' glow on the faces of children, friends, and family helps to give perspective to life.

For someone who is separated from his or her family and is spending Kwanzaa with people who are not blood relatives, it's a time to realize that we are all related, that our common heritage unites us in a special family.

But Kwanzaa also means the same thing to everyone. It is a time to reflect on black history and accomplishments. It is a time of joy and sharing. It is a time to ponder, discuss, and engage the principles: Unity (Umoja), Self-determination (Kujichagulia), Collective Work and Responsibility (Ujima), Cooperative Economics (Ujamaa), Purpose (Nia), Creativity (Kuumba), and Faith (Imani).

And it is a time to commit to putting these principles into practice in our lives—not just for a week, but throughout the year.

MENUS

A Down-Home Kwanzaa Buffet for a Crowd

Spinach-Leek Dip with Crudités
Charleston Crab Spread with Benne Crackers
Oven-Barbecued Drumettes with Dee Dee's BBQ Sauce

Baked Ham with a Secret Glaze
Sweet Potato Pudding
Sheila's Three Mixed Greens
Black-Eyed Peas Salad with Basil Vinaigrette
Put-Up Dilled Green Beans
Pickled Spiced Peaches
Grandma's Creamed Cornbread

Peachy Bread Pudding
Sue's Lemon Puddingcakepie

Eggnog with Vanilla Ice Cream Float

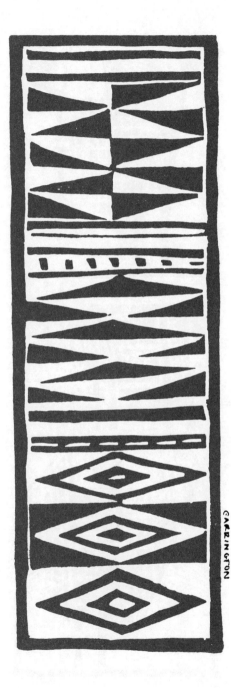

An African-Style Buffet

Curried Lamb Samoosas with Chutney Dip

Yassa
Babotie
Steamed White Rice
South African Vegetable Casserole
Fresh Greens and Apples with Curried Yogurt Dressing
Ginger Custard Ice Cream
Tanzanian Fruit and Cashew Salad with Rum Cream

Mavis's Pineapple-Papaya Punch
Assorted Chilled Beers

An Elegant Brazilian Dinner

Caipirinhas

Avocado Mousse with Shrimp Sauce

Moqueca, Pirao, Molho de Pimenta

Passion Fruit Mousse with Tropical Fruits

A Tropical Caribbean Supper

Chicarrones de Pollo

Chilled Caribbean Shrimp on Seasonal Greens
Jerked Pork Chops with Fresh Papaya Chutney
Cou Cou
Herb-Stuffed Christophenes

Coconut Mousse with Rum-Soaked Cherries

West African Ginger Beer

A Southern Fish Fry

Fried Catfish with Zippy Cornmeal Crust and Rémoulade Sauce
Alice's Potato Salad
Margaretta's Hush Puppies
Long-Cooked Green Beans, Tomatoes, and Bacon

'Nana 'n' Cookie Pudding

Real Lemonade

GLOSSARY OF FOODS

Achiote oil: A rusty-red oil made from the seed of the annato tree, used mostly for coloring. Found in most Hispanic, Mexican, and Indian markets.

Allspice, whole and ground: Also known as Jamaican pimento, allspice is so named because its flavor and aroma are reminiscent of cinnamon, nutmeg, mace, cloves, and other spices. Available whole— the berries are pepper-sized—and ground.

Annato seeds: Used to make *achiote oil*.

Avocado: Pear-shaped fruit usually sold hard and ripened at home until interior is pale green and creamy. Skin varies from green and smooth to black and rough, and size ranges from tiny—comparable to a small pear—to quite large, as big as a small melon.

Bananas, green: See *plantain*.

Banana leaves: Used by many cultures to wrap foods prior to cooking; usually sold frozen in Asian and Hispanic markets.

Basil: An aromatic herb reminiscent of tarragon and mint. Fresh basil is always preferable to dried.

Bay leaves: The leaf of the mountain laurel, grown in California and the Mediterranean; almost always sold dry.

Black beans, dried: Small, pea-shaped beans with creamy flesh and a meaty flavor; often served with rice, as in Moors and Christians.

Black-eyed peas: A staple of the American South, these ivory-colored beans, each with a single black spot, can be bought dried or canned.

Buttermilk: Traditionally, the liquid that remains after churning butter (modern techniques make buttermilk by lightly fermenting whole milk). A perfectly acceptable substitute can be made by mixing 2 teaspoons white vinegar or lemon juice into 1 cup tepid milk; let stand 5 minutes before using.

Calabaza: Also known as West Indian pumpkin, this yellow-skinned squash can be found—usually cut in slices because of its great size—in Hispanic and Caribbean markets.

Callaloo: Usually the greens of a Caribbean yam, callaloo may also refer to amaranth leaves, and to a soup made with greens. May be found in spring and early summer in Caribbean markets. Spinach and Swiss chard make fine substitutes.

Cayenne: Properly, the name of a fiery red pepper. More commonly, however, the generic name used for any powdered red pepper.

Celeriac: A variety of celery eaten for its delicious, bulbous root. Peel the thick skin well before using.

Celery seeds: A bitter seed taken from wild rather than cultivated celery. Use sparingly.

Chayote: This pear-shaped fruit comes in a number of shades of green, with a consistency somewhere between avocado and zucchini and a flavor not unlike cucumber. Also known as christiphene, mirliton, and cho-cho. Found in some supermarkets and Hispanic and Caribbean markets.

Chile peppers, fresh: Although most often used for their heat, chiles are also valuable for their flavors, which are distinctly different according to variety. Remove seeds from all peppers before using. **Scotch bonnet:** Tiny, hat-shaped pepper, generally considered the hottest. Excellent flavor when used in moderation. **Serrano:** Small green chile, important in the making of green sauces. **Jalapeno:** Short, fat green chile; moderately hot.

Chili peppers, dried: Usually cayenne, serrano, or jalapeno, these vary widely in their level of heat. Best cooked whole or with seeds removed.

Chili powder: Usually a mixture of ground chili pepper, cumin, oregano, and salt.

Chives: Grasslike leaves of the onion family. Use fresh if possible.

Cilantro: Powerfully scented leaves of the *coriander* plant, also known as Chinese parsley. Important in many cuisines. Dried coriander has a different flavor; do not substitute.

Cinnamon: The bark of the tree native to Sri Lanka and India. Sold as sticks and powder.

Cloves: From an evergreen tree that thrives near the sea in Africa, Asia, and the Caribbean. Sold whole or ground.

Coconut: The best fresh coconuts are heavy for their size, and slosh with milk when shaken. Dried coconut is a great convenience; use only the pure, unsweetened kind.

Conch: Large, spiral-shelled mollusks, also known as whelk, which are related to snails and clams. Whole conch should be refrigerated and used quickly; frozen meat should be used within a month of purchase.

Coriander seeds: Used sparingly, this dried spice has a mild, almost citruslike flavor. See *Cilantro*.

Corn, dried, cracked, and hulled: Also known as hominy, a food widely used by native Americans, especially in the Southwest. Ground, it becomes *grits*, the base of the breakfast cereal favored in the Deep South. Whole hominy is available cooked and canned, in supermarkets and dried in health food and specialty food stores; grits are sold in supermarkets.

Curry powder: There is a naturally occurring curry leaf, but the term curry powder refers to a combination of other spices, such as ginger, cardamom, coriander, pepper, turmeric, fenugreek, cayenne, and so on. **Curry powder, Jamaican:** This is similar to the Madras brand of curry powder and includes thyme and allspice.

Fenugreek: A common ingredient in most pre-mixed curry powders, fenugreek is quite bitter and only rarely used by itself.

Ginger: This aromatic rhizome is used freely in almost all non-European cuisines. Dried ginger is on every spice rack, and its more aggressive flavor is sometimes preferred. Fresh ginger, sold in most supermarkets, is milder and more pleasant-tasting; grate or mince before using.

Greens: A generic term for members of the brassica family that must be boiled (or otherwise cooked) before eating, including, but not limited to: **Collards:** One of the favored greens of the Deep South, collards are tough and dark green, and were probably first cooked here by African-Americans; they are still popular in West Africa. **Kale:** Dark green, curly leaves; a form of cabbage without a heart. **Mustard:** This strong-tasting green can be found wild everywhere, even in the middle of cities. Cultivated varieties are considerably milder. **Turnip:** So sweet-tasting that many varieties are now grown only for the green and not for the root.

Grits: Also known as hominy grits. See *Corn.*

Ham: The rear leg of a pig. Usually brined and smoked; "country" hams (such as Smithfield) are salty and strong, used primarily for snacks or flavoring. Supermarket hams are milder and sweet.

Hot pepper sauce: Usually an infusion of peppers in vinegar, varying in strength from one brand to another. Mostly for table use.

Hot red pepper flakes: Crushed dried chiles; essentially coarsely ground *cayenne.*

Liquid smoke: A strong natural flavoring made by condensing the elements of wood smoke.

Malanga: Also known as yautia, this shaggy brown yam with starchy yellow flesh is a Caribbean staple, usually boiled and served as a side dish. Readily available in Hispanic and Caribbean markets.

Mango: One of the world's great fruits, mangoes are ripe when soft to the touch. Using a mango is always a messy proposition: cut it in half, remove the pit as best as you can, and scoop the meat out of the skin with a spoon.

Mango chutney: A hot-sweet condiment made from raw ground mango, herbs, and spices.

Manioc flour: Dried meal made from the tubers of a tree that grows in Africa and Central America; also known as cassava or *yuca*, and widely available in Caribbean and Hispanic markets.

Marjoram: This mild-flavored cousing of oregano is almost always sold dried. Since its flavor is destroyed by heat, it is best to add marjoram just before serving.

Meats: Salted meats: Strongly salted meats, once a staple of sailors, remain common in Caribbean cooking, but may be difficult to find in the United States outside of Caribbean markets; substitute corned beef or lean salt pork. **Flavoring meats:** Inexpensive cuts used to season other dishes, such as pig tails and snouts; pig feet and fresh (unsmoked) ham hocks may also be used. **Goat (or kid):** Increasingly available, even in supermarkets; lamb is the best substitute.

Millet flour: Ground grain that is made into porridges and cakes; sometimes called poor man's wheat.

Molasses: The thick, dark syrup that remains after sugar is refined. There are three varieties: sulfured, unsulfured, and blackstrap, which is made during the final stage of the refining process and is the darkest.

Nutmeg: In its whole form, nutmeg—another of the famous spices of Southeast Asia—keeps indefinitely, and should be grated in small amounts just before using. Powdered nutmeg is an inferior substitute.

Okra: Often used as a thickener in Creole gumbo, okra is thought to be African or Asian in origin. Choose small okra whenever possible; larger ones are likely to be tough.

Old Bay Seasoning: A patented seasoning mixture used for seafood, especially boiled crabs.

Olive oil: Extra-virgin, made from the first pressing of the olives, is preferred.

Oregano: Like its milder cousin, *marjoram*, this is usually sold dried.

Palm oil: Saturated cooking fat from a tree native to West Africa. White in color and pleasantly mild in flavor. Available in Caribbean markets.

Papaya: Or paw-paw. A sweet tropical fruit with green skin and orange-yellow flesh. Its juice is a natural meat tenderizer, and it is occasionally used in Caribbean cookery for that purpose.

Paprika: This familiar, bright orange-red powder is, or should be, ground from select Hungarian peppers, some sweet, others hot. Paprika becomes stale quickly.

Passion fruit: Native to South America, this small, purple fruit is now grown in tropical areas around the world. Its intense flavor is incomparable.

Peanut butter: The best—for eating and cooking—is made from nothing more than peanuts and salt.

Pepper: Black and white pepper come from the same plant. The unripe black peppercorns are green when picked and darken as they dry. White pepper is peeled.

Pickling spices: A mixture containing some combination of the following, mixed with brine to produce pickles: peppercorns, garlic, shallots, onion, ginger, tamarind, bay leaves, cloves, cinnamon, chiles, cumin, coriander, fenugreek, turmeric, mustard seeds, horseradish, dill, fennel, sage, savory, and more.

Pigeon peas: Dried peas grown in tropical lands, ranging in color from white to brown to black.

Plantain: Also known as green bananas, this staple of the Southern Hemisphere is eaten at all stages of ripeness. Green, it is sliced and sautéed or boiled and mashed. Yellow, it is pan-fried and served as a sweet side dish. Black, it is baked in stews and casseroles. Sold in urban supermarkets and Hispanic and Caribbean markets.

Preserved peppers in vinegar: Any pepper can be brined, but most bottled peppers are hot. Found in many supermarkets and most ethnic markets.

Raw sugar: Crude brown sugar as it is shipped to the refinery; contains molasses. Dark in color and with larger crystals than refined sugar. Found in Caribbean markets.

Recato: A seasoning paste, used extensively in Mexico and Central America and usually sold bottled. Contains achiote, garlic, cumin, vinegar, and other spices.

Rice: Long-grain: Especially popular in the United States and India; grains remain separate during cooking. **Short-grain:** Widely used in Asia, Europe, and much of the rest of the world. Sticky and usually slightly sweet. **Popcorn, Basmati, Texmati:** Aromatic long-grain rice that cooks with a sublime nutty fragrance.

Rosemary: Piney, strong-flavored herb that dries well.

Rose water: Fragrant liquid made by distilling rose petals. Use sparingly. Most easily found in Indian and Middle Eastern markets.

Rum: Sugar-based liquor made in dark, light, and gold varieties.

Salt cod: Preserved cod essential for making cod cakes. Soak in several changes of water before using.

Shallots: Mild-flavored member of the onion family that grows in large cloves and has excellent flavor.

Soffrito: Tomato-based sauce, prevalent in Puerto Rican cooking, which contains peppers, onions, garlic, cilantro, and chili powder. Sold in bottles in most Hispanic markets.

Sorrel: Perennial herb with tantalizingly sour flavor. Use fresh.

Soy margarine: Used in strictly vegetarian recipes; made from soy milk.

Soy sauce: Fermented soybeans, sometimes with wheat. Tamari and shoyu, available in health food and Asian markets, are the most natural and delicious varieties.

Thyme: Basic herb essential to many cuisines. When fresh, dried thyme has good flavor; replace it often, however, as it does not keep especially well.

Turbinado sugar: Partially refined, with some molasses remaining. Tan in color, with larger crystals than white sugar. Sold in health food and specialty stores.

Turmeric: Mild flavored relative of ginger that is used more for its bright yellow color (and as a cheap substitute for saffron) than for its nondescript flavor. Almost always sold dried.

Ugli fruit: A hybrid cross between grapefruit, orange, and tangerine. Bumpy, misshapen, and sometimes quite delicious.

Wonton wrappers: Flat sheets of wheat flour dough used to encase savory foods. Sold in supermarkets and Asian markets.

Yam: *Not* a sweet potato, but another of the starchy tubers of the Southern Hemisphere, and a staple wherever it is grown. Typically boiled or baked, it is extremely bland.

Yucca: A starchy, bland root, also known as cassava or manioc. Used in stews as a side dish, and to make flour. The source for tapioca.

MAIL-ORDER SOURCES

This mail-order list will help you find some of the more unusual ingredients in this book.

General Ingredients

Rafal Spice Company
2521 Russell Street
Detroit, MI 48207
(800) 228-4276

Dean & DeLuca
560 Broadway
New York, NY 10012
(800) 221-7714
In New York: (212) 431-1691

PERMISSIONS

CARRINGTON

Page 55: From *Sky Juice and Flying Fish* by Jessica B. Harris. Copyright © 1991 by Jessica B. Harris. Reprinted by permission of Simon & Schuster, Inc.

Pages 76 and 324: From *The King's Drum and Other African Stories*. Copyright © 1962, 1990 by Harold Courlander. Reprinted by permission of the author. Published by Harcourt, Brace Jovanovich.

Page 79: From *To Praise Our Bridges: An Autobiography* by Fannie Lou Hamer. Jackson: KIPCO 1967. Reprinted and adapted by permission.

Page 154: From *A West African Cookbook* by Ellen Gibson Wilson. Copyright © 1971 by Ellen Gibson Wilson. Reprinted by permission of the publisher, M. Evans & Co., Inc., New York.

Page 170: Adapted with permission of Atheneum Publishers, an imprint of Macmillan Publishing Company, from *Staking a Claim: Jake Simmons, Jr., and the Making of an African-American Oil Dynasty* by Jonathan Greenberg. Copyright © 1990 by Jonathan Greenberg.

Page 173: "The Flying Contest" is from *Suriname Folk-lore* by Melville J. Herskovits and Frances S. Herskovits in *Afro-American Folktales: Stories from Black Traditions in the New World*, selected and edited by Roger D. Abrahams. Copyright © 1985 by Roger D. Abrahams. Published by Pantheon Books, New York.

Page 253: From *Where Did Your Love Go: The Rise and Fall of the Motown Sound* by Nelson George. Copyright © 1985 by Nelson George. Reprinted by permission of St. Martin's Press.

Page 256: From *Bantu Tales* by Patti Price. Published by Dutton in 1938.

Page 271: From *Crusade for Justice* by Ida B. Wells, edited by Alfred Duster. Copyright © 1970 by the University of Chicago Press. Reprinted by permission of the publisher.

Page 276: From *More Tales of Uncle Remus* by Julius Lester. Copyright © 1988 by Julius Lester. Used by permission of the publisher, Dial Books for Young Readers, a division of Penguin Books USA, Inc.

Page 281: From *The Black West* by William Loren Katz. Copyright © 1971, 1973 by William Loren Katz. Published by Open Hand Publishing, Seattle, Washington. Reprinted by permission of the author.

Page 322: From *Black Ice* by Lorene Cary. Copyright © 1991 by Lorene Cary. Reprinted by permission of Alfred A. Knopf, Inc.

INDEX